Shop stewards in British industry

Shop stewards in British industry

J. F. B. Goodman
*Lecturer in Industrial Economics,
University of Nottingham*

T. G. Whittingham
*Staff Tutor in Industrial Relations
Department of Adult Education
University of Nottingham*

McGRAW-HILL · LONDON

New York · Toronto · Sydney · Johannesburg · Mexico · Panama

Published by

McGRAW-HILL Publishing Company Limited
McGRAW–HILL HOUSE
MAIDENHEAD, BERKSHIRE, ENGLAND

94210

PRINTED AND BOUND IN GREAT BRITAIN

Preface

This book was written during the period that the Royal Commission on Trade Unions and Employers' Associations was considering the whole question of industrial relations in Britain. During this time, widespread attention has been given to problems in this area, but at the time of writing both the Report of the Royal Commission and its large-scale Survey of Workplace Relations had still to be published. These appeared, however, while the manuscript was with the printers, and summaries of their findings have been added as postscripts to Chapters 5 and 10.

Shop stewards in Britain have received extensive popular attention, and have been the subject of much comment, most of it critical. In an interview, Mr Aubrey Jones, Chairman of the National Board for Prices and Incomes, suggested that the problem of shop stewards was half the problem of British trade unions. Professor H. A. Clegg has suggested (See *Personnel Management*, December, 1965) that the power of shop stewards in Britain is greater than that of workshop representatives anywhere else. Mr Allan Flanders has distinguished the challenges the present industrial relations system faces both from above and below, stressing that the challenge from below—in the shape of shop stewards' activities—can disrupt the existing structure as well as present problems in developing an incomes policy. Indeed, an incomes policy is likely to necessitate changes at workplace level if the national interest is to be adequately expressed at this increasingly important collective bargaining level.

Most of the problems of present concern involve the roles

and interests of both management and unions, for both must influence shop steward behaviour and guide their future development. Management and union policies will be influential in determining, for example, the functions of workplace representatives and how they are formally accepted; and the strength of the link between unions and stewards in relation to unofficial strikes and less newsworthy industrial action; the extent, form, and direction of workplace bargaining; and the limitation of cost-push inflation at plant level, etc. Some of these topics illustrate the problems which arise from conflict of interest between stewards and management (and possibly their unions) in the regulation of employment relationships, though other difficulties arise from a shared preference between stewards and managers for the internalization of their dealings. Encouragement of shop stewards by management is an important but often overlooked element in workplace bargaining. At the same time, the reluctance of management to take the initiative in labour relations has been highlighted by strong workplace organization among its employees, and thus now represents an area of considerable opportunity for contemporary managements.

Essentially, our objective is to examine the nature, causes, and manifestations of the 'challenge from below', to assess the problems facing unions and management, and the institutions they have established jointly, as a result of the increased decentralization of industrial relations activity.

More precisely our aims are:

1. To study the factors responsible for the increased importance of shop stewards, and for variations in it.
2. To describe their present roles and the pressures and constraints which influence them.
3. To draw together information and hypotheses from specialist fields in the social sciences generally and industrial relations in particular, and to relate this specifically to workplace representatives.
4. To analyse the effects of the changed role, status, and functions of shop stewards on trade unions, management, and collective bargaining arrangements in relation to current needs in the labour relations field.

Thus, it is proposed to underline the position of the shop steward as a focal point of many related trends in industrial relations, and in so doing to break down the fragmentation of study in this field. Consequently, we shall outline and interpret the forces operating on, and in part generated by, the British system of industrial relations.

We have endeavoured to collect findings from published material directly concerned with shop stewards, and other work of more indirect bearing on their position. Much is available only in academic journals or in publications dealing only incidentally with shop stewards. In addition, we undertook a number of research projects to illuminate certain topics but, due to the limitations of our samples and of the case study approach, they have no claim to being definitive.

The study is informed by our experience in industry, including time spent on the shop floor in the motor industry, and as management representatives dealing with stewards. More generally, we have discussed the role, functions, and behaviour patterns of stewards with managers, personnel officers, full time union officials, foremen, stewards, and rank and file union members—though these discussions took place over a long period and in a way not easily reported statistically. Finally, we have had experience of teaching on broadly educational and specifically constructed training courses for stewards, which give some insight into the problems from the stewards' point of view. In consequence, this book is both a report of new research findings and a review of other research, as well as involving commentary on recent economic and social changes.

Our subject is large, diverse, and full of temptations to generalize. However, in our experience, variations exist between *and* within different plants of the same company, different industries, unions and between all these at various points in time. The problems raised by shop stewards therefore vary enormously in situation and time, and we anticipate that future research may reveal differences of which we are unaware. Like all issues of a human and economic nature, this is a dynamic one.

It is our contention that the importance of stewards in regulating industrial relationships is not widely understood.

Shop stewards attract emotional and often extreme opinion, and seem more prone to examination in stereotype than others in the field of employment relations. Moreover, it appears that the role of stewards is likely to develop, as they become increasingly significant to unions, managers, and the country at large. Yet, there has been no coterminous movement to incorporate them formally within the rules of the industrial relations system. The existing rules which attempt to regulate their behaviour are inadequate, and often irrelevant. Shop stewards appeared initially as minor workplace supplements to the organizing and administrative hierarchy of the unions, as recruiters and reporters rather than as principals with representational functions. Since the Second World War, they have emerged as a force independent of existing institutions. Pragmatically, they have built up practices and organizations which have eroded old established arrangements. Yet 'independent' is perhaps too strong. Stewards are not independent of their unions, though the distance between them is often great. Nor are they independent of management, whose behaviour can be important in determining their behaviour and attitudes. Thus, their attachment to the unions is often flimsy, while the degree of 'supervision' exercised by their constituents is also variable. Increasingly, the stewards, with the support or acquiescence of their constituents, cannot be controlled or even greatly influenced by union or management. This combination of stewards and constituents represents a relatively new and quickly developing interest group in the industrial relations scene, for which the traditional external mechanisms do not adequately cater.

Like other institutions, employers' associations and trade unions tend to acquire their own institutional life and interests, tending, in time, to gain a justification separate from the original purposes. This process is also apparent in the joint institutions and old established procedures through which they conduct their relationships. Additionally, if the institutions cling rigidly to existing patterns, their relevance diminishes and they are bypassed. Thus, individual managements and groups of union members (with their workplace leaders) have grown away from external institutions, though carefully preserving access to them where and when this is felt appropriate. The 'parent' bodies, employers' associations and trade unions, have become progressively less able (and often unwilling, due to the risk of further alienation) to regulate the behaviour of their members, though both occasionally issue threats or force resignations. Consequently, the validity of their claims to constitute the single voice of their members has been undermined, and their value to members often reduced.

Despite the more unified ideas of trade unions in comparison with employer associations and their more centralized authority, the trend of *actual* power and initiative is downward. Indeed, it would not be false to describe the relation of workplace organizations and the body of the unions in federal terms, with members paying low taxes, receiving poor services from and having only infrequent contact with the centre, and admitting only a few major decisions by the federal authority. Traditional concepts of union structure, of the functions of employers' associations, and of collective bargaining arrangements, appear less and less tenable. The institutions and their procedures are no longer comprehensive, nor perhaps appropriate. Managements are widely subject to 'domestic' claims, and have their actions, performance, and values scrutinized by stewards. Many managements have fostered this process, preferring to build up their own pattern of labour relations. Union officials seem little perturbed by the drift of events, and many district officials rely on stewards to relieve them of their duties—especially in 'reasonable' firms with 'reasonable' managements. In practice, many accept decentralization, and liberally consider that the union exists for its members, or even that 'the members are the union'. If to this view, we attach the widely held opinion (and fact!) that to many members 'the steward is the union', then the significance of members and stewards in relation to union hierarchies is apparent.

The trend is therefore towards decentralization: from union executives, full time officials, and branches, to stewards, and sometimes beyond stewards to other, informal, workplace leaders; and from employers' associations to company managements, plant and departmental managers, and labour specialists.

Needless to say, these processes have not been of equal

incidence in the diverse arrangements which constitute the so-called industrial relations system.

We would like to express our gratitude to the numerous trade union officers, shop stewards, managers, and supervisors who have answered our questions and referred both candidly and at length to their own experience. Several companies and unions gave us full facilities to conduct our investigations on their own premises, and we are greatly indebted to them.

We would like to thank the Department of Adult Education, University of Nottingham, and the WEA East Midland District, for allowing us to reproduce material from a booklet which appeared before this book was published. We would also like to express our thanks to the editor of *Personnel and Training Management* for permission to reproduce material in Chapters 4, 5, and 9 which was previously published in the journal.

Our thanks are also due to many of our colleagues in the University of Nottingham, particularly Professor F. A. Wells, for their comments and advice. Finally, we would like to thank Mrs M. Brown, who typed the book with both patience and care.

J. F. B. Goodman
T. G. Whittingham

Contents

Abbreviations Used in the Text

AEF	Amalgamated Engineering and Foundry Workers Union (until recently the A.E.U.)
ASE	Amalgamated Society of Engineers
ASLEF	Amalgamated Society of Locomotive Engineers and Firemen
ASPD	Amalgamated Society of Painters and Decorators
ASSET	Association of Supervisory Staffs, Executives and Technicians, now . . .
ASTMS	Association of Scientific, Technical and Managerial Staffs
AScW	Association of Scientific Workers
ASMM	Amalgamated Society of Metal Mechanics
ASW	Amalgamated Society of Woodworkers
AUBTW	Amalgamated Union of Building Trades Workers
AUFW	Amalgamated Union of Foundry Workers
BEA	British European Airways
BEC	British Employers Confederation
BISAKTA	British Iron, Steel and Kindred Trades Association
BMC	British Motor Corporation
BOAC	British Overseas Airways Corporation
CAWU	Clerical and Administrative Workers' Union
CBI	Confederation of British Industry
CEU	Constructional Engineering Union
CM	Corresponding Members
CSEU	Confederation of Shipbuilding and Engineering Unions
CWU	Chemical Workers Union
DATA	Draughtsmen's and Allied Technicians' Association
EEF	Engineering Employers Federation
ETU	Electrical Trades Union
FOC	Father of the Chapel
HDEU	Heating and Domestic Engineers Union
ICI	Imperial Chemical Industries

IPM	Institute of Personnel Management
JCC	Joint Consultative Committee
JPC	Joint Production Committee
JSSC	Joint Shop Stewards Committee
JWC	Joint Works Committee
LDC	Local Departmental Committee (on the railways)
NACODS	National Association of Colliery Overmen, Deputies and Shotfirers
NASDS	National Amalgamated Stevedores' and Dockers' Society
NATSOPA	National Society of Operative Printers and Assistants
NBPI	National Board for Prices and Incomes
NCLC	National Council of Labour Colleges
NFBTO	National Federation of Building Trades Operatives
NGA	National Graphical Association
NJIC	National Joint Industrial Council
NJNC	National Joint Negotiating Committee
NSMM	National Society of Metal Mechanics
NUBSO	National Union of Boot and Shoe Operatives
NUFTO	National Union of Furniture Trades Operatives
NUGMW	National Union of General and Municipal Workers
NUPBPW	National Union of Printing, Bookbinding and Paperworkers
NUPE	National Union of Public Employees
NUR	National Union of Railwaymen
NUS	National Union of Seamen
NUSMW & C	National Union of Sheet Metal Workers and Coppersmiths
NUVB	National Union of Vehicle Builders
PIB	National Board for Prices and Incomes
PKTF	Printing and Kindred Trades Federation
POEU	Post Office Engineering Union
PTU	Plumbing Trades Union
SOGAT	Society of Graphical and Allied Trades
TGWU	Transport and General Workers Union
TUC	Trades Union Congress
TWU	Tobacco Workers' Union
UPOW	Union of Post Office Workers
USDAW	Union of Shop, Distributive and Allied Workers
WEA	Workers' Educational Association

Note: In several instances, unions have changed their titles consequent on amalgamation. We refer to the old titles in the text where these are appropriate to the time of our research, to union policies, or to union publications.

1
Shop Stewards: An Introductory Survey

Definitions

The diversity of trade union structure, rule books, and practice makes it difficult to establish a definition of a shop steward inclusive of the men and women it is sought to define, without becoming so loosely phrased as to be indefinite. Many collective agreements introduce the term 'shop steward' to describe 'representatives appointed from the members of the unions employed in the establishment to act on their behalf . . .'.[1] This description is perhaps most common, that the shop steward is the representative of union members in the workplace, being acknowledged as such, by the management and by his trade union, but who is neither a full time officer nor a branch official whose workplace representational function derives solely from that office. This acknowledgement is usually shown by the workplace representative's function in the early stages of in-plant negotiations, which is frequently included in the procedural sections of collective agreements.

One problem arising from the definition of a shop steward as the representative of union members employed in the establishment where he himself works is that it is confusing in some industries. Here, this function is performed by a person like the workplace representative, but who does not, strictly, come within the definition. For example, in coal mining, the basic administrative unit of the National Union of Mineworkers is the branch, based on NUM membership at

1

a *colliery*, rather than on the colliery village. This identification of the basic unit of the trade union with the workplace is the exception rather than the rule, but where it exists it implies difficulty in determining the duties a branch secretary may have as a result of his tenure of this office and which are the result of his, occasional, election as workplace representative in the above sense. This complicated picture is illustrated by the definitional problems posed by the hardworking trade unionist in one motor vehicle plant who was simultaneously a shop steward for a section of workers, the convenor of shop stewards in the plant, and branch secretary of his union's newly established local (workplace based) branch. Management, in this case, recognized him in the first two positions, but gave him no facilities from holding the branch secretaryship. This example indicates the reduced significance of branch positions in the settlement of industrial relations problems, though this decline is not of equal incidence in all industries and unions. Generally speaking, the functions of branch officials tend to coalesce with those of the workplace representative only where there are workplace based branches, or where unions are, or aspire to be, industrial unions.

This book is concerned with shop stewards, using a working definition of the shop steward as:

(a) A representative of trade union members at the place of work where he himself is employed.

(b) Someone who is tacitly or explicitly accepted as such by management and his trade union.

(c) Someone who has a *de facto* responsibility for the conduct of the initial stages of negotiations in the workplace. (This must not be interpreted as all embracing. There are occasions, in practice, when local full time officials initiate discussion on topics affecting the plant. Similarly, many procedure agreements emphasize that any employee who has a complaint must, initially, refer to his foreman before approaching his shop steward.)

(d) Someone, however, who is not a recognized full time official of his trade union and whose recognition is not the result of his, possibly, holding branch office.

2

However, not all workplace representatives who fulfil these conditions are called shop stewards. This is explained by lack of standardized trade union terminology for their workplace representatives. Most widely known is 'father of the chapel' in the printing unions, a title which indicates both the old established nature of this position and the importance of tradition. Other titles used include those of 'corresponding member' in DATA, 'staff representative' in the CAWU, 'local department committee representative' on the railways, and in the Civil Service 'members of the Staff Sides of Local Whitley Committees'.

A further point is the position of convenors of shop stewards. A convenor is usually the senior shop steward in a plant, or of a union in it, and he is normally elected by his fellow stewards. A convenor's responsibilities vary but he is often acknowledged by management to have considerable influence over other shop stewards, and is frequently able to advise stewards within the plant on factory-wide practices and possibly policy. Often, the title convenor is given to the secretary of a shop stewards' committee formed by stewards of one union, and works convenor to the occupant of the equivalent position on the joint (i.e. inter-union) shop stewards' committee for the whole factory. The convenor in a large factory may be influential in the progression of disputes. He may join a steward in negotiations at a certain stage or may raise points of a plant-wide nature *ab initio*. He will usually become quickly involved if an issue is urgent. The convenor may retain his duties as a shop steward to a section of union members, and then it is easy to include him in our definition of a shop steward. However, when a convenor gives up his duties in favour of this higher position, his inclusion becomes more problematical, though we feel justified in allowing it—for the change is one of degree rather than kind. It is generally an extension of his representational function in the workplace rather than exclusion from it, though again it is necessary to emphasize variations.

We have sought to define the shop steward in terms which may be applied to any employment situation rather than to catalogue duties or functions. The only function regarded as essential to our definition is that of responsibility for the initial stages of in-plant negotiations, necessary to avoid confusion over the position of 'collecting' stewards. The collection of union dues and the checking of membership cards was one of the earliest duties of the workplace representative, although some union rules do not allow payment of dues at places other than the local branch. The increased role and activities of shop stewards in some industries have involved a division of labour, and some unions, e.g. NUGMW, appoint collecting stewards additionally, to be responsible for the collection of union dues. Where this is the limit of the collecting steward's activities, we will not be concerned with him. Only where he has progressed to a representational role would he come within our definition.

Shop stewards, or perhaps more usually convenors, have occasionally found that their representative duties have so developed that they become occupied with plant industrial relations for much of their working week. It is important to distinguish between representatives engaged for the whole working week on industrial relations problems in the workplace and the full time officials of the trade unions.

Shop stewards, or convenors, usually rank as lay officials of their trade union, but generally receive little or no remuneration for their services. In the two largest general unions, stewards who collect dues are paid a commission, $7\frac{1}{2}$ per cent in the T & GWU and 10 per cent in the NUGMW. The basis of payment for the shop steward or convenor whose representational activities, initially subsidiary to his employment, have in time virtually come to replace his nominal occupation with the firm, varies between companies. Management may formally recognize the position and pay the convenor for his duties, but probably will leave the position undefined and pay the convenor as if still engaged in his nominal occupation. Alternatively, where a firm refuses to pay a steward for time spent away from his 'normal' job, a steward's members may well contribute to make up his wages. The full time trade union official, on the other hand, is a paid employee of the union, his salary deriving from central funds, he being answerable in the normal way to his superiors.

Within the framework of our definition, it might be possible to refer to *the* shop steward, implying a basic uniformity of all

shop stewards. Obviously, any definition describes characteristics shared by all included within it, but with shop stewards
the common denominator is fixed at a fairly low level. There is
great diversity in different industries, and even between different plants of one firm in one industry. Managerial, company-wide policies, and similarly guiding lines postulated by a
union for its stewards, become subject to local pressures,
traditions, and interpretation by individuals. Such factors, *and*
many others, determine whether the steward can extend his
activities within and possibly beyond our basic definition.

The difficulties in deriving an inclusive but specific definition of a shop steward are indicative of a major contemporary problem. Practice varies, but generally trade union
rule books are vague in defining a shop steward; many evade
the issue either by introducing the term without definition,
or by wholly omitting to mention stewards or their equivalent.
A close definition of stewards, of their actual duties and functions, is a first step towards the clarification of problems which
their existence presents in industry.

The role and functions of shop stewards

Role has been defined as 'the actions performed by a person
to validate his occupation of a position. The role is linked to
the position and not to the person who is temporarily occupy-
ing it'. (See *Handbook of Social Psychology*, ed. G. Lindzey,
Addison-Wesley, 1954, Chapter VIII.) This definition may
be applicable for a closely defined role, but that of shop
steward is not usually precisely defined. Elliot Jacques (in
The Changing Culture of a Factory) observes that rigid adher-
ence to the role required by each situation becomes possible
only when the role itself has been precisely defined. This is
clearly not true of shop stewards, for the nearest approach to
role definition may often be found in the Shop Stewards'
Handbook (in those cases where they exist) and, with one
exception, these are certainly not meant to be definitive. Role
is therefore defined in this study as the actions performed by
a person to justify his occupation of a position (which is
usually imprecisely defined). The role is linked to a collection
of variables rather than to the position itself.

5

The role of a shop steward varies between workplaces and unions, and within both. Its content also depends on which of the interested parties is describing the stewards' role.

Unions tend to regard stewards chiefly as union administrators, as voluntary assistants within often large-scale organizations. Historically, they have been the chief recruiting agents, and so influence the numerical and organizational strength of the unions. They must maintain membership, and frequently collect weekly dues and check cards. They are also sources of information about shop practices and changes, and are expected to pass on information to their branch officials. Conversely, they disseminate information about the union, explaining policy to the rank and file. Moreover, they should ensure that union rules and the terms of collective agreements are observed, and report irregularities. They are involved in the event of accidents, and advise members of benefits and services available through the union to meet such eventualities.

If incentive payment schemes are in operation they should defend members' interests, discussing grievances with management. If a member cannot resolve a grievance, or if the problem is collective, the steward should assist in representations to management. In the event of continued dispute, the steward will be relied on to brief the full time official.

Management similarly regards the shop steward's role largely as a communications link, passing information between his constituents and management. He will be expected to state grievances arising from the shop floor and, having reached an agreement with management, will be expected to carry his members with him. As such, management may have a vested interest in his strength, regarding him as both representative and advocate. Additionally, he will be expected to lead, as well as reflect, shop floor opinion. The steward's representational role may be further emphasized by participation in joint consultative committees, about which he should also disseminate information. Finally, the steward will normally be acknowledged to assist with complaints between workers and management. Management may however endeavour to minimize this role, attempting to restrict the influence of the steward by stressing its own receptiveness to an individual's complaints and by pursuing policies which attempt to identify the interests of the firm and its employees.

Such, then, are the historical stereotypes of the steward's functions. They see the steward predominantly as a neutral agent, carrying information between union and management hierarchies. He is regarded as a recruiter and servicer of union members, a guardian of national agreements, and a useful aide in solving minor problems between management and members in the workplace, thus relieving busy, full time officers. His role in communications is assumed to be of an almost catalytic nature. However, these stereotypes do not accord with practice in many industries. The steward, while a lay official of the union, acknowledged by management as an accredited representative, is elected by union members in his shop, and usually feels primarily responsible to them. Though non-branch attending members may look to the steward for information about the union, their prime concern is with his ability to protect and advance their interests. As such it is their expectations, rather than union rule books and management conventions, which influence his behaviour, though other influences are numerous.

With full employment and buoyant product markets, workgroups have enhanced their influence, largely through the agency of shop stewards. Management styles have, by design or necessity, come to be more consultative than the old autocratic methods. Labour scarcity, expensive training, rapid technical change, and the teachings of human relations doctrines have emphasized the desirability of this style. In the last resort, the added impact of sanctions available to employees has induced management to lead rather than to drive, the consent of organized employees being necessary to continued operations. In large plants, obtaining consent demands a representational system, and thus places the occupants of this representative role in a strategic position. With the support of their members, shop stewards can determine the terms and conditions of consent. These developments have enabled shop stewards to emerge as a semi-independent force in the industrial relations system, with tenuous ties with the old established machinery. They have achieved bargaining functions on a multitude of directly and indirectly pecuniary topics, and on issues

7

concerned with workers' status and rights, which cumulatively have a powerful influence on the total working environment. This change, unevenly consolidated within British industry, partly reflects and is partly a cause of the changing power structure within and beyond the workplace.

The employment relationship is basically (though not exclusively) one of economic expediency, and within the workplace groups come together to further their own interests. These interests may not coincide with those of other groups, nor will they be identical with management's interests or those of their trade union, though all are to varying degrees interdependent. Thus, just as management needs the acquiescence of its labour force, so union full time officers need the support of their members. In practice, they rely on the advice of shop stewards, as well as on their own position and direct contact with members. Stewards are generally better acquainted with their workmates' views, can assess likely reaction to a given proposal, and it is they who supervise the day to day working of any agreement from the union side. Indeed, this fact has often brought stewards into negotiations with management on topics previously the exclusive province of district officials. Stewards have been largely responsible for extending the area which is subject to joint (i.e. union/management) regulation, and thus have developed negotiating or consultative rights on topics on which management would not previously accept the legitimacy of union officials' representations, let alone those of stewards. Their importance in some cases has meant that stewards negotiate at length with senior management, as they are beyond the competence of lower levels of the management hierarchy. Thus, the steward has engendered two separate but related changes—extending the range of topics on which his constituents can legitimately express their views and exert influence on management's decisions, and secondly in dealing with increasingly senior levels of management. The effect of both is to enlarge the competence of stewards and to enhance the status of the steward.

Continuous and detailed promotion of members' interests in day to day employment relations is not possible from outside the plant, and so close attention is inevitably left to workplace representatives. As noted, the parochial and short term interests of members do not necessarily coincide with those of the union. When in disagreement, work groups have felt and been free to pursue their objectives independently. This has meant that occasionally workplace leaders ignore the union, or act against the advice of its officials. The unions, for their part, seldom exercise sanctions against the opposition of a body of their members, for to attempt coercion is thought to risk the unions' future influence over their membership.

Thus, the emergence of powerful shop stewards places the unions in a dilemma. If they take action to restrict stewards' functions they will, in effect, reduce union influence over the working conditions of their members, and forfeit opportunities for gaining improvements. The advance of stewards is inextricably bound up with the achievement of the unions' central purpose, i.e. to advance their members' interests, for inevitably, in obtaining benefits for members, stewards increase their status in the eyes of the membership. Full time officials are overworked, their access to factories frequently restricted, some problems are urgent, others are long term. The increased volume of 'business' has meant, in practice, the devolution of wider functions to shop stewards. This is not an act of union policy, of explicit delegation, but rather a consequence of institutional rigidity in the changed post war environment.

The sources of shop stewards' power

(1) Trade union structure

British trade union structure has followed no preconceived pattern of development; British trade unions have developed to cater for different needs, in differing circumstances, and at different times. The result is a complicated structure reflecting little method and a multiplicity of organizational bases. Most prominent is horizontal organization, of either a certain occupation in different industries, or of categories of workers irrespective of industry or occupation, although a few incipient 'industrial unions' have tried to organize vertically. The implications of the occupational/general form of organization and its piecemeal development are that several different unions will have members in a factory, and a union's membership will cover many, possibly unrelated, industries. While the union may try to follow uniform policies for all members and all stewards, the variety of their workplaces will exert different influences, making standardization of other than minimal conditions and functions impossible.

The presence of members of many unions with different interests makes it difficult for outside full time officials to develop common policies and apply close supervision to one plant. Rivalries may inhibit their co-operation locally. Also, if plant-wide topics arise, it is difficult to ensure the simultaneous availability of the officials of several unions, thus making it expedient for management to deal with stewards. While some inter-union conflicts, e.g. over membership and demarcation, may affect or be generated by stewards, they frequently form joint stewards' committees to overcome the deficiencies of the union structure. The bond of common employment, experience of the employer, and the presence of bargaining opportunities within the plant stimulates joint organization, which thus facilitates concerted approaches to the employer. The committees' multi-union composition means that no single union can supervise its activities, and it may follow policies contrary to those of some unions or in defiance of all.

(2) Branch organization

In contrast with the generally haphazard development of trade unions, their internal administration especially at local level is not dissimilar. Rank and file members belong to a branch, and are able to participate in its policies by attending meetings, joining in discussions, and voting on resolutions and for officials. In practice, union branch meetings, like evening activities of many voluntary associations, are poorly attended. Professor Roberts states that, in large unions, branch attendances range from 3 per cent to 15 per cent, with a concentration between 4 per cent and 7 per cent in most cases.[2] A more recent sample survey of AEU and NUGMW branches revealed that average attendance at branch meetings was 9 per cent and 5 per cent, respectively.[3] The functions of the branch have been eroded over the years, being now predominantly administrative. Union members, it seems, dislike administra-

10

tion, and the democratic participation and control outlined in the rule books are not fully exercised.

For reasons of history, tactics, and economy, union branches are typically based on the place of residence rather than the place of work. Workmates in the same factory seldom belong to one branch unless they live in the same area and, even if these two coincide, the branch will normally be concerned with issues at other factories also. So, without a deep interest in union affairs, or an urgent problem at their factory, attending the branch is not an attractive proposition. Their steward will normally attend, and let them know what has transpired. Thus, direct contact between the union hierarchy and members is cut.

Secondly, stewards are often held responsible to the branch and its officers. However, unless membership is based on employment at one workplace, in which case branch officials may themselves be stewards, contact let alone co-ordination and control is usually minimal. Stewards' reports are records of past events. So, the low level of attendance, the preponderantly residential basis of branch membership, and increasingly close affinity of union members with fellow employees rather than fellow unionists elsewhere all emphasize the workplace as the centre of their attention, and the steward as the focus of union-type activities. The declining significance of the 'standard union wage rate', the sterility of branch activities, and the unity inspired by a common employer have contributed to this trend, revealing an institutional gap in trade union organization which the steward has come to occupy.

(3) Collective bargaining institutions

Typically, though not universally, collective bargaining is based on industry-wide institutions representing employers, formed into employers' associations, and the trade unions with members in these same undertakings. Bargaining is based on an industrial form of organization and is centralized, the terms of agreements being therefore generalized. As agreements cover many different employers, they cannot take account of the individual circumstances of each firm and offer opportunities for supplementary bargaining in the workplace. Indeed, collective agreements are not, of themselves,

11

legally binding documents and they can be supplemented to suit local needs. Although some employers' associations have continued to persuade their members not to exceed nationally negotiated basic wage rates, they have been unable to prevent other variations in workplaces. The national agreements provide the unions with guaranteed minimum conditions, which does not prevent employers providing more favourable conditions. Secondly, national agreements are not comprehensive, omitting many important topics, and providing only permissive guidance on others. Clearly, external machinery, understandably, fails to provide more than the framework for the regulation of employment relationships. It leaves innumerable topics to be settled locally—or more accurately, on a plant or company basis. The sketchy nature of national agreements ensures a role for workplace representatives who will be able to exploit any peculiarities of their immediate situation and thereby develop into bargainers.

(4) Union rule books

Union rule books vary in the provision they make for shop stewards, particularly in relation to their functions *vis à vis* management. All withhold authority to initiate industrial action, but most rule books, and the supplementary handbooks of the larger unions, leave to the steward's discretion which problems he passes to his branch or district officials, and when. Most imply that the steward should not negotiate agreements or reach 'understandings' prejudicial to national agreements, but leave him free to improve on them. Stewards are able to enlarge the vague 'job description' contained in union rule books as circumstances permit. Their scope varies, but, as in all human relationships, niceties distinguish apparently similar cases. Clearly, multi-industry trade unions find it difficult to prescribe the duties of their stewards *vis à vis* management strictly and comprehensively. While rule books *may* provide for the election, period of office, union administrative duties, and liaison with the branch and its officials, they largely fail to reflect the actual functions of stewards as bargainers. It is questionable how much influence a rule book exerts on a steward, other than for example his attendance at union meetings. His role is much more likely to be affected by his relations with other stewards, including those of other unions, with full time officials, by the nature of his constituency and constituents, and management itself.

(5) Full time officials

The history and militant image of shop stewards' movements frequently makes higher union officials apprehensive of the semi-autonomous position of shop stewards. The unions exercise a parental authority over them, almost invariably defending them from external attack, but are unable always to make them conform. The supervisory role of union officials is becoming increasingly difficult. Figures published for the early 'sixties show that the ratio of full time officials to members has been fairly steady over the post war decades, but the proportion of stewards to full time officers and of stewards to members has been rising dramatically in some unions.[4] The frequency of contact and the quality of informal relationships are very influential in determining how stewards are integrated into their unions, yet district officials can often establish only superficial acquaintanceship with their stewards. The problem is exacerbated when officials have stewards in many different and possibly small factories, and when turnover of stewards is high. Increased industrial relations activity in the workplace, and the overloading of full time officials, necessarily allows stewards increased discretion, as well as inducing them to forego assistance whenever possible. So, although stewards are lay officials of the union, they can continue, assuming stoppages are avoided, with very little supervision from full time officers.

(6) Work groups

For the rank and file, the shop steward is often the only contact with the union. It is common for members not only to think of the steward as the union, but to refer to him as such. The steward may have persuaded him to enrol, collects his dues, provides advice, spreads union news, advances complaints to management, sits on joint committees, etc. To other members, perhaps better versed in union affairs, his advice may not have the same predictability as that of the full time official, nor its implications of delay engender the suspicion that he has other more urgent problems. Unlike the steward,

13

the full time official is not on the spot, and cannot apply himself fully to the problems of one department or one factory.

The crux of the power of any shop steward is his ability to carry his members with him in a course of action. Without the tacit support of the work groups he represents (which may be several and diversely composed), the steward is impotent, and from management's point of view he may be a hindrance to the development of a good representational system. A steward may be closely watched by his members and his performance of the job assessed, but the pressure exerted on him by his members will vary in frequency, direction, and intensity. They may apply direct pressure for specific objectives, or allow him to interpret their implicit expectations. In some shops, the position may be keenly sought, in others it may be difficult to find someone to do the job. However, if a steward is to lead, he must be responsive to the changing needs and expectations of his group, for failure to respond—in the absence of complete apathy—will lead to his effective replacement.

The traditions, behaviour, and atmosphere of a factory may induce a certain kind of steward to emerge, and to adopt a certain attitude. However, the steward is not necessarily a mere reflection of his members and their views of management. He has his own personal qualities, may be able to anticipate their requirements, and use his initiative to project them. A successful record will help him maintain his position, though his tactics may not always command unanimous support. His leadership is strengthened by his superior knowledge, his access to information, and his participation in negotiations with management. He may persuade members by quoting information and circumstances they cannot challenge. The information available to rank and file members is at best imperfect and at worst non-existent, a source of security and power to stewards, though occasionally reacting against them. Stewards usually have few facilities to speak to their members collectively, and risk the distortion of messages circulating through the shop. Between mass meetings, which often have a large emotional content and activist tendencies, the steward may exercise his own discretion and members have little opportunity to form a consensus view. Information put out

14

by management may be ridiculed simply because of its source, particularly when there is conflict. The shop steward's leadership is reinforced by the almost inbred solidarity of trade unionists and the social consequences of non-conformity. Confidence in a steward may derive from his previous performance, and the steward can therefore expect to be followed, at least initially.

Thus, the steward's strength stems from his leadership being accepted by the work groups he represents. He cannot retain his leadership if he fails to fulfil their implicit or explicit requirements. He may be closely scrutinized by some of his constituents, but even where this occurs—and it may not be widespread—his position allows him discretion to lead as well as to reflect. The extent of this discretion depends on his experience, record, and personality, but may be extended by apathy in the workplace and the imperfect facilities for checking with, and being checked by his constituents, especially in the short run.

(7) Management

Whether as a positive policy, or as the unconsidered concomitant of decisions on other topics, management may enhance the scope, power, and authority of shop stewards. Historically, many managements would have preferred unions to develop along lines internal rather than external to the workplace. Being on the payroll means that union representatives are subject to the sanctions of the firm and enables the management to exert some influence over them. However, the results of the recently developed internal system have been somewhat different from those previously anticipated, for the labour market has changed and stewards can appeal for external support if necessary. Managements often prefer to deal with shop stewards rather than full time officials. Stewards are available, better informed of the history, facts, and implications of a shop floor dispute, and may obtain the acceptance of an agreement by their members more reliably. They will be concerned with its implementation, which may be easier if they have participated in its negotiation, while their continuous presence enables management to build up informal as well as formal relationships with them. Nor are all factory issues raised by stewards. Management, too, may initiate discussions and negotiations over changes in production, working arrangements, etc., and may seek their acceptance by stewards before making a change. If problems are important and urgent, management may prefer to involve stewards rather than outside officials.

On the other hand, management is often placed in a dilemma over what facilities to give stewards, on which topics to allow stewards' representations, which to disallow, and which to confine to outside officials and their associations. The tendency has largely been to keep issues within the workplace. Similarly, management faced with implicit threats from stewards who 'can't hold their members much longer in the absence of concessions' has to decide where to draw the line, on which issues and at which times resistance is justified 'at any cost'. The balance of comparative costs is always a fine one, but continuous surrender to stewards, especially over issues on which the claims of full time officials have been rejected, provokes little sympathy when management appeals to those officials to control their members. If a management is thought only to understand force, then a premium is placed on its use, and concessions to it make it a viable exercise. Such a management is adding to the power of militant stewards, and inducing its frequent demonstration.

Some management policies, and the absence of policy, add to the power of stewards. Decentralized supervision of payment schemes, procrastination in dealing with problems, inconsistencies of treatment by different managers, and arbitrary actions all facilitate the development of strong workplace representatives, all afford opportunities for militant activities. Management has quite widely fostered the growth of shop stewards, and promoted their wider areas of responsibility. How this enhanced role is exploited is often dependent upon management's behaviour. Encouragement of stewards has often reached the level of active policy. In many instances, it is a realization of the influential position which labour scarcity and the institutional structure afford the stewards. However, many managements are reluctant to accept the division of authority and loyalty epitomized by stewards, and regard the representatives of this division as an intolerable challenge to

16

their right to manage. Many resent the time consumed by acknowledging the existence of a pluralist system internally, regarding such time as non-productive and as a secondary part of the manager's job.

Any generalization about relations between stewards and managers is subject to qualification, but mostly they co-operate satisfactorily. Many managers go to great pains to achieve, and subsequently take pride in, cordial relations with their stewards. This relationship is often a personal one, in which both sides respect the individuals they are dealing with, rather than being achieved through the domination of one side by the other. However, their relationships involve conflict, for their objectives are dissimilar. Stewards will try to derive benefits from any situation, will seek to extend their own influence while limiting the freedom of management. They will strive for the most favourable interpretation of agreements and precedents, and in so doing enhance their own role. Thus, there is a nearly continuous struggle for power and influence, not only between stewards and management, but often between stewards and their unions externally. Both have their own dynamic, and are never settled in any final sense.

The challenge of shop stewards and its problems

Behind the institutional and behavioural features which have facilitated the development of the steward's role is a background of labour scarcity, of buoyant product markets, and the attitude that cost increases can be passed on to the consumer. Thus, in as far as the activities of stewards involve cost increases they are of public concern, particularly in the export industries. The incidence of wage drift reflects the success of stewards' pressure, though such indexes do not indicate all the stewards' activities. Not all disputes are about wages, and many issues which arise have only indirect effects on costs. However, increased bargaining in the workplace has implications for the development of centralized economic planning seeking to influence prices and the distribution of rewards. In certain industries, wages systems and structures, and the organization of work facilitate workplace bargaining. Others afford fewer opportunities, thus ensuring that equality of central influence and of sacrifice will be difficult if not impossible to achieve. Unions, and particularly stewards, are being asked to restrain the exercise of their local bargaining strength.

Wage drift not only affects labour costs, it also reduces the significance of industry-wide collective agreements. Between new agreements, decisions determining major components of earnings are taken at plant level, and so transfer both unions' and members' attention to this level. The widening gap between earnings and wage rates demonstrates this tendency, and the failure to consolidate improvements gained at workplace level into national agreements perpetuates the failure in regulation by external negotiators. Industry-wide bargaining has become unrealistic on the earnings and hours equation. Collective bargaining remains the principal method used by trade unions to achieve their objectives, but its location is increasingly decentralized. In some industries, it is open to question whether industry-wide negotiations are not now subsidiary. Because shop stewards are partly the agents of wage drift[5] they can jeopardize incomes *and* prices planning in individual workplaces, as well as undermining traditional bargaining institutions. The stewards present a challenge to both.

Another feature of their challenge is increasing unofficial industrial action, notably strikes and overtime bans. In present conditions, the power structure of trade unions more closely resembles an inverted pyramid, than the orthodox structure of their formal organization. Power, as opposed to formal authority, rests with the rank and file who may entrust it to external officials or seek to exercise it themselves. Unofficial action demonstrates the autonomy of union members and shop stewards, and its persistence illustrates the inadequacy of both union and management sanctions.

However, unofficial strikes and similar pressures are an almost inevitable consequence of the present devolution of bargaining activity to the workplace. Bargaining assumes sanctions available to both sides and, given full support, shop stewards can imply—if they do not always apply—measures to coerce management. Not all unofficial action is regarded unsympathetically by the unions, though some leaders have persistently led strikes in defiance of advice. Most unofficial

18

strikes are contrary to agreed procedures and may, as the Devlin Committee felt, 'be best explained by the fact that (in the post war period) men have felt freer to follow their own inclinations and to strike . . . if they want to.'[6] The causes of such strikes are seldom susceptible of exhaustive analysis. They may be analysed as practical exercises of bargaining strength, or emotional outbursts of moral indignation, as a safety valve for accumulated frustrations, as aggressive actions in support of new claims, or as a responsive defence of rights in the face of management encroachment. Strikes stem from causes which differ not only in their ostensible explanation, but in their more fundamental purposes.

The identity of stewards and the leadership of unofficial strikes is probable rather than invariable fact. It is not unknown for a steward's advice to be ignored by his members, nor is the unobtrusiveness of most shop stewards publicly recognized as a testament to their often steadying influence in workshop crises. However obscure the link between stewards and unofficial strikes, they in fact are often closely connected. As elected representatives of their members, stewards cannot fail to be involved in any industrial action affecting them. The economic damage caused by unofficial strikes cannot be measured easily, but they do represent the most apparent manifestation of the steward's independence. This freedom from trade union control exists potentially in most workshops, but despite increasing unofficial strikes (especially outside the coal industry) it is comparatively seldom exploited to the point of stoppage. The available power of the unofficial strike does much to enhance the influence of workplace representatives, compensating for the uncertainties induced by the absence of detailed and realistic agreements over their roles.

A similar manifestation of a steward's only partial reliance on his union is the formation of inter-union committees of stewards for an establishment, company, or for different companies in the same industry. The first two types fulfil a real organizational need, while the last is the logical extension of them. Joint stewards committees in the workplace commonly take on policy making activities, either ignorant of their union's position, to fill gaps in the official policy, or in defiance of it. Such a committee cannot be held answerable to any single union, though the union federations in the engineering, ship-building, and building industries have tried to integrate them. The similarity with strike action is apparent. Individual stewards may call strikes independently of their union or may use this as a last resort, but the potential freedom of committees to ignore union advice is even greater than a steward's to defy his union. Joint shop steward committees may pursue policies not sanctioned by the unions to which their members belong, and undermine union policy making bodies. Certainly, there is little guarantee that their policies will be acceptable to all the unions. On the other hand, stewards' committees often act as a focus for union activity in the plant, enabling management to solve plant-wide problems, and senior stewards to influence less experienced colleagues. By the same token, some committees have exacerbated problems for political as well as 'selfish' motives. The present system permits, or rather risks, abuse. It is surprising, and heartening, with the failure of unions and bargaining institutions to accommodate these developments, that irresponsible behaviour is not more common.

Stewards are concerned with the intricacies of workplace relationships. The tardy reaction to their emergence has left them much initiative, which may be welcomed or resisted by the management concerned. They have discretionary power, independent of their union, though their own values and their constituents' expectations prevent them operating in a vacuum. Their accountability is divided; they may make themselves variously answerable to their electorate, to branch and union officials, or to the need to retain the respect of their fellow stewards. Usually, regulation is exercised not by rules, nor by legal prohibitions, but by the social constraints of human relationships. This reliance may be insufficient though it will continue to determine the quality of day to day relationships.

Society's expectations of the system of industrial relations are changing. Industrial peace and the prevention of exploitation remain highly valued, but the freedom of the parties to pursue self-interest and reach 'private' agreements is no longer sacrosanct. Wages affect prices, one agreement affects another elsewhere, unofficial strikes cause widespread concern, and restrictive practices are widely condemned even if both sides are relatively content. All these workplace problems involve shop stewards, and any change which is sought necessarily affects them. Success will depend on an understanding of their position, and an appreciation of their difficulties as well as their faults. The challenge posed by shop stewards is not simply that of discouraging their less desirable activities: it is also to harness positively the forces their emergence reflects, and the opportunities it provides, to the benefit of both sides of industry, and of the community.

References

1. Handbook of Agreements in the Engineering, Shipbuilding and Ship Repairing Industries.
2. Roberts, B. C., *Trade Union Government and Administration in Great Britain*, G. Bell and Sons Ltd., 1957, p. 95.
3. Royal Commission on Trade Unions and Employers' Associations, Research Papers, No. 1. *The Role of Shop Stewards in British Industrial Relations* by W. E. J. McCarthy, HMSO, 1966, para 68.
4. Clegg, H. A., Killick, J., and Adams, Rex, *Trade Union Officers*, Basil Blackwell, 1961, p. 40. See also Marsh, A. I., and Coker, E. E., 'Shop Steward Organization in the Engineering Industry', *British Journal of Industrial Relations*, June, 1963.
5. See Chapter 7 for a definition and discussion of wage drift.
6. Final Report of the Committee of Inquiry into Certain Matters concerning the Port Transport Industry, HMSO, Cmnd 2734, 1965, para 17.

2

The Early Growth
and Development of
Shop Stewards

The British system of industrial relations, and its largely voluntary institutions, have evolved to meet immediate needs rather than being of planned or of revolutionary origin. The democratic political background to the emerging system ensured the rejection of revolutionary methods by most trade unionists, even when social conditions provoked deep discontent. Thus, for example, it was completely in character for the movement to turn to a new, democratically based political party when its very existence was threatened by the House of Lords' decision in the Taff Vale case in 1901. While their fellow trade unionists in France talked of revolution, British unionists sought constitutionally to achieve their aims.

Developments in industrial relations have been largely piecemeal, as unions and employers adopted expediency in dealing with problems as they arose, and solved them pragmatically. Consequently, *ad hoc* solutions to problems have created institutions and behaviour which quickly became entrenched, and, although much is of lasting value, trade unions' evolution and subsequent rigidity have raised problems. For example, some believe that the TUC (which originated to articulate the trade union voice and to act as a pressure group) should be given powers of leadership which the trade union movement in the late nineteenth century thought neither necessary nor desirable. So, too, with shop stewards, since their early duties consisted of checking the cards of new-comers, urging new staff to join the union, checking that exist-ing members were paying their dues, keeping a watch generally on the observance of union rules and practices in the shop, and making a periodic report to the district officer and his com-mittee.[1] Since this time stewards have enlarged their roles, but no parallel movement has brought their enlarged roles within the rules of our industrial relations system. The reasons for this lie not solely, however, in the British system, but also in the historical development of the steward's position.

Early developments

There has probably always been a spokesman for the unions inside an establishment once organization has started. Apart from those in the printing industry, however, these were not official. In printing, the unions have organized on the basis of chapels for a long time,[2] and the father of the chapel has always performed at least some of the functions of a modern shop steward, although not until the end of the last century did he engage in negotiations. In other industries, however, the history of shop stewards goes back to the period 1824–31. At this time, delegate meetings were held by the Foundry Workers' Union (then the Friendly Ironmoulders' Society) in districts in Scotland; each shop sent two delegates, one elected by the shop, one by the meeting itself. In addition, a financial delegate was elected in each shop to collect con-tributions, to give 'leaving lines' (i.e. certificates of employ-ment and union membership) to members leaving, and to see that new workers were union members.[3] At this time, also, the cotton unions exhibited at the local level some of the features of modern trade unions. 'There is the same federal superstructure—the shop steward (head shop men or "box stewards") forming the local committee.'[4]

These stewards appeared, however, to be largely content with collecting contributions and inspecting the cards of those starting work.[5] But, possibly unrecorded, their duties might have come to be representational, although with no extant records probably it was only on a minor scale. At the end of the nineteenth century, a powerful shop steward movement was built up in the Amalgamated Society of Engineers, which in 1878 gave its district committees power to appoint stewards. Not until the 'nineties did these stewards appear in any great numbers.[6] Their growth seems to have originated in the change in industrial techniques and workplace management, especially the introduction of piece rate, incentive systems, and high speed machine tools. So, a local representative with an intimate knowledge of the workshop was necessary to represent employees, since full time officials found it increasingly difficult to keep up with the bewildering variety of developments. These workplace representatives, however, aroused some suspicion from full time officials, who feared that they would make independent agreements with employers cutting across union policy, and that they might be used by employers to reach agreements which the official union policy could not support.[7] Probably, however, most stewards contented themselves with checking the cards of newcomers, urging newcomers to join the union and other day to day responsibilities listed above.[8] In the Amalgamated Society of Engineers, stewards were for many years unknown outside Scotland and Belfast, and their functions were limited to ensuring members were in benefit and that newcomers were Society men.[9]

The administrative duties of stewards were not all however. H. A. Clegg[10] notes that, as early as 1872, the Tees District of the Tyneside and National Labourers' Union reported that 'The shop stewards have worked like niggers and several disputes between the platers and platers helpers have been satisfactorily settled'. He notes that this suggests that the stewards' functions were being extended from recruiting members and collecting contributions to taking part in negotiations. Professor Clegg states that, within a few years, it was accepted practice for the official delegate to take the steward into the office when he went to talk to the employers. Also, in the case of the Amalgamated Society of Engineers, evidence suggests that stewards were trying to enlarge their scope to include negotiating functions. The Glasgow and District Engineers' and Boilermakers' Association in a minute of 1896 referred to 'Members of the newly formed Vigilance Committee of the ASE known as shop stewards' and complained of cases 'where individual men were quite satisfied with the pay and increases they had received but yet were practically driven out of the shop' by stewards.[11] This conflicting evidence suggests differences in the duties of stewards according to union, industry, job, location, personality, etc., and probably the behaviour of management and the vicissitudes of the trade cycle.

In the coal mines, factors such as management attitudes, militancy of the union, and the need for a check on work led to a local representative at an early date. Since 1845, when the Miners' Association of Great Britain was a vigorous force, miners had been demanding a representative to check the weight of their output, but were unsatisfied until 1860 when an Act of Parliament provided for a permanent official in each lodge to act as a checker of weights, or 'checkweighman'. This official became specially important in the miners' unions owing to a growing lack of correspondence between the membership of the district council and the groupings of workmen. As early as December, 1860, a miners' circular stated that such people negotiated, for it said: '. . . having a man of our own in every pit would render free access to our employees at all times and on all occasions reason would do the work of strife and contention.'[12] The Mines Regulation Act of 1872 slightly strengthened the position of the checkweighman and, despite bitter struggles with some employers, the numbers employed in at least one part of the country, West Yorkshire, rapidly increased.[13] Contemporary writers spoke of some of the fathers of the chapel in printing receiving similar powers,[14] and here, with the branch based on the workplace, communications with full time officials were better than where it had a residential basis. Indeed, the rule of geographical rather than workplace location of branches added to the difficulties of communication already created by local variations in technology and the increasing variety of industry.

The development of the shop steward was thus spasmodic and patchy, constituting a development in industrial relations which occurred piecemeal and pragmatically and which varied according to a variety of factors. As with other union developments, it became entrenched before the problems involved could be examined by the parties concerned and the public at large. Policy during the war, aimed to achieve other objectives, actually speeded up the movement towards workshop representation. At the same time, it provoked some activities which were long to colour the attitudes of the major interested parties towards stewards.

It was during the First World War that the fears of union officials, that shop stewards might disrupt and challenge the authority of the full time officials, were realized through the growth of the Shop Stewards' Movement.

The shop stewards' movement

Change through revolution is not readily acceptable in a democracy. Here, social institutions in the democratic framework affected by change should themselves broadly concur with a new direction being consciously adopted. This axiom is supreme in British industrial relations with its high regard for the voluntary principle. Consequently, advocates of revolutionary change are regarded with suspicion by the major parties in collective bargaining—the trade unions, management, and government. The Shop Stewards' Movement was so regarded, and it is pertinent to ask how such a revolutionary movement developed in a country so dedicated to constitutionalism, except for a small minority. G. D. H. Cole[15] traces two factors underlying the growth of the movement. He points to the disarmament of the official union movement in the face of the international situation, and the fact that the outbreak of the First World War led to the suspension of the ordinary sanctions behind trade union bargaining. Secondly, he instances extensive industrial unrest, and its mobilization in organizations readily capable of workshop form. These dissatisfactions were later accentuated by the dilution of labour and the relaxation of some customary trade practices, following the Treasury Agreements of March, 1915.

The Shop Stewards' Movement was firmly rooted in the engineering industry, and usually the local workers' committee consisted of workshop representatives.[16] Its rapid expansion was brought about by dilution and other changes calling for effective workshop organization, by the weakening of the engineering unions following the Treasury Agreements, and by widespread industrial unrest during the war.

26

The Movement originated on the Clyde, its powerhouse being the Clyde Workers' Committee—the rump of the Central Withdrawal of Labour Committee—which remained in being after the Clyde strike of February, 1915.[17] Clydeside had been among the areas in which, before the war, union members had been most active in seeking to appoint shop stewards. Also, several unofficial and semi-official bodies based on steward and workshop organization had come into existence there before 1914. The Socialist Labour Party was influential, always stressing in its industrial propaganda the importance of workshop organization in obtaining control in industry. More generally, the prewar neglect by the unions of the growth of workshop organizations[18] especially on the Clyde with its dearth of full time officials, also contributed. This neglect allowed local, unofficial movements to develop and encouraged attitudes more local than national. The background to this development was the increases in the number of stewards immediately before 1914. Many unofficial stewards were elected, in unskilled as well as skilled unions, though the former remain inadequately represented in the wartime Shop Stewards' Movement.

The war transformed the position of shop stewards since many, especially those officially accepted by their unions, became negotiators and representatives in dealing with the foremen and management on many workshop problems.[19] In effect, the Treasury Agreements and Munitions of War Act of 2nd July, 1915, by introducing dilution of labour and 'leaving certificates' (employees could not leave their jobs without the consent of their employers) demanded such representatives, since a union official was needed to implement these concessions. They were also able to negotiate as technology advanced apace under the impetus of war and as piece rates became more prevalent. Ironically, therefore, it was the three main parties to wartime collective bargaining, Government, management and unions, who speeded up the advent of shop stewards. Yet, certain developments in fact caused the alienation of the three major parties.

The spark which set the movement alight was the strike called by the engineering shop stewards on the Clyde against the Treasury Agreements. For a fortnight, under the leadership of the Central Withdrawal of Labour Committee (the nucleus of the Shop Stewards' Movement) 8,000–10,000 engineers struck demanding a wage increase to keep pace with the increased cost of living. They attracted, however, the wrath of the Press and of public opinion by disturbing the supply of munitions and acting against the advice of their full time officials.[20] The Committee, however, won most of its immediate aims, though remaining concerned about abuses in the dilution of labour and in the system of leaving certificates. This discontent was not allayed by the Amending Act of January, 1916, which stated that dilutees (unskilled workers replacing the skilled) should receive skilled men's pay and laid down safeguards in the use of leaving certificates. The Committee struck unofficially early in 1916 against the government's policy, some receiving prison sentences.[21] Undeterred, however, an unofficial strike committee remained in being, linking with others to form a National Workers' Committee Movement to oppose compulsory arbitration and create industrial unionism and workers' control of industry.

From the beginning, the movement spread. Workshop committees of local stewards sprang up around the country, usually covering a big city, such as Sheffield, or a wider area, such as Merseyside. Most were content to take their lead from the Clyde Workers' Committee, to accept its policies and constitution. This Movement was strengthened since most employers, wishing to operate dilution and leaving certificates schemes smoothly, were forced to grant *de facto* recognition to shop stewards and the workshop committees.[22] Stewards reported to their organizations on all introductions of dilutee labour, readjustment processes, reduced wages or threats to established union customs; but it was the steward in the workplace upon whom the ordinary member increasingly relied. The majority of shop stewards were not members of the Movement, however, contenting themselves with detailed workshop readjustments.

Many stewards in the Movement were not content merely to negotiate but were also fed on a diet of political ideas by numerous political movements. Thus, the Socialist Labour Party, a Marxist body, counted all leading members of the

Clyde Workers' Committee as adherents except William Gallacher (then in the British Socialist Party) and David Kirkwood (who belonged to the Independent Labour Party). The Socialist Labour Party believed in revolution with an industrial take-over by the workers and the dissolution of Parliament instigated by Socialist members. It regarded existing trade unions as bulwarks of capitalism to be destroyed. Consequently, it wanted the Movement to form a new industrial union, and became very critical when its demands were not met.

The influence of the Guild Socialists was far less direct than that of the Socialist Labour Party. They advocated ownership of all means of production by self-governing committees, which would then hand them over to be administered by the workers organized in national guilds. These would, in turn, pay rent to the central co-ordinating organ of society. This last would be a Guild Congress, which would co-ordinate national economic development, settle disputes between guilds, and co-operate with bodies representing consumers. All these managing bodies from the workshop to the Guild Congress were to be democratically elected and subject to the control of their constituents. Their establishment was to be by 'encroaching control' accomplished by union pressure to be applied peacefully. These doctrines, depending on gradualism, alienated the Shop Stewards' and Workers' Committee Movement; consequently it, and the Guild Socialists, moved apart in the period 1918–19.

The Syndicalist influence was not strong, only being found in Amalgamation Committees, groups of stewards favouring a distinct revolutionary union movement and calling for violent industrial action. These were disintegrating by 1915.

The Clyde Workers' Committee itself sought control of engineering establishments by workers and management representing the state (not absolute control along Syndicalist lines). The main instrument was to be an all grades committee, composed of representatives of all grades of workers within an establishment. Its desires were revolutionary in involving the abolition of private ownership. The constitution of the committee put its objectives in the following order:

(*a*) To obtain increasing control over workshop conditions.

(*b*) To regulate the terms upon which the workers shall be employed.

(*c*) To organize the workers upon a class basis and to maintain the class struggle until the overthrow of the wages system, and the freedom of the workers and the establishment of industrial democracy, had been obtained.

'It was,' says Pribicevic, 'perhaps the first major workers' organization to put workers' control in the form of an immediate demand instead of an ultimate objective.'[23]

The Movement believed that emancipation of the workers was to be achieved by themselves, rejecting the state Socialist ideas of nationalization and progressive state action leading to industrial unions as instruments to overthrow capitalism. It left unargued the state's role and whether its industrial organization could administer industry, nor did it examine the mechanics of the struggle for power except to suppose it would be confined to, and decisive in, industry. They presumed that the state would disappear after the fundamental change.

After the 1917 Bolshevik revolution in Russia, the influence of Russian Communism over the Movement increased. Writing in the Movement's journal *Direct Action*, in December, 1919, Gallacher and Campbell stated that the social and industrial organizations would have to 'fight the capitalist state, not to take possession of it but to smash it', and the task of the workers was to develop repressive functions which would 'reduce the capitalist minority to political and social impotence'. These ideas were borrowed directly from Lenin who expounded them in *The State and the Revolution*. The Second Congress of the International enthused the shop steward delegates with the Communist ideal, and in *The Worker* of 14th February, 1920, joint control was repudiated, the National Conference officially declaring workers' control to be the objective. In 1921, the National Conference adopted a clause in the Constitution of the National Workers' Movement stating that 'the objects of the organization shall be the overthrow of capitalism and the setting up of workers' control and management of industry shall be developed'. Only the

30

engineering section of the Committee, its administrative apex, queried the practicability of these ideas and proposed an interregnum of state appointed managers.

During the war, the engineering and allied industries took the lead, but later the mining industry took over. In 1918, the Miners' Federation of Great Britain had defined its fundamental demands as nationalization and the concession of a partial control of the mines to the workers. Indeed, at the beginning of 1919, a threatened national strike over these and other demands was only averted by the establishment of the Royal Commission on the Coal Industry. Among the miners' demands to it were the establishment of a representative Mining Council, and of coalfield and pit committees, to which management under public ownership should be entrusted. Later developments led to the General Strike.[24]

The railways were also centres of militant organization, and numerous national or local 'Vigilance Committees' or line committees were formed to guard the interests of sections of workers and to ensure that their grievances received quick attention from the union. These Vigilance Committees were ready centres for the ideas of the Movement as they were unofficial and not subject to union control; together with the vehicle builders of the locomotive shops, they made railwaymen active in the Movement. Thus, it was predominantly workers in engineering, railways, and the mines who chiefly supported it.

Yet, by the early 'twenties, this revolutionary Movement had petered out. There was no realistic means of attaining its ends, and the idea of one industrial union, based on the workshop and workers' committees and envisaged as a weapon to smash the state, was bound to fail. There were no 'industrial' unions in the country. Secondly, there was little thought about the role of the state in the proposed general strike, it being assumed that it would 'wither away' as Marx predicted. Again, the unions would not have had sufficient technical expertise to run industries and to fulfil their functions of representation, protection, and education. In an established democracy, they had to remain free and voluntary, which was hardly possible if they were to run industries. British unionists have been traditionally suspicious of becoming involved in management

31

since they dislike the idea of facing their own representatives directly or indirectly in collective bargaining. In any case, since the unions were at the basis of the politically democratic labour movement, there was no hope of securing such control unconstitutionally. Indeed, the whole ethos of the Movement ran contrary to the traditional approach of the union movement and most parliamentarians to problems of social change. In a country where constitutionalism was so firmly embedded it was unrealistic to expect unions and workers to use their industrial power against the legal government on such an issue. Yet the authorities became concerned by this Movement, thinking it more typical of the feeling of the rank and file than it actually was. It was felt that the popular demand for 'workers' control' might be moderated if national, local, and workshop committees discussed not only wages and conditions of employment but also problems of efficiency and management.[25]

The very real problems of industrial relations of the prewar years, accentuated by the Shop Stewards' Movement, served as a background to the setting up by the government in 1916 of a committee, under the chairmanship of J. H. Whitley, to recommend permanent means of improvement in relations between employers and workers. The Reports of this committee are landmarks in the history of British industrial relations; of specific relevance here is that supporting the establishment of joint committees at the workplace. These works committees were to represent employers and workers, and to promote industrial harmony and efficiency. However, after spirited growth between 1917 and 1922, most collapsed, those surviving being more restricted in scope than as envisaged by the Whitley Committee. The composition and functions of this shortlived attempt at workplace consultation varied widely, and unfortunately there is no evidence of the role played by stewards, nor whether they modified more extreme demands for workers' control. However, a lasting hierarchy of Whitley Councils was set up in some sectors, notably in the civil service and the post office. Perhaps the most important long term effect of the Shop Stewards' Movement was to tarnish the shop stewards' image as being revolutionary, and therefore made it extremely suspect. This image persisted through the inter-war period, and was exacerbated by events in the early part of the Second World War. After the First World War, the leaders of the Movement became even more extreme politically, many becoming connected with the Communist Party in Great Britain, formed in 1920, and directing their energies to its cause.

Partly because of these revolutionary tendencies, some unions brought stewards within the scope of their rule books in order to control them. This is true, for example, of the Amalgamated Society of Woodworkers and the Amalgamated Society of Engineers. Some employers also moved towards formal recognition. In engineering, stewards had no nationally recognized rights in workshop negotiations until the end of the First World War. The Engineering and National Employers Federation and a number of engineering unions, including the Amalgamated Society of Engineers, concluded shop steward and works committee agreements in 1917 and 1919. These agreements, consolidated in the Procedure Agreement (in force today and applying to thirty unions) provided that, in federated establishments, any society party to the agreements might appoint stewards for shops, and that their names and their unions should, on election, be indicated officially to the management. These national agreements did not include recognition of 'grades' of steward or joint shop steward organization in the workplace, with the exception of works committees, and still do not do so. The convenors of shop stewards authorized by the Amalgamated Engineering Union in 1920, and the Joint Shop Stewards' Works Committees and Confederation stewards sanctioned by the Confederation of Shipbuilding and Engineering Unions twenty-seven years later, do not enjoy formal recognition by federated engineering employers, though individual managements can negotiate with them. Yet the 1917–19 agreements represented 'a most important incentive for engineering stewards',[26] since they gave them the basis of formal status in the factory 'even though this was not as comprehensive as some of them may have desired'.

Even this process of constitutionalization could not, however, prevent the disappearance of many representatives *qua* representatives during the period 1920–35. 'Successive reports by the AEU's executive council suggest that the breakdown in domestic negotiations was widespread though not necessarily complete. The evidence shows however that many firms were no longer prepared to tolerate the activities of stewards.'[27] Given the stewards' image in general, it is not surprising that during the depression of the 'twenties and 'thirties, firms ended negotiations with stewards, and that the Amalgamated Engineering Union's full time officials failed to strengthen their stewards' position beyond the agreement of 1922.

In 1920–35, there appears to have been little shop steward activity beyond 'minimum' union administration, and no evidence is available either from union histories or published works on the General Strike. Firstly, with the onset of recession in 1921, and the depression, union organization in the workshop was badly hit. Largely, representatives either ceased to exist as such, or were reduced to being watchdogs, merely ensuring that employers complied with minimum terms and conditions of employment. With labour markets favouring employers, stewards could attempt little but to maintain the *status quo*, and were presumably often victimized. Even in those industries which traditionally had stewards, such as printing, the fathers of the chapel, although still existing, had few opportunities to be other than defensive in their dealings with management. Also, the radical characteristics of the Shop Stewards' Movement probably alienated many union leaders, who may have countenanced even the disappearance of some stewards rather than fight employers on the issue. This attitude might have been buttressed by the opinion that the way to economic recovery was by cutting wages to reduce prices, thus making goods more competitive. Such an atmosphere was hardly conducive to strong workshop representation. Finally, although important during the war, stewards had not long been accepted in industry, not being considered as essential as they are today. Their disappearance would not therefore have created much opposition.

The Second World War and after

With the improvement in the trade position in the later 'thirties came a revival in the numbers of stewards. Evidence from the AEU shows[28] that numbers increased since average payments to stewards in 1935–8 were nearly three times as great as for the preceding four years. However, it was not until the Second World War that this increase became really marked. It is widely, though not universally, accepted that, during the 1939–45 period, stewards channelled their energies into more constructive activities *within* the official framework than in the First World War.[29] Mrs Inman[30] notes that, during rearmament and early war years, an unofficial stewards' organization developed in the engineering and shipbuilding industries, and as early as 1936 there were signs of a movement in the aircraft industry. Workers in this industry were to be the vanguard as the unofficial movement developed during the war.

Early in April, 1940, the first meeting of a national shop stewards' council took place in Birmingham and planned to develop nationally. Political aims were not mentioned, the council concentrating on wage grievances among munition workers, and particularly those in shipbuilding. Apparently, some of the rank and file wanted to follow such an organization, and the author notes feeling among them against the union officials who once again were drawn into official collaboration with the government, which was considered by some members as tantamount to 'selling out to the bosses'. An aggravating fact was that educational work to explain government and trade union policy to the rank and file had not been extensively developed by the union movement. Further, experienced trade union officials at headquarters and in the districts had accepted jobs in expanded government bodies, their successors lacking experience and being often less effective. This contributed to the growth of workplace bargaining, as stewards became more numerous and important in order to cope with dilution problems and quickening technological changes, as in the First World War. Indeed, this process was extended as the branch declined in importance due to difficulties of attendance at branch meetings.[31] Opportunities were therefore plentiful for stewards to act independently of the unions, as well as facilitating the growth of the unofficial organization.

Yet, in practice, the influence of the unofficial shop steward movement over ordinary members was severely limited. This can be illustrated by the number of strikes, which increased after 1941 despite being condemned by the Communist Party, which had much influence through its members in the unofficial shop steward movement. As Professor Turner has observed, these figures appear to convict the Communists of agitational incompetence.[32]

The strength of the movement was the aircraft industry in the Midlands and the engineering shops and shipyards on the Clyde. Twice, in the winter of 1940-1, shop stewards on the Clyde settled strikes through the intervention of men well known in public life, in each case bypassing the constitutional negotiating machinery. Inman notes that these disputes indicated that the movement drew strength from the tactless and highhanded actions of some foremen and managements, and from lack of co-operation between managements and men. Finally, in the engineering industry, stewards did not always pass grievances to the Confederation Committees, not being represented on them, and many stewards took care to negotiate as much as possible themselves.

The impact of the unofficial stewards' movement was marginal, for two principal reasons. Firstly, the Communist Party encouraged the war effort after the invasion of Russia in June, 1941. Secondly, to ensure better co-operation at plant level, joint production committees were organized under the auspices of the government, after—but not necessarily as a consequence of—the Engineering Shop Stewards' National Council meeting in London during October, 1941. These committees were supported by the Engineering and Allied Trades Shop Stewards' National Council largely through *The New Propeller*, the organ of the unofficial organization in the aircraft industry. The functions of these committees varied widely. Sometimes, they took the lead in discussions with management, even on questions normally reserved for the collective bargaining procedure, such as wage rates, and the role of the stewards other than as committee members was small. Elsewhere, the committees' discussions concerned technical and production questions, others being left to the stewards. The committees varied in strength but the best were where trade union organization was strong, where the stewards actively supported the committee with the aim of winning the war, where representatives were technically able, and where the stewards joined them to discuss problems and solutions.[33] Certainly, shop stewards did much constructive work during the war, and this had many byproducts. For example, Jefferys observed that 'the prodigious growth in membership and influence of the AEU was by no means an automatic process. It rested largely on the painstaking work and feats performed by the stewards up and down the country who gave up much of their limited spare time and evenings and fre · quently sacrificed their earnings to devote their attention to improving the condition of their workmates'.[34]

This attitude encouraged unions to appoint stewards more freely, and accounts for their increased numbers during the Second World War. More fundamentally, however, such factors as technological developments, necessitating changes in jobs and job rates, the dilution of labour, the relaxation of trade union custom and practice, and innumerable new regulations to be explained to members all brought an increase in steward numbers. Further, the increasing numbers of women in trade unions during the war demanded shop stewards to represent this special group, women stewards again swelling the total. Marsh and Coker noted that the AEU's survey of 1947 revealed that almost 5 per cent of stewards were women.[35] In addition, the Engineering Employers' Federation agreed with some unions, including the AEU, that steward approval had to be sought by federated employers before labour was diluted in any establishment.[36] This increased the importance of stewards.

The numbers of stewards have also increased since the war. After examining AEU records, Marsh and Coker[37] suggest that the increase was about 50 per cent between 1947 and 1961. They showed that the increase in federated engineering establishments was proportionately greater than overall, a possible explanation being that the 1919 Agreement makes recognition of stewards obligatory on federated firms, firms outside having no such duty. However, as the AEU relies more on its stewards than some unions, its growth of shop steward numbers may be somewhat higher. Marsh and Coker indicate that the numbers of AEU shop stewards in federated establishments increased three times faster than that of manual workers in such establishments in 1947–61.[38]

The total of shop stewards in the United Kingdom has been variously estimated at 90,000, 100–120,000, and 200,000. The first figure was suggested by Clegg, Killick, and Adams in 1961, though admitted as 'little better than a guess'. Marsh and Coker suggested the second in their article referred to, and the third is taken from the TUC Annual Report of 1960. All are estimates and it is not possible to do more. Our own approximation, whose basis is elaborated in Chapter 5, is of between 125,000 and 133,000 shop stewards or their equivalent.

Over the post war decades, the ratio of full time union officials to union members has improved little, against a dramatic increase in the number of shop stewards. This means that officials have to cope with increasingly large numbers of stewards, which clearly complicates the problems of union control of workplace activity. The supervision of full time officials must often be minimal, and wide responsibilities are in practice now carried by stewards. In many cases, the continued functioning of unions rest on their voluntary efforts. This strengthens many shop stewards *vis à vis* their unions, and emphasizes the problem of controlling them. With imperfect and inadequate official union links with the workplace, the precise relationship between workplace representatives and the unions externally becomes important. A useful starting point is the instructions to stewards in union rule books, and the advice in handbooks published for their use, for these documents outline the formal relationship between stewards and their unions.

References

1. Phelps-Brown, E. H., *The Growth of British Industrial Relations*, Macmillan, 1959, p. 297.
2. The earliest mention of the chapel system is to be found in Joseph Moxton's *Mechanical Exercises*, 1682.
3. Fyrth, H. J. and Collins, Henry, *The Foundry Workers*, Amalgamated Union of Foundry Workers, 1960, p. 26.
4. Turner, H. A., *Trade Union Growth, Structure and Policy*, George Allen and Unwin, 1962, p. 85.
5. Fyrth and Collins, *op. cit.*, p. 128.

6. Jefferys, James B., *The Story of the Engineers*, Lawrence and Wishart, 1945, p. 137.
7. Roberts, B. C., *Trade Union Government and Administration*, G. Bell and Sons, 1957, p. 58.
8. Phelps-Brown, *op. cit.*, p. 287.
9. Jefferys, *op. cit.*, pp. 165–6.
10. Clegg, H. A., *General Union in a Changing Society*, Blackwell, 1964, p. 27–8.
11. Quoted in Clegg, H. A., Fox, Allan, and Thompson, A. F., *A History of British Trade Unions since 1889*, Vol. 1, Oxford University Press, 1964, p. 432.
12. Machin, Frank, *The Yorkshire Miners*, National Union of Mineworkers, 1958.
13. *Ibid.* p. 248.
14. Webb, Sidney and Beatrice, *History of Trade Unionism*, Longmans, Green and Co., 1950 edition, p. 299.
15. Cole, G. D. H., *Workshop Organization*, Oxford University Press, 1923.
16. See Pribicevic, B., *The Shop Steward Movement and Workers' Control*, Basil Blackwell, 1959.
17. Cole, G. D. H., *op. cit.*, pp. 28–35.
18. *Ibid.*, p. 36.
19. *Ibid.*, p. 42.
20. Pelling, H., *A History of British Trade Unionism*, Penguin Books, 1963, p. 151.
21. *Ibid.*, pp. 154–5.
22. Cole, G. D. H., *op. cit.*, p. 66.
23. Pribicevic, B., *op. cit.*
24. Cole, G. D. H., *op. cit.*, p. 127.
25. See Pelling, H., *op. cit.*, p. 160.
26. Marsh, A. I. and Coker, E. E., 'Shop Steward Organization in the Engineering Industry', *British Journal of Industrial Relations*, June, 1963.
27. Marsh and Coker, *op. cit.*, p. 175.
28. Jefferys, *op. cit.*, pp. 241–2.
29. Marsh and Coker, *op. cit.*
30. Inman, P., *Labour in the Munitions Industries*, HMSO and Longmans, Green and Co., 1957, p. 401.
31. Inman, *op. cit.*, p. 400.
32. Turner, H. A., *The Trend of Strikes*, Leeds University Press, 1963.
33. Inman, *op. cit.*, p. 388.
34. Jefferys, *op. cit.*, p. 201.
35. Marsh and Coker, *op. cit.*
36. *Ibid.*
37. *Trade Union Officers, op. cit.*
38. *Ibid.*, p. 40.

3

Unions, Shop Stewards, and Rule Books

A common problem facing a shop steward is that of reconciling his role as a representative of union *members* with that of representing the *union* in the workplace. The unions, as institutions, face a similar dilemma in regulating their stewards' activities without stifling initiative. This chapter examines the nature of the instructions and advice given to stewards by different unions' rule books and in some shop steward handbooks. As will be seen, their provisions are sparsely and vaguely worded, though a primary source of reference for all union officers. The failure of some rule books to define realistically a steward's function and responsibilities may reflect the attitude of a union to workplace representatives. Some unions appear to want to play down their significance, others deliberately leave their role relatively undefined to allow enlargement as dictated by local circumstances. In other cases, such brevity may merely reflect the difficulties of making rules for the wide range of industries and workplaces involved. Further, there are variations between unions in the method and degree to which executive leadership is balanced by lay control. However, contact between a union's higher officials and its stewards can take many forms, and unions may well prefer informality. Nevertheless, few rulebooks have been amended to cover the new roles of stewards, or to build in additional facilities for them within the unions' administrative and policy forming (or informing) *machinery*.

We first outline in detail the provisions made for stewards

in the rule books and handbooks of seven unions. The dates of the rulebooks are given where possible, and occasional reference is made to the procedural sections of some collective agreements.

The Transport and General Workers Union (1962)

The union issues a handbook of some eighty pages to shop stewards, but its rule book deals with them in a few lines. Rule 11 provides that 'shop stewards shall be elected wherever possible by the membership in organized factories, garages, depots, wharves and on building jobs', but it does not list their functions. Rather, it goes on to assure stewards of the union's 'fullest support and protection'. Emphasis is given by the provision that '. . . immediate inquiry shall be undertaken by the appropriate trade group committee into every case of dismissal of a shop steward with a view to preventing victimization either open or concealed'. The same rule, alternatively, allows a branch to appoint collectors and/or shop stewards to gather members' contributions. Those who undertake these duties are remunerated in accordance with General Executive Council regulations—currently $7\frac{1}{2}$ per cent of contributions collected. The union formerly debarred members of the Communist or Fascist Parties from holding either lay or full time office.

Shop stewards are supervised by their branch, defined in the members' handbook as 'the place to which the member takes his problems . . .'. The subordinate role of stewards to branch officers is further emphasized in the Members' *Handbook*, viz.: 'Where collectors are appointed they operate under the supervision of the branch secretary. This also applies, in certain cases, to shop stewards, who have the responsibility for dealing with minor matters arising at their members' place of work.'

The shop steward's Handbook

The *Handbook* offers advice to T & GWU representatives in all industries, acknowledging that the steward *is* the union as far as members are concerned, being thus responsible for the image of the union. The need for unity and loyalty is stressed, and stewards are asked to help members with grievances and problems, either personally or via the union. Stewards are reminded of their responsibilities to recruit new members, maintain membership, and turn 'card holders into trade unionists'. They are advised to know their agreements and the procedure, never to depart from the latter and, if in doubt, to consult the district officer. Informal agreements, custom, and practice are stressed as no less important.

In relations with managements, stewards are counselled not to bypass the foreman, for tactical as well as courtesy reasons. Skill and honesty rather than noise and sharp practice are recommended in negotiations. Stewards should build up the loyalty of their members by their handling of grievances, to keep them informed, etc., to be confident of support and room for manœuvre in negotiations. Stewards should pass on union news, circulate the union journal, stimulate interest in branch activities, and encourage participation.

Looking after members' problems in the workshop is put forward as the steward's main function, but close liaison with the district officer is again firmly recommended, particularly at all stages of major developments. The *Handbook* stresses that he is normally necessary in important negotiations. A systematic plan for progressing grievances is recommended, emphasizing the need to obtain and check the facts, to follow procedure and the manner in which to approach management, reporting back to the member concerned, other members, and the branch, etc.

The *Handbook* then outlines the major features of the Factories Act, and the steward's role in its enforcement. He is advised to press for and support joint factory safety committees, to report all accidents and, with management's permission, to check the accident book. The pamphlet outlines the procedure for claiming, and the level of, state and union benefits.

Six pages are devoted to joint consultation and its uses, outlining the topics normally acknowledged as appropriate to it, and recommending it as a source of information as well as a body which may rectify some grievances. Some differences of function between negotiation and consultation, and the consequent need for different approaches, are explained. Stewards are advised to report to the branch officer anything arising on a JCC which appears to conflict with union policy or rights, and the union explains that for these reasons it likes to control the nominations for worker representatives.

The *Handbook* tells stewards how to recruit new members, how to write letters, make reports, and claim union financial benefits. It then outlines the structure of the union, sources of information within it, educational facilities, and covers local Trades Councils and the TUC.

The National Union of General and Municipal Workers (1965)

The NUGMW makes provision for collecting stewards, under the direction of the Branch Secretary and the Branch Committee, and shop stewards, who fall under the District Committee. (Often one member holds both positions.) The collecting steward can sign membership cards, receiving 10 per cent as commission. In addition, 'he shall, in a legitimate manner, see that the workers at any place of work become members of the union', and 'shall notify the Branch Secretary of any infringement of the rules of the union coming to his notice'.

There are several methods of appointment or election of NUGMW shop stewards, depending 'whichever is the most suitable in a particular case'. This can be by majority vote on a show of hands, or by ballot, of the members at the workplace, or 'by a majority vote on a show of hands at a branch meeting', or 'by common consent among the members that the office shall be filled by a member appointed by the District Secretary'. Stewards must give the District Committee 'an undertaking to observe the rules of the union, and at all times act in conformity with the decisions and policy laid down by the governing authorities of the union'. District secretaries are to be informed of all appointments. With the permission of District Committees, branches may levy members to provide funds for negotiating stewards for loss of earnings not otherwise provided for.

The NUGMW is unique in that its rule book states that shop stewards' duties shall be as defined in the shop steward's *Handbook*.

The shop steward's Handbook

This emphasizes the recently extended work of stewards, particularly in joint consultation. Their organization and protective function in the workshop is acknowledged. Stewards are expected to set a good example by observing union rules, attending branch meetings regularly, and keeping informed of union activities and policies. A thorough knowledge of agreements, of PAYE, National Insurance, and bonus calculations is desirable. The union's educational facilities are recommended. The *Handbook* covers methods of election, recruitment, and collecting duties—stressing the aim of a 100 per cent membership.

Stewards must take an interest in members' welfare, from individual grievances to safety, and the Factories Act. Poor attendance at branch meetings is deprecated but acknowledged, and the consequent value of stewards as linking the union's machinery and the rank and file is stressed. They are asked to publicize the union's activities and services, particularly in passing on information during national negotiations. Conversely, they should 'report all matters of consequence on organization, members' requirements, grievances settled and practices of management that may affect working agreements' to the branch secretary.

On handling members' complaints involving negotiations with management, the *Handbook* says that 'no hard and fast line can be drawn between cases that come within his power to deal with and those which should be referred to the Branch for action by District officials. In the absence of specific instructions from the District Secretary he should be guided by the custom and practice of the industry.' However, the *Handbook* suggests that the following can usually be dealt with at shop level—breaches of agreements or established working conditions, piecework and rates subsidiary to agreements, overtime working, holidays, canteens, and general factory welfare, and personal matters affecting individual employees.

The *Handbook* then emphasizes that 'any question implicating the terms of a signed agreement or which can be properly regarded as a subject for such an agreement must be reported without delay to the branch secretary who will refer it to the

District office. This applies also to important questions of principle by which a number of members would be affected.' The steward is reminded that he has no power to sanction strikes, and that, should his members suddenly stop work, he should ascertain the cause, advising an immediate resumption. He should then start the procedure to discuss the grievance with management. Stewards are told always to approach management accompanied by the member concerned in any question, or by another shop steward. Moreover, before any approach, he should know that the member, or the majority of members, approve of the action he proposes.

The *Handbook* refers to the inter-union workplace machinery of the CSEU, but where none exists, shop stewards 'should nevertheless consult and co-operate with stewards of other unions if joint action appears to be advisable'. They should attempt to reach agreement with other unions' stewards particularly on questions of demarcation, but any attempts by such stewards to persuade the unions' members to transfer must be reported immediately.

Joint consultative machinery is recommended to stewards, whose potential contribution to its effectiveness is underlined. The importance of safety, and of recording all accidents is stressed. The *Handbook* then briefly outlines the structure and organization of the union, concluding with copies of the procedural sections of three collective agreements.

The Amalgamated Engineering Union (1960)

Like many other craft and ex-craft unions, the AEU is characterized by considerable decentralized and lay authority, this being embodied in the District Committee. AEU shop stewards are authorized by the District Committee, and are responsible to it.

Rule 13 provides that 'District Committees shall authorize the appointment of shop stewards and shop committees in Works and departments in their respective districts . . . and committees [are] to be under the direction and control of the District Committee'. Stewards elected by the members cannot function without the District Committee's approval. Moreover, 'the powers and duties of shop stewards and shop committees shall be defined by the District Committees with the approval of the Executive Council . . .' . The union allows that 'stewards or shop committees may appoint a convenor, who must himself be a shop steward . . .', but again the District Committee defines his powers and duties.

Shop stewards, as lay officials, are strongly represented on the District Committee, thus helping to define their own powers and duties and those of other stewards. Rule 13 states that 'shop stewards shall be directly represented on the District Committee on the basis of one shop steward for every 5,000 members or part thereof . . . elected at a meeting of shop stewards called by the District Secretary in December'. The District Committee must convene the shop stewards and convenors at least once a quarter, paying 10s to stewards and 12s 6d to convenors attending. Smaller fees are paid to those who only submit written reports to the meeting.

Rule 13 lays down four minimum duties for AEU shop stewards, shop committees, and convenors:

(a) To examine and sign the contribution cards of all members at least once a quarter. Members refusing to show their cards to the shop steward are to be reported to the District Committee. This also applies to pay tickets.

(b) 'To use every endeavour to see that all men starting are duly qualified trade unionists.'

(c) To see that all persons are complying with the practice of the shop and district, and receiving approved rates.

(d) 'To report to the District Committee any case in which the position is not satisfactory and cannot be adjusted within the shop.'

Stewards are to 'interview' foremen or other management representatives on questions arising in the shop 'only when accompanied by another member . . . provided that no question involving a principle, change of practice or stoppage of work shall be determined in any shop until it has been reported to and ratified by the District Committee, and that in all matters shop stewards, convenors and shop committees shall act within the rules and principles laid down by the District Committee and the Executive Council . . . and in national or district agreements.'

Stewards must have twelve months' adult membership, with discretion for new shops. Rule 29 permits payment of dispute benefit for 'members discharged for acting on legitimate shop deputations, authorized, or afterwards sanctioned, by the Branch or District Committee . . .'.

The shop steward's Manual

The *Manual* aims to guide stewards in general principles, and emphasizes the trust placed in him by his members. The *Manual* assumes that the steward will represent them for the next twelve months in matters connected with their employment. Stewards' representation on the District Committees and their quarterly meetings is used to illustrate special channels open to them in the union.

The AEU divides the steward's job into two, placing recruitment and maintenance of membership before the 'maintenance of the best possible wages and working conditions for our members', although the *Manual* devotes more space to the latter. The aim suggested is that of 100 per cent membership via at least quarterly card inspections, but in recruiting stewards are told that a volunteer outweighs a 'conscript'. Stewards should keep members interested in the union's work, encourage branch attendance, and circulate the union's journal. Special sections detail the recruitment of juvenile and women workers. On promoting members' interests, stewards are advised to ensure that wages, etc., at least equal those provided for by collective agreements, if necessary by examining payslips, and if they fall below these to report to the convenor or district secretary. 'Justifiable grievances' are to go through normal procedures, and stewards are reminded that many of these involve members first approaching the foreman. Frequently raising trivial matters with the foreman is regarded as bad tactics, and stewards should be sure always to have a witness. Any settlement is to be reported immediately to the convenor or district secretary. Stewards' bargaining opportunities are described thus: 'Remember that you, at shop or factory level, have the best chance to settle any grievance. The higher the stage in procedure, the more difficult it becomes to reach mutual agreement. One of the employers' most familiar arguments at national level is "we cannot grant you this for the workers at this firm, because your members all over the country will want the same".'

The procedure for fixing piecework prices or times in 'federated' establishments is then covered; stewards in doubt should, again, consult the convenor or the district secretary. The role of the convenor is outlined, all correspondence to the district secretary going through him. Stewards should fill in quarterly report forms, and also inform the convenor and district secretary of developments concerning wages, conditions, or membership.

The function of a Joint Shop Stewards Committee under the CSEU is mentioned, with the need for constant co-operation between various union workshop representatives. Joint production committees, and the steward's role in the event of accidents, are explained.

Finally, the *Manual* advises stewards to be firm but flexible, to remember they do not function separately, and should never decide nor act in isolation. Supporting services, from the convenor and District Secretary to specialists in the head office, are impressed on him, as is his responsibility to keep them informed. The union recommends its own and external educational courses, and gives a reading list. The final section contains procedural and other agreements with the EEF and the AEU rules relating to shop stewards.

The Electrical Trades Union (1965)

The ETU rule book places its stewards explicitly under the (elected) area full time official, ordering them to obey the executive council (Rule 17). 'In each shop, yard and undertaking of any description a shop steward shall be elected at a meeting convened for that purpose . . .'. An existing steward must call such a meeting annually for the elections. All voting is by show of hands, with a second vote between the two leading candidates, failing an absolute majority. In the event of a tie '. . . the candidate to be elected shall be determined by lot'. Area secretaries are to be notified of the election of a steward.

The union provides for senior stewards 'in large undertakings where there are shop stewards in several departments'.

These *may* be appointed by the stewards themselves, or 'if they consider it necessary then a meeting of all the members employed in the shop . . . shall be convened for the purpose'. The senior shop steward must already be a shop steward, and is annually re-elected.

The rank and file can call a meeting of all members in the shop. A shop steward may do this '. . . at such times as he thinks proper and whenever requested to do so by one quarter of the members so employed . . .'. Members are to produce their cards for inspection or periodic collection by the steward on notification. Any member refusing, and failing to give good reason to a *meeting of members* on the job, is to be reported by the steward to his branch secretary.

Unusually, the ETU provides for the co-operation of their members 'on jobs where less than four members are employed and a shop steward of another trade has been appointed . . .' with another union's steward, in inspecting cards and maintaining of union conditions.

The ETU rulebook outlines a comparatively detailed list of duties. These include reporting to the area secretary on card inspections, or violation of rates, conditions, and customary privileges at the workplace, and all cases of overtime work. He is to interview the foreman or a manager on any question arising on the job 'provided that no question involving a principle, change of practice or stoppage of work shall be determined by the shop steward or other members on any job until the matter has been reported and the decision has had the approval of the appropriate Area official or . . . the Executive Council'. He is to ensure that union rules are observed in any strike or lockout. He can only accept conditions on a job where members have given prior approval, and if conditions comply with union rules, agreements, and policies. The ETU emphasizes inter-union co-operation in the workplace, in that the steward is to work in conjunction with other shop stewards and works committees. However, he cannot commit his members to any joint decision without their consent, or contrary to the policies of the union. Finally, the steward is to perform any other duties required from time to time by the area official or executive council.

Rule 10 clarifies the role of the steward in relation to the individual member. The member is to report to his branch any matter of the conduct or business of the union, or the conduct of any of its officers or members, but any matter concerning his employment to his shop steward, or failing one, with his area official.

Stewards must have one year's membership and male stewards must be over 21, but women qualify for appointment at 18. Members of the Communist Party cannot hold office (Rule 9). While the payment of contributions is the responsibility of each member, twelve or more employed together may appoint a money steward, with branch approval. He is paid 5 per cent of his collections.

The ETU has recently improved its communications machinery, and Rule 18 provides for national and area meetings of shop stewards (and others) on industrial lines. National Industrial Conferences are to be convened between each Biennial Delegate Conference of delegates from electrical contracting, electricity supply, shipbuilding and ship repair, engineering, and other industries. Secondly, area secretaries are to convene annual Area Industrial Conferences of shop stewards from the same industries, to elect delegates and submit motions to the National Industrial Conferences. Further, area officials may call meetings of stewards in a given section of industry, to aid communication on issues as they arise. The executive council consider such meetings to be of benefit to the members concerned.

The National Graphical Association (1964)

The NGA makes the formation of at least one chapel and the appointment of a father of the chapel obligatory on members in all offices recognized by the union, if there are four or more members. The members are to draw up rules for administration, to be submitted to the appropriate branch for approval. Chapel collectors are to be appointed by the chapels, and the FOC must sign monthly subscription lists, indicating those in arrears, before dispatch to the branch.

Part time union officers, whether branch secretaries or presidents or fathers or clerks of chapels, are given special compensation against victimization. They receive benefit at the rate nationally agreed for their job, unless all members are affected by a strike or lockout. Ordinary members receive one third or one half the minimum grade rate of the branch, depending on how many are involved.

The rule book emphasizes the role of the branch, rather than of the chapel and its officials, in rectifying breaches of union rules, encroachments on the customs of the trade, the regulation of apprenticeships, hours, wages, etc. Where settlement is impossible, branches and regions must refer to the executive council.

The British Iron, Steel and Kindred Trades Association

Works representatives in BISAKTA are branch officers, elected at special meetings each December. The branch committee is to supervise ballots. 'Any member refusing without reasonable cause to take office in a branch when nominated shall be fined 2s 6d.' Rule 9 further provides that 'No person . . . who has been guilty of . . . acting in any way injuriously to the Association should be permitted to hold any office whatsoever in the branch . . . or hold any position as an officer or representative of the Association'. The executive council has wide discretion in interpretation here.

Works representatives are 'to interview employers when instructed by the branch committee on matters arising in the works affecting the terms or conditions of employment' of branch members. However, if 'the matter is one of urgency the works representative may, after consultation with the branch secretary, arrange to interview the employer's representatives before receiving the instructions of the branch committee, but the case must be reported to the branch committee without unnecessary delay. The works representative should, as far as is practicable, be accompanied by the branch secretary, together with a small deputation of . . . members concerned.' The Association explicitly withholds allowance for loss of work from deputation members, except for works representatives and branch secretaries, for whom allowance is made only for unavoidable loss. Such claims go forward to Central Office only after the approval of the branch committee.

The procedural role of the works representative is given in Rule 19, which states that should a dispute arise 'which in any way might lead to a stoppage of work, arrangements shall be made for the works representative accompanied by a deputation to interview the employer or his representative. . . . Failing a settlement by this means the branch secretary shall without delay report the whole facts of the dispute to the divisional officer. . . . It shall not be permissible for any member(s) to strike employment without the authority and sanction of the Executive Council.'

When payment of contributions at branch meetings is impracticable, the executive council may authorize other arrangements through branch stewards, who are paid quarterly on an incentive basis.

Rule 31 allows for the payment of 'victim benefit' to any member dismissed for taking active part in the affairs of the Association. No handbook for works representatives is published.

The Draughtsmen's and Allied Technicians Association (1965)

DATA provides for the annual election of an office committee of at least three members, the number of members permitting. The committees are to ensure the observation of all company, local, or national agreements and to report difficulties to the branch secretary or divisional organizer. In disputes, it is their first duty to report to the branch secretary and divisional organizer to obtain advice on how to conduct negotiations. The committee is thus responsible for all negotiations between the office and management, 'unless it is considered advisable that such negotiations should be conducted through the branch or divisional council or through the executive committee'. The committee is to report the results of negotiations to members, and to the branch council on its exercise of its functions, ensuring that the corresponding member carries out his duties satisfactorily to members and the council. It is to form the nucleus to represent members on joint committees with other workers. The committee is to be 'linked up' with the Branch council, kept informed of Association affairs, and to meet fortnightly, although special meetings of the committee or office may be convened.

The corresponding member has to place all correspondence and information dealing with the Association before the committee. A corresponding member is to be elected annually in each office, retiring members being eligible for re-election. DATA lays down that, in large offices, there shall be at least one CM for approximately every thirty members.

A single CM is to act as secretary and treasurer of the office committee; otherwise, the committee selects one of the CMs to act in these capacities. The corresponding member is to collect members' subscriptions, circulate the union's journals, notices, leaflets, etc., and maintain records required by the Association. He is to advise the branch secretary and divisional organizer of any changes in office conditions, wages, etc., and must attend meetings of CMs convened by the branch council. Committee and corresponding member's expenses are paid by the branch secretary, after approval.

In offices with insufficient members to form an office committee, the members are to appoint a CM being themselves responsible for the functions of a committee.

Conclusions

A glimpse at these union handbooks and at the response to our questionnaire shows that union rule books are not exhaustive in providing regulations for shop stewards. This is a common and accurate supposition among students of industrial relations, though this survey shows that union rule books display wide differences in approach and comprehensiveness. Some unions, such as USDAW and NUFTO, which have shop stewards, fail to mention them; others, notably the ETU, have made efforts to outline their position and duties and also to cater for their increased importance. Therefore, it may be useful to summarize the major provisions made for stewards, noting issues on which rule books are silent.

In addition to those analysed above, the rule books and *where issued* steward handbooks of another twenty-three unions have been studied,[1] being referred to below. Some of these unions have recently amalgamated, but their rule books nevertheless indicate the different approaches to, and provisions made for, workplace representatives.

(1) The presence of shop stewards

Although, in practice, most stewards are elected by the members they are to represent, this is not always made clear. Some rule books prescribe that stewards are to be elected, e.g. T & GWU, CWU, AUFW, ETU, but few provide for suitable special meetings. Others simply state, unspecifically, that they 'be appointed'. Two, the NUGMW and the CEU, allow the district official or union executive to appoint stewards in certain circumstances. Unions vary in their requirements of when stewards are to be present. Some state that they 'shall' or must be appointed or elected, e.g. the ETU, NUSMW, CEU, DATA, Bakers, CWU, etc.; others lay down that there 'shall' be stewards 'wherever possible' (TGWU) or 'wherever necessary' (NUGMW), and others that there 'may' be stewards, e.g. HDEU. As noted, some unions make no provision at all. Perhaps the greatest emphasis on workplace representatives is among the printing unions, and those with a large proportion of members in the building industry. The NUPBPW and the NGA insist on the formation of a chapel and the appointment of a FOC when there are, respectively, two or four members employed. The ASW and the PTU oblige the first member on a site to act as steward, pending the employment of more and an election. In the latter union, the district secretary can convene a meeting for this purpose, issuing credentials immediately on the site. If there is no steward in a bakery, the 'senior man' is to organize an election; in the ETU and the ASW, the 'retiring' steward has this responsibility. Among the white collar unions, DATA members must undertake the duties of corresponding member and office committee failing sufficient numbers for normal elections. The method of election and the electorate are rarely specified, though the ETU stipulates a show of hands, laying down procedure if there is no overall majority. The common practice appears to be a show of hands by the members of the union to be represented,[2] but in some cases, e.g. BISAKTA, elections are at branch meetings.

Although, in practice, most stewards are eligible for repeated re-election this is infrequently stated. Some unions do not state a period of office, e.g. AEU, NUSMW & C, but many specify twelve months, e.g. NUPBPW, ETU, PTU, and AUFW. Fathers of the chapel in NATSOPA are subject to quarterly re-election, and the NUFTO *Handbook* recommends twice yearly elections.

The qualifications of those eligible to stand are rarely mentioned. Among others, the AEU, ETU, and rubber workers make one year's union membership a condition (except in new factories), while the CEU recommends three years at the trade where practicable. The ETU is the only one to stipulate a minimum age, and the HDEU alone in explicitly debarring those holding supervisory positions. Members of the Communist Party or Fascist Parties are not eligible in the ETU and HDEU by rule, while members or supporters of 'prescribed bodies' are ineligible in the CAWU as are 'members acting injuriously to the Association' in BISAKTA.

The NUPBPW and the Bakers' allow for deputies on different shifts, as does the CEU in other circumstances, but only the Bakers and DATA recommend specific maximum limits to constituency size, though the AUFW does this more generally.

Only one union, the Bakers, *explicitly* allows for stewards to be removed by shop meetings while in office, though the confidence of members and union executives is a *sine qua non* to most stewards. In several unions, the executive body can replace a steward 'in the interests of the union'. The emphasis on obeying rules implicitly makes any steward in breach of any rule liable to lose his credential, though by whose authority is seldom specified.

(2) Collectors

Practically all the unions studied, except, notably, the AEU, either permit the appointment of collectors or make this a function of the shop steward. In practice, many stewards hold both positions, and no union prohibited this. Generally, the procedure for collecting and paying dues is outlined in detail, often fairly severe penalties being provided for any breach. The commission paid to collectors varies widely, from $2\frac{1}{2}$ per cent in NUFTO to 10 per cent in the NUGMW and NUPE. Most ex-craft unions pay 5 per cent, while the Tailors and Garment Workers rewards collections from female members more highly and the BISAKTA operates an elaborate incentive scheme.

While stewards may benefit from being collectors, few rule books provide for specific payment to stewards for their other duties. NUBSO provides for loss of earnings to be covered by the branch, NUGMW branches can levy members to cover stewards' 'loss of earnings', the NUSMW & C allows 8s 6d per hour for employment lost, the PTU allows a nominal sum for out of pocket expenses, the CWU payment of an honorarium by the branch, ASSET covers any loss of salary, and chapel funds in NATSOPA have to 'pay the FOC for his services'. The AEU pays stewards 10s and convenors 12s 6d for attending quarterly meetings. Thus, rule books do not provide for stewards' remuneration other than to cover loss of earnings and expenses, though some do not explicitly cover this. BISAKTA emphasizes this financial constraint to works representatives and deputation members.

(3) The answerability of stewards

In few unions could a steward give a straightforward reply to a question on this topic. His reply would vary with the problem he faced and, while for example he might normally report to his branch secretary, this may be only monthly. But the secretary himself would be subject to both the branch meeting and, between meetings, the branch committee. The frequency of such meetings varies, and the branch is not always coterminous with the factory.

Though responsibility to the district committee is stressed, e.g. by the AEU, NUGMW, PTU, and ASW, a distinction must be drawn between these predominantly lay committees and the full time district officials.

Stewards often have a choice of contacting a part time branch official or a full time union officer in an emergency, while sometimes informing both. Some unions stress reporting to and being instructed by shop or factory committees, or shop meetings. In others, stewards, *ex officio*, carry the status of branch officials. Given the democratic checks and balances in

56

most constitutions, it is often impossible to define answerability clearly, and informal arrangements are doubtless of much greater significance than rule book provisions. The relations with the various officials 'above' the steward may determine the pattern of communication; so may the ratio of stewards and members to these officials.

In practice, the room for manœuvre within the rules varies widely between unions. For instance, the AEU rules are vague about stewards' negotiating responsibilities, but the *Handbook* specifically emphasizes their unique opportunity for improving members' conditions, encouraging them to bargain at this level. Moreoever, stewards are responsible to the district committees, which have very strong steward representation. The ETU stewards are directly responsible to the area full time officials, rather than to a committee consisting predominantly of lay members and, as the rule book is more specific about stewards' duties, they may therefore operate closer control. Bargaining activities at factory or site level are encouraged in the ASW *Handbook*, stewards again being responsible to a largely lay management committee. In these and other unions, there are strong traditions of membership control over full time officials. They are subject to periodic re-election, which further weakens their powers *vis à vis* the stewards, who can influence support or opposition to officialdom.

In other unions, the position of stewards, on paper and in fact, is not so strong. For instance, the NUGMW particularly emphasizes obedience to the rule book, allowing district secretaries to define matters which may or may not be dealt with by stewards. In fact, district secretaries have a commanding position in relation to both stewards and district committees. The union has expelled stewards for unconstitutional action.[3] The T & GWU operates fairly close control over most stewards' activities, made easier by a low ratio of members to full time officers. Having investigated ten (federated) engineering firms in Birmingham, Derber[4] showed that T & GWU officials were in frequent contact with members and stewards, often being asked for advice as well as negotiating. He concluded that T & GWU stewards were subject to much closer control by their district officials than were AEU stewards. Thus, while the traditions of the industry or the plant may exert pressure towards uniformity, union affiliation affects the degree of their autonomy in practice.

BISAKTA seeks to control its stewards closely, particularly insisting on the improvement of branch officials in their negotiating activities. Expulsions have occurred for disobedience of the rules. In the printing industry, the close liaison between FOCs and branches, and the orderly pattern of chapel rules, helps regulate the duties of FOCs. Moreover, the existence of a labour supply closed shop adds to the authority of the unions' full time officials.

(4) Local officials

Local full time officials are extremely important to the shop steward, often constituting his direct point of contact with the union. Furthermore, they are able to interpret union policy on local matters and deal with local problems. Their power and responsibility under union rules therefore closely affect that enjoyed by stewards. For instance, in the AEU, the district committee's powers limit those of the district secretary considerably, and here the official will often only enter into bargaining if the stewards cannot succeed. In addition, they are re-elected every three years, which inhibits 'unpopular' control over stewards or the district committee. Similarly, ETU area officials are periodically re-elected, their responsibilities being limited to 'such duties as the Executive Council, or branches in their area with the consent of the Executive Council, entrust to them'. (ETU Rulebook, Rule 12.) In other unions, e.g. BISAKTA and NUGMW, district officials have much greater power; in the former, they are not even encumbered by elected district councils or committees, being directly under the jurisdiction of the executive council.

However, the formal constitution of a trade union is only the skeleton, and it is impossible to specify the exact position of a full time official since the experience and personality of individuals influences their power. Without examining individual cases, it is therefore difficult to estimate the influence of local full time officials, even within the same union. Moreover, the writers are acquainted with AEU officials who exercise considerable influence over their stewards and members, and T & GWU officials who with difficulty avoid repudiation by their membership, despite their very different constitutional positions. In practice, many members regard full time officials as mediators, between the stewards and management, and as legal claims experts rather than as their representatives.

Immediately, stewards consider themselves responsible to the members who elect them, but seldom do rule books prescribe regular meetings in the factory or on site to obtain mandates or authorization. The NUGMW (*Handbook*) and the ETU require stewards to have members' approval before taking action or accepting conditions of work. A few rule books enjoin stewards to call shop (or equivalent) meetings when a proportion of the members so request: e.g., ETU one quarter, PTU, unspecified, and NATSOPA, an agreed proportion. The NUFTO *Handbook* recommends frequent and regular shop meetings, but generally provisions for democratic processes are scanty. The Bakers' Union *Handbook* constantly recommends extended communication with individuals, but only NUFTO is explicitly confident of employers regularly providing facilities for frequent instructional meetings. Some unions compensate by emphasizing the importance of shop committees, looking to them to supervise stewards' activities and to keep them in touch with the members, and with union rules and policy, e.g. CWU, AUFW, Hosiery Workers, and the Office Committees of DATA.

(5) Internal communications

Many unions examined provide for special meetings of stewards. AEU stewards attend quarterly meetings of the district committee, having special representation on it. The PTU and NUSMW & C hold quarterly meetings of stewards in the different areas. These are provided for at unspecified intervals in the ASW and DATA, while the ETU area secretaries must now call annual area industrial conferences of stewards in several industries, and may convene stewards merely *ad hoc* to improve communications. Other unions, of course, also do this, but are seldom explicit in rule books. The ETU rules include national conferences of stewards from defined industries. Of the unions examined, only the ETU and the Tailors and Garment Workers' rules specify the organization of meetings between stewards at different plants of the same firm, though this is mentioned in the ASSET *Handbook.*

The Chemical Workers' general secretary is to send copies of correspondence relating to their shops to stewards and branch secretaries. The executive council of the AUFW can explicitly communicate direct with stewards; all NATSOPA correspondence is to go through FOCs, and HDEU full time officials visiting a factory must contact stewards before meeting management.

(6) Convenors

Only the AEU, ETU, PTU, and AUFW provide for the appointment of convenors or senior stewards, although both ASW and CAWU *Handbooks* recommend it. Of these, only the PTU says that a convenor 'shall' be appointed but does not state how. In the AUFW, the shop committee 'decides', in the ETU the senior steward may be elected by and from the stewards, or from them by the membership, while the AEU allows stewards or shop committees to appoint one. A few unions, though not defining the position, allow for a system of seniority among members of shop, factory, or office committees; e.g. Hosiery Workers and NUFTO *Handbook.*

(7) Duties and functions

As shown, many rule books make stewards responsible for collecting union dues. Allied to this, many emphasize their duty of gaining new members and maintaining membership, particularly in the need to approach new employees. The maintenance of members is, in part, provided for by the holding of card inspections, which most craft and ex-craft unions stipulate. These may be monthly, as in the HDEU and ASW, or quarterly. Usually, members in arrears are to be reported to the branch or district officials, but the ETU and ASW provide for those in arrears to appear before meetings of members on the job.

Several unions, e.g. the AUFW and the NUSMW & C, stress the duty of informing members of branch meetings, while the HDEU insists that stewards always attend. More generally, union rules often charge the steward with disseminating information from both branch and other sources to the membership. On the other hand, the steward's duty of passing information about workshop conditions, wages, hours, etc., is more often stated, and periodic reports in writing are usually to be supplemented by reports of all changes. Any violation of rates, customs, privileges, agreements, or union rules is often specified for immediate report to branches, branch, or district committees or full time officials. Some stewards are required to check that all members receive union rates, and follow union or district practices. Others provide that stewards keep the relevant local body informed 'on all matters', or maintain close contact.

Some unions, notably the TGWU and USDAW, do not list any functions for stewards in their rule book, while those in printing provide for chapels to draw up rules and duties for the FOC, but give an outline in the rule books. A few, e.g. the AEU, ETU, and DATA, allow for the performance of duties 'delegated' to stewards. Others, often individually, allocate additional duties specifically. Most common is to report accidents, but others include reporting overtime, NUSMW & C and ETU; keeping lists of piecework prices, AUFW; ensuring the observation of union rules during strikes, ETU; notifying job vacancies, Chemical Workers and the printing unions; handling legal claims, etc. At least two, the NUSMW & C and the AUFW provide for a shop or pricing committee, rather than individual stewards, to handle piece-work or incentive schemes.

The predominant impression is that most unions, though there are exceptions, do not issue a detailed job description in their rule books. The duties mentioned emphasize the steward as a recruiter of members, a contribution collector, and card checker, a custodian of agreements and practices together with a communications responsibility, particularly in passing information out of the factory. The steward's representational and negotiating role is often unmentioned and, where mentioned is constrained rather than promoted by the rules. But some, notably the white collar unions and some with a craft tradition, are relatively open in allowing this function. Two manual unions, the Bakers' and NATSOPA, protect the steward by giving him an exclusive position in progressing members'

61

complaints, grievances, and disputes, but many others provide members with alternative channels.

The most frequently encountered rule about the steward's negotiating role is that taking up grievances with management representatives is permissible provided no question of a *principle* or *change of practice* or stoppage of work shall be determined without prior external approval. Some ex-craft unions, e.g. the CEU, leave the situation undefined and few prescribe which topics come within the steward's competence, or otherwise. Several unions, e.g. AUFW and Chemical Workers, insist on stewards being closely superintended in negotiations by shop or office committees, while others, e.g. the Hosiery Workers, ASSET, and DATA, allocate this function to committees rather than individuals. Others require stewards to be accompanied, or to inform the convenor and, in a few cases, stewards are to take up issues only under instruction from the membership or branch committees. The ETU and NUGMW (*Handbook*) appear to require the consent of the members before any settlement is accepted.

Clearly, the rule books offer little from which to glean the steward's bargaining functions in day to day factory life. The less formal *Handbooks* give more indication, though a few are at pains to play down this role in relation to recruitment. As they offer advice on conducting negotiations they now appear to accept that this is a major stewards' function. It is difficult to account for its scanty coverage in rule books. Certainly, the unions know of the real dangers of stewards not taking opportunities, or making bad agreements, or breaking union rules, but some seem even more afraid of promoting, or acknowledging, a shift in the balance of power in the unions' central activity—that of bargaining.

(8) Relations with other unions

Only three unions studied provided for building up contact with stewards of other unions. Of these, the ETU goes furthest in enjoining stewards to work with other stewards and to join in joint shop steward committees. DATA's office committee members are to represent members on joint committees with other employees, though again there is vagueness. The CAWU allows its representatives and committees to co-operate with other unionists for common purposes, and the NUGMW *Handbook* which contains rules rather than advice recommends inter-union co-operation at the workplace. Otherwise, this topic is unmentioned, though many unions approve of joint workplace committees. In view of the proliferation of joint shop steward committees, this reticence again indicates the inadequacy of rule books in guiding stewards.

(9) Shop steward handbooks

For many stewards, the union's rule book and handbook are the only formal guidance received. Only one union, the NUGMW, makes its handbook binding on stewards, others being issued principally to offer advice about parts of the job, his responsibilities, his priorities, and how to function successfully. Often, the advice is very similar, e.g. in how to prepare a case before negotiating with management and how to conduct such negotiations. However, several interesting points emerge from the composition of these handbooks. In some, e.g. USDAW's, the recruiting function is very heavily stressed, in others, e.g. the ASW's, the representational role. Unions place different explicit emphasis on loyalty to the union, and when and on what topics stewards are to refer to external union officials varies quite widely, e.g. AEU and ASW stewards compared with those of USDAW and the CAWU. Some describe union constitutions fully; others outline financial benefits at the expense of guidance on other topics. Practically all emphasize the duty of consultation when in doubt, and a steward's duty to pass information to members, to 'turn cardholders into active union members'.

There is very little evidence about internal communications between unions and their members. A Gallup Poll conducted in 1959[5] found that 140 union members replied to the question: 'Where do you get your information about the affairs of your union, or don't you bother about it?' in the following way:

Shop stewards	35	Circulars	17
Notice board at work	34	Other ways	5
Talk at work	27	Don't bother	4
Union journal	18		

This admittedly slight evidence implies that information and discussion is concentrated on the workplace, rather than on the often poorly attended branch, and the steward's duty in informing members' discussions appears enormous. While this, and consequent emphasis on the steward's communication function in handbooks is not surprising, it is perplexing that so few unions provide other methods of informing either stewards or members directly of the union's affairs. Similarly, while only three unions refer to inter-union co-operation at the workplace, a further six mention it encouragingly in their handbooks.

Some handbooks are clear and concise on stewards' duties, e.g. NUFTO; others leave contentious problems open, but stress the need of external advice. Clearly, the assistance given by these handbooks is variable, but, without detailed study, their actual readership and impact cannot be estimated. At least, most are more attractively presented than the average rule book.

References

1. The other unions whose rule books and handbooks (where issued) have been studied are as follows: USDAW (1961); PTU; ASW; NUFTO (1964); ASSET (1964); CAWU (1964); AYFW (1964); NUPBPW (1960); NATSOPA (1960); HDEU (1963); NUSMW & C (1965); CEU (1963); NUBSO (1965); NUPE (1965); POEU; UPOW; AScW; ASLEF; NU of Hosiery Workers (1963); NU of Dyers, Bleachers and Textile Workers; NU of Tailors and Garment Workers (1963); Chemical Workers Union (1961): United Rubberworkers (1963); AU of Operative Bakers; and the Amalgamated Weavers Association.
2. Constituencies are normally based on union membership. The practice at the Ford Motor Co. Ltd., of basing constituencies for non-skilled workers on geographical workplace zones irrespective of union affiliation, is exceptional.
3. See Clegg, H. A., *General Union*, p. 113 and pp. 124–33.
4. Derber, Milton, *Labour Management Relations at the Plant Level under Industry Wide Bargaining*, University of Illinois, 1955.
5. Quoted in Selvin, David F., 'Communications in Trade Unions: A Study of Union Journals, *British Journal of Industrial Relations*, February, 1963.

4

Shop Stewards and Work Groups

Union rule books and handbooks constitute *one* guide for stewards' behaviour, though their comprehensiveness varies between unions. So, too, does their influence over day to day activities. A more immediate influence is the relationships between stewards and members in the workplace.

Relationships between stewards and their constituents are complex and variable, ranging from constituents allowing a steward wide discretion to interpret their requirements to specific pressure for defined improvements. A steward's activities may, continuously, be a subject of interest to only a few members, and pressures on him may derive chiefly from individuals. For example, an aspirant to his position may seize every opportunity to press points he knows to be popular with constituents. Dissident members may repeatedly raise trivial or even imaginary problems, and strong personalities may criticize his failure to be sufficiently militant. Clearly, many issues a steward raises with management will be of a largely individual nature, others having broader implications to involve *all* members. Sociologists have repeatedly emphasized the primary work group as an important determinant of behaviour, suggesting that informal leadership is bestowed on those most close to the norms and values which bind the group. Thus, while day to day pressures on stewards may stem from individuals, in the longer term they are influenced by the need to avoid repudiation by or, more positively, to maintain the approval of, their members collectively. In our experience, stewards take this as axiomatic, regarding their constituents as their primary source of reference. Consequently, recent theories of social organization in the workplace are important in an understanding of the relationship between stewards and their membership.

The group in industry

The importance of the primary work group in industry is now almost universally recognized. Perhaps the most positive recent recognition has come from Mr Allan Flanders, who has gone as far as to say 'under conditions of full employment trade unions may enter into agreements which neither they nor management have the power to enforce. They meet with resistance on the shop floor which cannot be crushed because neither party has sanctions strong enough to override the interests of the work group, enjoying as it does a life and authority of its own.'[1]

This recognition arose initially from the findings of the Hawthorne experiments, refined, but in many ways substantiated, by more recent research. Before the Hawthorne experiments, industrial psychology had been focused on the *individual* worker—by F. W. Taylor, Frank Gilbreth, and others, who studied the worker as an isolated unit of production, exaggerating the importance of the economic factor in work. From this, techniques of work measurement were developed, calculated to maximize the individual's efficiency, with similar attempts to optimize his environmental working conditions. They attached great importance to effective movements while working, sufficient rest periods, effective lighting, and suitable economic incentives to stimulate maximum effort. They concentrated attention on the worker primarily as an isolated production unit, regarding him as principally, if not exclusively, motivated by economic factors. It was supposed that he could be enticed to maximum productive effort simply by promises of reward or threats of punishment.

These simple theories were challenged by the work of some early sociologists and social psychologists, Elton Mayo being most important. He discovered that the primary work group was an essential element in work life, and argued that this group life could lead to contented workers prepared to co-operate in production for the good of the company. Mayo and his researchers created a new attitude to labour–management relations which stressed the great importance of group relations and led away from economic deterministic theories. This thought has been supported by many post war writers.

Some developments in primary group theories

More recent developments of industrial group theories have come from the United States. Significantly, L. R. Sayles postulated[2] that the primary work groups on the factory floor are not only important, but largely *determine* the quality of workplace relations. By far the most significant factor in determining the nature and composition of work groups is technology. For example, Sayles says, 'The technology of certain plants can predispose the total worker/management relationship towards a high degree of co-operation or towards the opposite pole—that of hostility. Other plants, due to the inherent strength of individual occupational groups, tread a middle ground. They have less potential for noteworthy co-operation but also less inclination towards the open conflict type of situation.' He suggests that groups formed by different technologies exhibit different behavioural characteristics which influence the industrial relations of individual plants. In particular, they differ in the methods they evolve to solve day to day problems, their response to management and supervisory behaviour, and the type of people they elect as leaders. It is these responses which produce the patterns forming the fabric of industrial relationships. As part of his novel theory, Sayles went on to classify the groups into four types.

The first type is *apathetic* groups with little skill and few grievances, who participate in union activities only sporadically. Common denominators are limited, there is practically no use of pressure tactics, and a lack of clearly identified or accepted leadership. Examples of workers forming such groups are floor sweepers or cleaners.

Secondly there are *erratic* groups. These consist of members with a high rate of interaction on the job, who make homogeneous crews, work on short assembly lines, with job descriptions and rates matching nearly perfectly, and the work is worker rather than machine controlled. Characteristically, these groups are easily influenced and inconsistent in behaviour, with often tightly centralized leadership, and are quickly converted to good relations with management. Examples include assembly line workers.

Thirdly are *strategic* groups. These are shrewd pace setters, articulate on every weakness in order to gain results, they have better jobs than the former but not the best within the plant. The job does not always have individual operation, and the operative element is important (they may be welders or pressers, etc.). Their behaviour involves continuous pressure, well planned and continuous grievance activity, a high degree of interaction, and sustained union participation.

Finally, the *conservative* groups are self-assured and successful, with a moderate internal unity. Their behaviour is to show restrained pressure for certain higher specific objects, and to manifest activity–inactivity cycles in terms of union activities and the plant grievance procedure. Examples of such workers are skilled craftsmen.

This thesis throws light on the industrial relations in certain industries. For example, the vehicle industry contains many erratic groups, which helps to explain the frequent unofficial activities of car workers which, according to Sayles, are inherent in the technology of the industry. This may be an important reason why the vehicle industry in many countries suffers from industrial unrest. On the other hand, the hypothesis does not explain the differences in activities between similar groups in various plants. It does not tell us, for example, why one motor company has better industrial relations than another, nor why the quality changes over time. The theory concentrates too much on technology and the resulting group structures, ignoring other factors—the quality of management, geographical location, attitude of the unions concerned, individual motivations, which all determine the behaviour of work groups. In addition, Sayles's research methods are not entirely convincing, for he relies on interviews only, adopting no corroborative methods such as questionnaires or work diaries. Even his interviews are suspect, since in about half the firms interviews with union officials were refused by management. His work, however, is a presentation of hypotheses, which he freely admits.

Work on primary groups has been taken further by James W. Kuhn.[3] He does not isolate one variable attributing overriding importance to it for, in his analysis, other factors are thought significant in affecting group attitudes. For example, he draws attention to:

(a) The services offered by the union, which can either help groups in grievance bargaining, or be so poor as to make little contribution. This encourages groups to act either officially with the union or unofficially without it.

(b) The traditions of industrial relations within the plant. For example, a tradition of using sanctions can cause pressure groups and stewards to continue applying them.

(c) The presence of Communists. This can accentuate problems in industrial relations, although Kuhn insists that, in his experience, they catalyse rather than cause problems.

(d) The nature of the industry. For example, there are industries in which redundancy is likely, such as shipbuilding, or those in which the labour market is tight such as printing, or where profits are high and the capital–labour ratio also high, as in oil refining. All are important in determining the behaviour of work groups.

(e) The quality of management. It is important whether they recognize problems or are slow to do so, thus inducing frustration among work groups.

Kuhn believes that technology is also important, but thinks it is only one factor influencing the behaviour of work groups. This appears more accurate, since similar technologies may produce different group reactions, which must be accounted for. Kuhn feels that, together, these factors determine the nature of inplant group activity, which largely influences how shop stewards behave. He notes that the local union, meaning the plant organization of the union, is a political body and partly the creature of the work groups. Its authority could crumble if it resists the groups too strongly. Since he believes that, consequently, shop stewards bargain as *leaders of these groups*, they may embrace unofficial activity and strike action because of the groups' behaviour. This view is relatively novel, it being often assumed in this country that shop stewards are primarily union officials able almost to dictate to members and having considerable personal freedom to manoeuvre. Under full employment, much attention has been focused on shop stewards, but until Kuhn's book was published in 1961, few had envisaged shop stewards as, partly, prisoners of the socio-psychological forces in the workplace. Arguing from the American collective bargaining structure, Kuhn suggests that, to prevent unofficial action, certain topics should pass into the purview of lower level representatives, shop stewards, instead of belonging to full time officials or convenors. This would be important in those technologies most conducive to plant bargaining.

These, he notes, have four aspects: They subject many of the workers to continual changes in work methods, standards, or rates, as they work at individually placed jobs. They allow workers considerable interaction with others in their technological groups. They group most of the work force into several, nearly equal sized, departments. They require continuous sequential processing of material into one major product. These categories are somewhat vague, and Kuhn does not specify exactly why they are so important. However, he argues that local representatives should discuss with foremen such subjects as rotation of jobs, overtime arrangements, seniority procedures, and other departmental problems. He believes this would help workers to obtain meaningful control over their jobs, and preclude attempts to secure it except through, official bargaining. The subjects he suggests for departmental bargaining omit major factors such as wage rates, but perhaps such problems must be included for workers to obtain a *real* measure of control over their jobs.

This, too, is an interesting thesis which has much to offer, but it can be said at once that it contains one obvious drawback. It assumes that shop stewards are *necessarily* acting democratically as leaders of small groups. This does not always follow. The personality of the steward or the particular question at issue (evoking apathy in the group, thus leaving

70

the steward comparative freedom of action)—may produce autocratic rather than democratic leadership. Kuhn is assuming that work groups, existing in workplaces and often consisting of few workers, naturally produce democratic leadership. This is, of course, an easy assumption, and many advocates of democracy, and of democratic organization, have also made it. Democratic theorists say that the smaller the unit, the easier is democracy, and the less likely is autocracy to develop. This is arguable, however, as a leading theorist of group behaviour reminds us: 'this word "democratic" may not be easily applicable to small groups . . . to talk about the "democratic" atmosphere or way of life of a group often leads away from careful reasoning so ill defined are these terms and it makes dictators happy by further muddying the meaning of "democracy", a result that they themselves have done their best to accomplish. The fact is that leadership in a group may be at one time abrupt, forceful, centralized, so that all the communications originate with the leader and at another time slow, relaxed, dispersed with much communication back and forth between leader and followers. Each mould is acceptable, appropriate and effective but each in different circumstances.'[4]

Given the varied circumstances of group formation, attitudes, and behaviour, it is impossible to generalize about stewards as work group leaders. On occasion, stewards themselves may formulate what the group accepts as its best interests; on others, they may be largely responsive to the group's wishes. The incidence of decisions made by the leader or the group will vary greatly according to its nature, whether 'apathetic', 'erratic', 'strategic', or 'conservative'; the personality of the steward, forceful or easy going, and the type of issue involved, important to the group which will therefore insist on making its wishes known, or of little interest and therefore left to the leader. W. E. McCarthy quotes the evidence of Dr G. Clack who took part in unofficial strikes when engaged in research. Clack notes that, generally, stewards were a restraining influence, although 'they could not afford to get out of touch with the feelings of the shop'.[5] In practice, it is impossible to use stereotype descriptions of group behaviour. Also, groups change their behaviour and attitudes with circumstances. All that can be said is that some lean more to

71

democratic forms and others to autocratic. Even this can be misleading in ignoring changing conditions and changing behaviour. Nor is it definitive, it being true at a certain period of time; evidence collected later might provide a different picture.

Despite this, Kuhn's theories are accepted by industrial relations experts in the UK, being the foundation of their approach to plant bargaining problems. For example, Mr A. Marsh[6] remarks that 'All current investigations into the workplace situation tend to lay stress on the notion that work groups find it natural to evolve norms or standards of behaviour and to produce leadership of their own whose principal aim is to defend these standards. Workers may well be content to follow the directions indicated by management until their norms are disturbed. Working pace, levels of earnings, allocations of work, methods of work, ideas of just treatment of individuals—all these considerations may, in varying degree and in different circumstances, seem to be of prime importance to work groups.' Marsh suggests that stewards reflect the wishes of the work groups, when he writes '. . . . Nor do they [i.e. recent writers] appear to doubt the position which the shop steward tends to hold in relation to the work group and its norms. He tends to be not merely a workplace representative but also a work group leader or, in more informal circumstances, merely recognized by the work group.' He does give another reason for the *effectiveness* of the steward: 'If the role of the steward can only be explained, at bottom, in terms of the work group, his *effectiveness* in that role and more recently his rapid rise in authority over the economy as a whole can only be explained in terms of general labour scarcity. Until recently the work group has only in exceptional circumstances been able to apply its working rules to the workplace so as to make its bargaining position felt by management.' Marsh stresses that the steward's position as a work group leader is good reason for encouraging the growth of workplace bargaining and, like Kuhn, is concerned that work groups, left out of workplace bargaining, may act unconstitutionally.

These views of primary group activity envisage them participating in collective bargaining, formally or not, and thereby acting in opposition to management. Some writers suggest

72

that they can be brought into *co-operation* with management, if encouraged to act as groups in consultation on matters of mutual interest with management. For example, J. A. C. Brown[7] writes, in his interpretation of the Hawthorne experiments, 'There are two lessons to be learned from this part of the Hawthorne research. Firstly that no collection of people can be in contact for any length of time without such informal groupings arising and natural leaders being pushed to the top. Secondly that it is not only foolish but futile to try to break up these groups; a wise policy would see to it that the interests of management and workers coincided to such an extent that the collection of informal groups which make up a factory would be working towards the same goals instead of frustrating each others' efforts.' This argument will be examined in the next section.

Some criticisms of primary group theories

One serious fault in interpreting the Hawthorne experiments is to read them as suggesting the feasibility of absolute co-operation between the work groups and management. The remarks of J. A. C. Brown above provide one example. Another can be found in the work of Stuart Chase, who says,[8] 'the worker is driven by a desperate inner urge to find an environment where he can take root, where he belongs and has a function; where he sees the purpose of his work and feels important in achieving it.' Chase sees Hawthorne as proving that management must provide such roots and security by encouraging primary work groups in industry. These arguments are questionable, in implying manipulation of the work force in the interests of management. This is likely to arouse the opposition of work groups, shop stewards, and unionists as such and, at least in strongly unionized factories, will prove difficult. Additionally, such arguments assume that conflict can be ignored—surely unrealistic when economic and status conflict is the basis of collective bargaining. This does not mean that conflict must inevitably result in strikes, overtime bans, go-slows, etc., since it can be constructively channelled. Moreover, even strikes are partially constructive, or at least not entirely destructive, sociologically. Indeed, a strike may be acknowledged 'necessary' by management as well as men. The conflict inherent in our system of industrial relations cannot be ignored. Kuhn realizes the implication of the conflict theory, suggesting that the groups be brought into the collective bargaining process as a counter to management's strength, and that conflict be channelled through the groups. This viewpoint, taken up in the UK by, for example, Flanders and Marsh, appears to be more realistic than the 'co-operation school'.

A second criticism of shop steward related work group theories is that writers of this school tend to refer to stewards as leaders of work groups, as if each steward was elected only by his work group constituents, representing them only in collective bargaining. This is unlikely, since work groups, certainly at the primary level, can be very small; probably, several make up the constituency of most stewards. Evidence from a detailed study of nineteen shop stewards in six different factories, five in the London area and one in North Wales supports this. The study was carried out by one of the writers by interviews with management and shop stewards, observation on the shop floor, and work diaries kept by the stewards during two months. Altogether, six months was spent investigating each plant. A variety of trade unions was covered, including the AEU, T & GWU, NUGMW, H & D, NGA, and ETU. Technologies covered included process production (oil industry) and batch production (print, photography, synthetic fibres, and engineering). This research showed that the median number of groups under each of the nineteen stewards was five. One steward represented ten different primary groups and another nine and, excluding these, the mean average was three. Therefore, it is more plausible to count shop stewards as leaders of work *groups* rather than as work *group* leaders. However, the research also revealed seven cases of informal leaders of individual primary groups putting pressures on the stewards, in two cases going over their heads to the factory convenor. Thus, some stewards may not even act as group leaders, being regarded as unsuitable for this role in not belonging to that work group. Other leaders may be 'appointed'. An excellent example of a *de facto* change in union leadership in a plant in changed circumstances is given in A. W. Gouldner in *Wildcat Strike*.[9] Here, he shows how an aggressive local union plant leader took over the leadership from his less forceful superior at a time when the members felt militancy was necessary. The picture is, therefore, more complex than suggested by the work group theorists, and it may be difficult or impossible to bring the work groups effectively into the collective bargaining process simply through shop stewards. In a recent study of the motor industry, Turner, Clack, and Roberts[10] note the emergence of the 'unofficial–unofficial' strike, i.e. one not approved by the official union hierarchy, and also not first approved by the shop stewards. They also observed in a series of strikes at a car assembly plant 'the shop stewards, and particularly the senior stewards' committee . . . attempting to control a number of pressures to which they are subject, including those from the management and outside union officials, but *especially including pressures from particular groups and sections of work people themselves. . . .* The stewards appear as attempting to minimize trouble; but when trouble seems inevitable, they *attempt* to assert their leadership, in order to maintain their authority over the operatives.' 'Stewards themselves had to be goaded into reluctant action by their electorates,' [our italics].

Stewards may not know sufficiently well the tasks of the work groups to represent them effectively in collective bargaining, and may even lack sympathy with the attitudes of some groups within their constituencies. Conversely, stewards may represent one group, e.g. in representing a small homogeneous group of maintenance craftsmen. More work is needed on this subject before the establishment of valid general theories. The evidence from our inquiries among the nineteen shop stewards also suggests that the importance of group activity can be exaggerated. Of the nineteen, fifteen were leaders of work groups, and were subject to little pressure from those they represented. None of the stewards at Photography felt such pressure, and even H., himself aggressive and dealing with an unco-operative manager, was responsible to ten apathetic groups and seized on individual not group problems. I. (90 per cent of whose constituents were women) and J. also dealt with apathetic work groups, covering individual not group matters. At Synthetic Fibres, K. and L. represented apathetic groups and again dealt with individual problems. Neither N., O., nor P. at Precision Engineering had anything but apathetic groups to deal with and at Printing, groups under O. and S. were not active. E., F., and G. at Wharfage, representing white collar workers, had apathetic groups, and finally, at Refining, C. was in the same position.

This would not of itself disprove the thesis of Sayles and Kuhn, had these groups been naturally apathetic. However, in about half the cases, this was not so. The groups under H. should have been erratic, since they manifested all the characteristics of this Saylesian type—high interaction, lower skill type, pay about middle range, short assembly lines, worker element important to the job. They were, for example, spirit preparers, magnetic strippers, and ammonia processers; J. also represented such 'erratic' groups of film slitters, perforators, packers, and labellers. At Synthetic Fibres, K. represented groups with exactly the same 'erratic' type characteristics in workers who were mixers, viscose cave attenders, mercerizers, and grinders. At Precision Engineering, P. had 'strategic' groups of welders and pressers and so had O. in mostly semi-skilled inspectors. At Printing, Q. and S. represented 'strategic' groups, doing jobs which often had individual operation with the operative element important in the job, with the job relatively important to the plant though not the best in pay or status within the plant. These men were compositors and letterpress operators. These seven stewards represented groups which should have been active but were not. Management and union officials confirmed that this impression gained during two months was typical. The stewards were not regarded as acting as representatives of the groups beneath them, but as taking up problems for *individuals*.

Thus, at Photography, H. dealt with the following matters: bonus queries for two individuals inquiring about their own job; he himself reported a door needing repair, nobody approaching him; again, he himself reported a faulty drinking fountain; he dealt with individual complaints about the attitude of one of the shift foremen; he answered two individual inquiries about a more senior job open to promotion; he answered an inquiry from an individual about the prospects of redundancy; he dealt with an individual's holiday query, and finally tried to answer a question from a constituent about the future of his job in the department.

J. spent his time collecting subscriptions, answering two bonus queries affecting individual constituents, and attending a discussion of the application of work study to a new (individual) job.

At Synthetic Fibres, K. dealt with an objection by a constituent about how the work load was distributed, and an individual's complaint of not receiving a day off in lieu of having worked during a holiday; he collected subscriptions and visited a man who was ill. On one occasion, he did discuss a problem of abnormal filtration affecting the viscose cave attenders— one of his work groups. But this was the only time he acted as a work group spokesman. Certainly, at monthly shop steward meetings he discussed problems affecting the whole plant.

At Precision Engineering, R. handled no departmental problems during this period, but dealt with matters of overall concern: the need for a new grievance procedure; a training scheme for apprentices, shift payments, a new sick scheme, a forty-hour week. O. dealt with similar matters, since the shop stewards' committee was meeting with members of management to discuss new plant policies. But he also dealt with matters in his department. These included the problem of a man not doing sufficient work, according to the departmental manager, two individuals often absent, and one concerning a bad timekeeper.

At Printing, Q., a full time FOC, dealt with seventy seven individual items. Suffice it to say that his constituents approached him as individuals with matters affecting themselves. One complaint about draught did affect part of the work group in one section, and the steward was therefore representing part of a work group. But this was untypical. For the rest, he dealt with complaints about the quality of individual's work; two operators complained about bad paper and one of the discourtesy of a deputy overseer to himself. S. dealt with ninety seven separate points, here again being pressed by individuals in his department. He had only one problem entailing the use of the grievance procedure, otherwise carrying out the routine administrative duties of the full time

FOC, including correspondence, absenteeism, and typing out notices.

The lack of activity of the other eight stewards' groups may be explained in their being either apathetic or conservative types. N., at Precision Engineering, represented skilled craftsmen with the best job status and pay in the plant (conservative), while F., at Photography, had as 90 per cent of his constituents women who were reported as very apathetic. The three Wharfage stewards represented white collar workers who appeared, for the most part, as too management orientated to press the stewards.

The groups of stewards A., B., D., and M. were active since there was a special common factor. All represented craftsmen operating as maintenance workers in process plants. At Refining, the three craft groups under A., B., and D. (respectively, engineering maintenance men, riggers, and crane drivers, and ventilating engineers) were concerned about pay differentials between themselves and process workers. A few highly skilled operators earned more than the craftsmen's consolidated rate. Although this was due entirely to the shift differential, the craftsmen were unhappy and pressed the stewards to effect a change. This involved group activity by the constituents. Similarly, the groups were concerned over demarcation problems. Stewards were very careful to negotiate to protect the spheres of activity of each group of craftsmen. During this period, problems arose between riggers and management at Refining, over the rights of a rigger to accompany rigging equipment in transit. Also at Refining, ventilating engineers insisted on performing work which had, till then, been done by pipefitters. Similar activity existed at Synthetic Fibres, where the pipefitters and the engineering craftsmen were in dispute over who should do certain work on extruded piping. Again, the engineering craftsmen were worried about pay differentials, since some skilled process workers could, with shift differentials, earn more than the engineers' consolidated rate. Here group activity occurred, as the engineering craftsmen pressed the steward very hard into getting an increase to rise above the few process workers earning more (before overtime) than they were. These examples illustrate the exclusive and jealous attitude of craftsmen described by Professor H. A. Turner.[11] With craftsmen, therefore, stewards may act as work group leaders on occasions, but evidence suggests this is confined to groups whose status is being threatened.

In conclusion, it is impossible to accept the generalizations about work groups without considering carefully the activities of groups in actual factories. A more realistic and inclusive theory of work group activity must take account of more varied behaviour than present theories appear to. With these provisos in mind, it is proposed to examine the implications of primary group theories in relation to collective bargaining in the UK.

The significance of primary group theories to shop stewards: some observations

Assuming the theories discussed are accurate in some cases, then on sociological grounds, explicit plant bargaining is advantageous, as Kuhn suggests, for without it groups may act unconstitutionally. In the USA, a 'shop steward's' responsibilities for bargaining on grievances arising from the plant contract are often narrowly circumscribed by it, and stewards usually cannot bargain above the level of departmental foremen or departmental management. In the UK, stewards are less constrained, their functions being rarely limited by formal plant agreements with disputes procedures explicitly eliminating stewards at an appropriate stage, except in so far as they inform full time officials of the facts. Most stewards have responsibilities limited only by custom and practice, the policy of management, which may encourage them to develop their responsibilities, the policy and structure of the union, plus other factors of greater or lesser importance from industry to industry. Generally, stewards in the UK are thought to have great power within their work units, some writers arguing that it should be curbed. Certainly, many stewards have acquired power to negotiate on a variety of matters some, such as piece rate schemes or the overtime permitted to individuals, being extremely important in determining earnings. Probably, in practice, many stewards' powers are not as great as is suggested. Milton Derber[12] shows from research done in 1955 in ten firms federated to the Engineering Employers Federation that the bargaining powers of stewards vary from union to union. He concluded that union influence depended on the degree of steward organization, while the steward's position varies with the union. He found, for the AEU, that stewards formed powerful groups and appeared largely self-sufficient in dealing with management. They utilized the services of full time officials only when the procedure required their presence, though other unions' stewards were subordinate to them. Derber found that the T & GWU controlled stewards more closely, noting that the local organizer of the T & GWU frequently contacted his members at branch and stewards' meetings, often gave advice to senior stewards, and occasionally met management to negotiate wage and other issues. Among the reasons for this closer control are higher membership and steward turnover, since labour mobility among semi- and unskilled workers is often higher than among craftsmen. Therefore, full time officials check on new stewards to see that membership is kept as high as possible.

It should be noted, though Derber omits to, that this was in a period of exceptional labour shortage, 0·5 per cent being the overall unemployment average in the Birmingham area where the firms were situated. This probably increased stewards' powers *vis à vis* management, possibly overemphasizing their typical nature. Even in the case of the AEU, which gives its stewards a large bargaining role, if there is relatively high local unemployment, then managements may be less prepared to bargain with shop stewards.

The NUGMW also restricts the bargaining powers of stewards, being known to expel stewards who take unconstitutional action and restricting its stewards' activities to those in its *Handbook*. In this union, the district secretary plays a large part in factory negotiations, while the NUGMW also has full time branch secretaries as active negotiators.

The BISAKTA has also expelled stewards for breach of its rules, and indeed its rule book limits their powers through the branch. Among other unions acting similarly are those in the printing industry. The T & GWU has about 25,000 stewards according to one estimate,[13] the NUGMW about 15,000. Together they have nearly a third of the shop stewards in the UK. If the works representatives in the BISAKTA and FOCs in printing unions are added, the number of stewards with bargaining activities subject to relatively close surveillance by their unions would reach about a third of the total number for the UK. Arguably, in workplaces with a multiunion structure, stewards from these tightly controlling unions would have more freedom following the example of, say, unions like the AEU. But there is no evidence to support this; indeed Derber's evidence challenges it. Possibly, also, the lack of common interests between craftsmen and noncraftsmen might inhibit close co-operation leading to an accretion of bargaining powers by non-craft stewards. In several cases known to us, stewards have complained of lacking the bargaining responsibilities of other stewards in their plant.

The group theories also have important implications for the behaviour of shop stewards within the plant. They imply, for erratic and strategic groups, that stewards' behaviour may be due to group pressure. Thus, it is unrealistic to condemn it without first studying the group concerned and the problems leading to specific actions. Of course, not all stewards' behaviour derives from full group activities since, as stated above, not all primary group activity is democratic. However, often stewards are pushed into activity by a group, their behaviour not necessarily reflecting their own views. These considerations should be balanced against approaches seeking to deal with stewards as culprits, and recommending such universal 'solutions' such as banning unofficial strikes. This could be positively harmful to industrial relations, easily exacerbating problems by leaving basic causes untouched, creating martyrs, and adding to bitterness in disputes. Similarly, the removal of particular stewards, e.g. by dismissal by management, is not necessarily effective in 'solving problems', though it may be a necessary prelude. The removal of one 'culprit' may lead to the election of another, the group choosing as leader that person who best reflects their mood. Bad management creating distrust and resentment is likely to produce a succession of militant stewards.

Where there are apathetic or conservative groups, and in unstable situations, stewards may have more freedom of manœuvre, and forceful leadership and demogogy may well produce the results desired by the leader. However, many other causes may affect steward behaviour. It would be inequitable to condemn stewards because their groups are apathetic, for the service offered by the union helps determine the activities of local leaders. The logic of this group analysis supports the creation of methods of investigation into the causes of disputes to forestall similar disputes in the future. Such experiments as the Joint Labour Council in the motor industry, which investigates industrial disputes to isolate basic causes, are to be welcomed. For example, many of its Reports criticized the application of incentive payment to changed and changing jobs. This experiment could be repeated elsewhere, especially in industries or firms prone to strikes and other unrest. Certainly, before final judgement, such investigations are needed, it being too easy to make remarks, on superficial evidence, which can only be damaging. Without such opportunities for investigation, we must rely on the evidence of the two sides, which is naturally likely to be biased. Rarely do newspapers or broadcasting services record the views of those involved in dispute. Accusations of irresponsibility directed at trade unions are doubtful, unless statements exist from all the parties and are reported by a neutral agency.

The formalization of stewards' roles

If the work group theories are accepted as applicable, the responsibilities of many stewards should be increased to bring the work groups they represent into the process of collective bargaining at plant level. This could be done in various ways. Perhaps the best way to recognize local situations, would be to define shop stewards' duties and responsibilities in a plant agreement which took account of the nature of the groups. Thus, the roles of stewards would be formalized in plant contracts, giving work groups an acknowledged position within the bargaining system. They could be drawn up by a committee of full time officials, e.g. branch and/or district officers, plus managers and stewards aware of behavioural patterns and plant structure. This would make more democratic the process of formulating grievance and bargaining machinery. As the structure of groups changes, e.g. with advances in technology, the plant contract can be revised and the role of the shop steward amended. Possibly, most managements would not wish to grant stewards such explicit powers, although some evidence on managements' attitudes[14] suggests that they prefer dealing with stewards rather than with full time officials. However, they may prefer to leave such bargaining on its present basis. Dr McCarthy[15] suggests four reasons why management prefers to avoid formal recognition of shop stewards' *de facto* facilities and privileges.

(a) For example, managers felt that *de jure* recognition would add to their status, their role being guaranteed by letter rather than acquired by custom or bestowed by privilege.
(b) Even if the present incumbents did not abuse the extension of *de jure* rights, managers were worried what advantage their successors might take.
(c) Some managers felt it better to confine stewards' rights as at present, for concessions over that might simply encourage even broader demands, to be extended *de facto* before consolidation.
(d) '. . . Management, particularly at board level, would not be prepared to admit publicly that they had been forced to accept such modifications in their managerial prerogatives and formal chains of command. For example, acceptance that no work change could be introduced without the prior agreement of shop stewards, or that a senior steward had immediate access to the works manager whenever he wished.'

From his experience, Dr McCarthy concluded that generally stewards 'do not seek to deny that their influence and status would be in some way advanced by a measure of modification of *de facto* procedural channels, one being quoted as saying, 'of course we would like to have the rules on our side—who wouldn't?'.

Objections could be expected from full time union officials, loath to agree increased or even formalized bargaining powers to their stewards, meaning irrevocably reduced powers for themselves. Their objection might be to the act of formalization, since they would be pressed to exclude themselves from areas of bargaining they might prefer to retain. Moreover, the approach of unions to the extent of stewards' bargaining activities varies, making it difficult for district officials to agree between themselves on the procedural rights of their stewards. Unless the officials could agree, management might recoil further from the formalization of existing practices.

Yet many full time officials are overworked and cater for thousands of members. Clegg, Killick, and Adams[16] found that the average hours worked per week by full time officials in their survey was 57·2. If they are to spend more time on the more important aspects of their job, they might be advised to delegate, where necessary and possible, responsibility to their stewards. This would overcome the problem of giving better service to their members, while being unable to persuade them to pay adequate union dues to provide it. By allowing stewards to provide more services, unions need not recruit more full time officials of the old style. The extra resources obtained from increases in dues might supply research and information locally, for example by the appointment of district research officers to assist full time officials and steward bargainers.

This would effectively reform trade union activities within existing practice in collective bargaining. It could be accomplished quickly and efficiently, not needing sweeping changes in structure or methods of financing, and would have the advantage of bringing union activities closer to the membership. Also, since most members who show themselves apathetic about trade union branch meetings, etc., tend to regard the stewards *as* the union, our proposals might encourage non-unionists to join. They would see the benefits of membership at first hand, rather than regarding trade unionism as something centred beyond, and remote from, their workplace.

But, in conclusion, more research is necessary on the role of stewards in relation to work groups before anything definitive can be said. Clearly, this relationship varies with many rather than one overriding factor. From our review, however, shop stewards cannot be categorized universally as work group leaders, there being wide variations in constituents' pressure and in their acceptance of the stewards' leadership. Sometimes work groups may throw up informal leaders to challenge the steward, or they may be comparatively uninterested in his activities. If work groups are to play an active part in determining industrial relations within a workplace through their representatives, the stewards *must* retain their confidence and support. Evidence suggests, particularly in large plants, that as stewards become accepted by management, and as they develop bureaucratic tendencies within their own stewards' associations, the senior ones become dissociated from the work groups they nominally represent. The fuller acceptance of stewards by management, and the definition of their enhanced status in agreements, stimulates greater interest in their activities by the rank and file. However, a means in the workplace for the regular expression of constituents' views and for more frequent reporting back by stewards will clearly be necessary if they are to remain representative and avoid this potential divorce of interests.

References

1. *The Fawley Productivity Agreements*, Faber & Faber, 1964, p. 140.
2. Sayles, L. R., *Behaviour of Industrial Work Groups: Prediction and Control*, John Wiley and Sons, London, 1958, p. 118.
3. Kuhn, James W., *Bargaining in Grievance Settlement*, Columbia University Press, 1961.
4. Homans, G. C., *The Human Group*, Routledge and Kegan Paul, 1962, p. 419.
5. Royal Commission of Trade Unions and Employers' Associations, Research Paper No. 1, *The Role of Shop Stewards in British Industrial Relations*, HMSO, 1966.
6. Marsh, A. I., *Managers and Shop Stewards*, Institute of Personnel Management, 1963, pp. 15–16.
7. Brown, J. A. C., *The Social Psychology of Industry*, Penguin Books, 1961, p. 82.
8. Chase, Stuart, in *Men at Work* and *The Proper Study of Mankind*, quoted in Brown (7.), pp. 72–3.
9. Gouldner, A. W., *Wildcat Strike*, Routledge and Kegan Paul, 1955.
10. Turner, H. A., Clack, Garfield, and Roberts, Geoffrey, *Labour Relations in the Motor Industry*, George Allen and Unwin, 1967, p. 222 and p. 214.
11. Turner, H. A., *Trade Union Growth, Structure and Policy*, George Allen and Unwin, 1963, Sect. 3–2.

12. Derber, Milton, *Labour–Management Relations at Plant Level Under Industry Wide Bargaining*, University of Illinois, 1955.
13. Roberts, B. C., *Trade Union Government and Administration*, G. Bell and Sons, 1956, p. 67.
14. Clegg, Killick, and Adams, *op. cit.*, p. 175.
15. Royal Commission Research Paper No. 1, *op. cit.*, para. 50.
16. *Trade Union Officers, op. cit.*

5

A Survey of the Duties, Responsibilities, and Attitudes of Shop Stewards

A study of primary work groups reveals an important source of pressure on shop stewards. We now turn to a survey of the duties and responsibilities of shop stewards as they appear in practice. The general paucity of evidence about shop stewards' duties (with the exception of the Clegg, Killick, and Adams survey, there is at present no substantial body of evidence published from direct sources), led us to devise and conduct a survey by means of questionnaires distributed to shop stewards. (The questionnaire is outlined in Appendix C. Both pieces of research were undertaken between 1964 and 1967.) *In addition,* an intensive survey of nineteen stewards was conducted by means of work diaries, in which we recorded their activities over a two-month period, in interviews and discussions with stewards and with management. Observations of shop floor activities were made periodically over a six-month period at each plant, covering stewards from the AEF, T & GWU, NUGMW, ASW, NGA, and ETU. The technologies covered included mass and batch production types. These detailed observations took place at six factories, five in the London area and one in North Wales.

The results of the survey

One hundred replies to the questionnaire were obtained, the following sixteen trade unions being represented: AEF,

NUR, NUGMW, BISAKTA, DATA, ASTMS, Hosiery Workers, NUM, ASW, NUSMW & C, T & GWU, ASMM, NACODS, ETU, NGA, and ASPD. Numbers for each union varied, with the AEU providing fifteen respondents and the ASPD, NGA, and NACODS three each. Industries covered included: engineering, tobacco, hosiery, British Rail, telecommunications, coal, steel, bicycle, shoe-making machinery, aircraft, printing, motor accessories, electronics, and the Post Office. Again, the distribution varied, ranging from fifteen in engineering to one each in electronics and the Post Office. All respondents came from either the Nottingham area (80 per cent), or Derby and Leicester (20 per cent between them).

The distribution of respondents by size of establishment is shown in Table 5.1.

Table 5.1. Size of place of work

Over 10,000 Workers	2–10,000 Workers	500–2,000 Workers	100–500 Workers	Less than 100 Workers
7	70	6	12	5

This table shows a heavy concentration in larger work units, especially the 2–10,000 worker group. This obviously affects our results, and we would not assume our findings indicative of the situation outside this work unit group.

Size of constituency

We attempted to define features of workplace representatives' jobs through a variety of questions, commencing with an analysis of numbers of constituents for whom the stewards catered. The results are presented firstly according to the union, in Table 5.2.

These figures show an interesting range of constituency sizes. For example, stewards in the AEF had many more members than those in the ASPD, the ETU, or ASW. The samples being small, however, constituencies were also estimated by union groups, as set out in Table 5.3.

Table 5.2

Union	Number in sample	Average size of constituency
All respondents	100	126·8
AEF	15	98·8
NUR	12	150·5
NUGMW	9	61
BISAKTA	9	61
ASTMS	8	181
DATA	8	71·9
NUM	6	150
Hosiery workers	6	131
ASW	5	36
T & GWU	5	180
NGA	3	100
ASPD	3	20
ETU	3	24
NACODS	2	43
NUSMW & C	2	71

Table 5.3. Size of constituency by union groups

	Number in sample	Size of constituency
All unions	100	107·5
Skilled	5	85
Ex-craft	30	105·7
Single industry	35	101
General	14	120
White collar	16	126·4

This shows, on the whole, a considerably smaller constituency size than found by Clegg, Killick, and Adams,[1] but our sample is just under half the size of theirs and excludes convenors. Our sample shows that the white collar group had the largest constituencies, though this group is restricted in our sample to DATA and ASTMS both providing eight respondents. DATA organizes its workplace representatives into office committees, several members carrying out some of the 'shop steward's' functions individually or as a committee. With ASTMS, the large number of constituents may derive from all our respondents working in large factories, which may not be typical.

The figures for the 'single industry' group are smaller than might be expected from the comparable Clegg, Killick, and Adams figures, being less than one quarter. Since theirs appears extremely large, however, it would be interesting to know how the inclusion of convenors affected it. Our average figure is smaller than theirs in both tables (see their Tables 45 and 46, *op. cit.*, p. 150) and again perhaps because they included convenors. But, interestingly, our respondents are predominantly from larger undertakings (2,000–10,000 range), theirs being predominantly from the smaller ranges (100–500 and 500–2,000). Our returns show almost uniformly smaller constituencies, suggesting that within large undertakings there is more than one steward to each department. Given such wide variations, however, it is perhaps more realistic to examine the median figures for all unions and union groups. These are presented in Tables 5.4 and 5.5.

The figures in Table 5.4 and 5.5 appear more realistic than those for arithmetical averages. For example, the figure for the NUM seems more credible. The NUR figure also looks

Table 5.4. Size of constituency by union: median figures

Union	Number in sample	Average size of constituency
All respondents	100	60
AEF	15	65
NUR	12	60
NUGMW	9	46
BISAKTA	9	70
ASTMS	8	35
DATA	8	64
NUM	6	128
Hosiery workers	6	90
ASW	5	20
T & GWU	5	60
ASMM	4	40
NGA	3	100
ASPD	3	20
ETU	3	35
NACODS	2	40
NUSMWC	2	68

Table 5.5. Shop stewards: size of constituency by union groups (median figures)

All unions	Number in sample	Size of constituency
All unions	100	70
Skilled	5	35
Ex-craft	30	73
Single industry	35	70
General	14	94
White collar	16	67

more convincing in Table 5.4 than in Table 5.2. Comparing Tables 5.3 and 5.4 with Clegg, Killick, and Adams's Table 46, we find consistently lower figures in our sample. The most convincing explanations are that we did not include convenors nor, except in the case of the NUM and NACODS, branch secretaries, and perhaps that our respondents were from larger work units than theirs.

With regard to numbers of shop stewards in the UK, it may not exaggerate to suggest that between three quarters and four fifths of British unionists are represented by shop stewards or their equivalents. With our median constituency of 60, the conclusion would be that there are between 125,000 and 133,000 shop stewards in the UK. This is, however, a very rough approximation.

Size of constituency, duties, and responsibilities

We examined the range of duties carried out by stewards, using the answers to Question 5 as the basis of Table 5.7. Secondly, we sought stewards' views of the relative importance of their different duties, and their responses are presented in Table 5.6.

The duties and topics covered are numerous, but stewards concentrated on only a few. From the tables, it appears that they spend their time dealing mainly with matters of pay, hours, policing agreements with management, or problems of hygiene, on questions arising from joint consultation, and attending branch and steward meetings. Other important duties include production queries and dealing with complaints about

Table 5.6
Importance of main duties
according to stewards
questioned*

Table 5.7
Range of duties

Duty	Number of times mentioned/100
Pay problems	36
Observance of agreements	33
Joint consultation	28
Safety	19
Union membership	15
Production queries	12
Complaints about management	12
Welfare problems	12
Branch meetings	11
Steward meetings	10
Hours	8
Branch committee meetings	7
Redundancy	6
Overtime	5
Demarcation	5
New works agreements	4
Apprentices	3
Discipline	3
Job performance	2
Victimization	2
Shift work	2
Holidays	2

Duty	Number of times mentioned/100
Pay problems	82
Hours	53
Observance of agreements	43
Hygiene (factory cleanliness, etc.)	34
Branch meetings	32
Safety	29
Joint consultation	28
Production queries	28
Complaints about management	26
Steward meetings	26
Union membership	23
Overtime	19
Welfare of constituents	17
Holidays	14
Dues	11
Redundancy	9
Job performance	8
Work study	7
Discipline	6
Victimization	6
Shift work	6
Staffing	6
Apprentices	4
Suggestions scheme	1
Terms of reference	1
Supervision of work	1
Demarcation	1

* Respondents were asked to list the seven duties they regarded as most important in order of priority. However, many listed less than seven.

management. One often forgotten element of the steward's job, highly placed in both tables though particularly in Table 5.6, is that of members' 'welfare' problems. Many members regard their stewards as sources of assistance on many welfare matters, especially those relating to social insurance benefits. In many cases, stewards are supplementing, if not supplanting, supervisors and welfare departments in this function. Surprisingly, dues were not as important in Table 5.7, and are not mentioned in Table 5.6, in which they had free choice of topics.

The study of nineteen stewards referred to in Chapter 6 suggests a similar pattern, with pay problems, hours, safety, and steward and branch meetings being the most time consuming duties.

Time spent on duties as a shop steward

The average time spent on duties by stewards of all kinds was 9·7 hours a week, 4·9 hours being at work and 4·8 hours in their own time. This is less than the Clegg, Killick, and Adams figure of nearly 11 hours a week, of over 6 hours at work and 4·5 in their own time. Results from the detailed research on the nineteen stewards were an average of 3 hours 55 minutes spent on duties per week. This low figure is probably because the majority of these stewards came from the general unions (T & GWU and NUGMW) which give less time consuming workplace duties to their stewards.

Reasons for standing for the position of shop steward

In answer to this question, most stewards gave reasons associated with social conscience, for 71 per cent stated that they were motivated to 'help their fellow workers'. The only other reason given with any frequency, 53 per cent of respondents mentioning it, was the desire to take on responsibility. If these answers are genuine, stewards have at least some of the qualities making for useful supervisors, and not surprisingly many managements regard them as potential supervisory material. Nearly half our respondents, 49 per cent, expressed interest in becoming supervisors. These same attributes are also important for full time union officials, and it is hardly surprising that many stewards obtain these positions also. Thirty seven per cent expressed themselves interested in doing so.

Election

Stewards were asked about the opposition they faced at elections and whether, in fact, they were subject to regular re-election. Table 5.8 provides a breakdown of the answers.

Table 5.8. Incidence of opposition to stewards at elections

Union group	Proportion subject to regular re-election		Proportion opposed at first election		Proportion opposed at subsequent election		Proportion with someone to replace them	
	Nos.	%	Nos.	%	Nos.	%	Nos.	%
All unions	73	73	32	32	24	24	64	64
Skilled	5	100	1	20	—	—	3	60
Ex-craft	16	53	8	26	5	16	14	46
Single industry	23	74	15	43	12	34	23	65
White collar	16	100	5	33	4	25	13	81
General	13	93	3	21	3	21	11	78

Many of our respondents are subject to regular re-election, but in practice opposition is limited and only in the single industry groups were more than 40 per cent of positions contested at first election. The white collar groups showed one third, as in the first election. Overall, contested elections are few. Many stewards retain office as long as they wish, and they are seldom challenged democratically after first election.

However, the replies to the question on replacement show a larger number of potential stewards than expected from actual elections. It may be that, though prospective opponents will not challenge the incumbent, they are prepared to wait until he retires. The returns showed an average time of 6·5 years, to date, spent as a steward. This suggests that the majority of stewards retire voluntarily, since their span of office gives plenty of time for opposition to manifest itself. However, this does not imply lack of resistance to existing stewards. Informal leaders may emerge temporarily though be unwilling to stand at elections. Sometimes, turnover of stewards creates problems for both unions and managements, and the figure may be as high as 30 per cent per year. Though our sample is not conclusive, it suggests that such instability is exceptional. One reason why stewards give up the job might be that of age, since the (mean) average age of our respondents was forty two and it is possible that, by the mid forties or early fifties, stewards wish to hand over to younger men. Also, they may have lost their desire for responsibilities outside homes and work.

Relations with management

We wished to assess the relationships within which the respondents were working, and especially the place of the departmental foreman, it often being assumed that first line foremen have little to do with industrial relations activity. In Chapter 9, an example shows how the virtual exclusion of foremen almost jeopardized an important productivity agreement. Moreover, lacking information, foremen may unwittingly hamper the development of good relationships at shop floor level.

We therefore asked about the range of subjects negotiated between stewards and foremen, obtaining the results set out in Table 5.9.

Some interesting features emerge from Table 5.9, particularly when examined against Table 5.7. Firstly, the number of times topics were mentioned is much higher in Table 5.9, perhaps because thinking of the issues in relation to foremen jogged our respondents' memories. The 'observance of agreements', i.e. the actual supervision of their day to day application, is by far the most important in the relationship between stewards and foremen, while this 'topic' was a poor third to pay problems and hours in the range of duties (Table 5.7). Indeed, 'pay problems' were mentioned by only fifty respondents in referring to negotiations with foremen, but by eighty two in Table 5.7, despite the larger response to Question 15. Similarly, 'hours' is high in Table 5.7, but much lower in Table 5.9, while mundane topics like safety, overtime, and discipline assume an importance in the latter table not revealed in the broader question answered in Table 5.7. Similarly, topics such as job performance, demarcation, dues, apprentices, and work study receive much more attention.

Table 5.9. Negotiations with foremen

Subject	Percentage of respondents who stated that they 'negotiated' on each topic with foremen
Observance of agreements	83
Safety	53
Overtime	53
Pay problems	50
Discipline	45
Hours	38
Job performance	33
Welfare of constituents	33
Joint consultation	31
Shift work	29
Demarcation	28
Victimization	25
Complaints about management	25
Dues	25
Holidays	24
Staffing	22
Apprentices	22
Redundancy	22
Work study	21
Hygiene	13
Union membership	10

The importance of 'shift work' and 'holidays' is perplexing, but may refer to rotas, exchanges, and allocation. Some distortion may arise from protracted negotiations over holidays and a shorter working week in one large factory immediately before this survey.

Table 5.10. Position of the foreman in collective bargaining

Scale: Importance of the supervisor in the collective bargaining procedure	Ratings of supervisory importance (%) rating
Very important	14
Important	26
Neither important nor unimportant	23
Not very important	27
Not important at all	10

Table 5.11. Relations with departmental managers

Scale: How well do you get on with your departmental manager?	Percentage response
Very well	38
Well	31
Neither well nor badly	23
Not very well	6
Very badly	2

However, the implication remains that there is differentiation between topics stewards discuss with foremen, and those on which their time is spent predominantly with management, some topics being beyond the foreman's authority. This seems the case with pay and hours. On other topics, stewards may feel that though 'negotiating' with foremen, the *degree* of negotiation and the significance of those *aspects* of the topic on which they negotiate determine the significance they attach to the foreman's negotiating role. Thus, the inconsistency of stewards' responses to Questions 20 and 21 of Table 5.10 may be more apparent than real. (We asked *stewards* to evaluate the foreman's position, not the foremen.) Our question held ambiguities, e.g. the interpretation of 'negotiate'. Stewards may deal with foremen over minor issues within a broad topic, but will not necessarily accept finality at that stage.

From answers to Question 17 (Why did you rate the foreman so?), many stewards regarded supervisors as staging points in bargaining procedure, important negotiations being carried out with departmental managers or above. Yet, a few more stewards placed foremen in the important/very important range than in the not very important/not important at all class. However, this does bear out others' findings that the supervisor's role in industrial relations is often of lesser significance than that accorded to him in procedure agreements, etc. For example, Thurley and Hamblin[2] found foremen arranging discussions with members of middle management for stewards, but that generally foremen were not involved in industrial relations matters.

From Question 14, we found that 36 per cent of our

respondents circumvented the foremen in matters thought too important for them. Here, the foreman was only approached for time off for discussion with higher management. The reasons for this virtual exclusion appear as follows. Firstly, senior managements discourage such bargaining, fearing that, left to themselves, foremen might create unwelcome precedents. Secondly, managers may doubt their ability in human and industrial relations. Finally, supervisors themselves may think it better not to get involved, with its possible danger of failure and recriminations. However, while these factors continue to influence the supervisor, the findings of Table 5.10 suggest a slight reversal of the trend of 'negotiations' away from foremen. Many larger firms have recently paid increasing attention to foremen, particularly in their human and industrial relations functions. This reallocation of responsibilities may explain our respondents' views of foremen, particularly as the sample is biased towards larger firms where supervisory training may emphasize these functions. This is not to argue that, often, contact with foremen is more than a first step. Two thirds of respondents knew departmental managers sufficiently well to say they got on either well or very well with them. Many preferred to bargain at this level of management.

The response does not, then, support a stereotyped image of the steward and his manager forever at loggerheads as the former aggressively defends his position or attacks the manager's. Similarly, in regard to the quality of industrial relations, most stewards indicated that, in *their* opinion, industrial relations were satisfactory.

Table 5.12. Quality of industrial relations

Scale: Description of industrial relations at the place of work	Percentage response
Very satisfactory	19
Satisfactory	43
Neither satisfactory nor unsatisfactory	19
Unsatisfactory	11
Very unsatisfactory	8

Table 5.12 does not show most stewards operating against a background of unsatisfactory relations at the workplace.

Good relations with management were further stressed by very few cases of victimization of stewards being reported. Only 8 per cent respondents mentioned such victimization as occurring within the last ten years. The remainder reporting no cases. Similarly, only 8 per cent of stewards considered that management imposed restrictions hampering them in their duties. Of these, three felt that insufficient time was allowed for these duties, one complained of being kept waiting unduly by management, one said management ignored procedure, one said he lost bonuses in being a representative, and another complained of not being allowed merit pay.

Factors affecting the shop steward

Though most stewards seek and achieve amicable relations with management, motives are mixed. Stewards may not invariably be acting as they would like, but are responding to various pressures. The steward has a difficult political position between the conflicting interests of management and men—answerable to a union outside the immediate conflict and subject to the pressures of the nature and traditions of the workplace. We must, therefore, go beyond a simple behaviourist approach, to inquire why the steward behaves in a particular way. Figure 5.1 presents some of the factors affecting shop steward behaviour.

An examination of these factors, and other relevant ones, is necessary before moral judgements are made on stewards' activities. It is interesting to note that stewards did not equate the quality of industrial relations with that of their personal relationships with management. Some respondents gave a high order to one, a low to the other. (See Tables 5.11 and 5.12.) Apparently, personal relations with managers are partly independent of, and above, stewards' views on industrial relations, and both parties may occasionally act in ways considered undesirable without undermining their relationship.

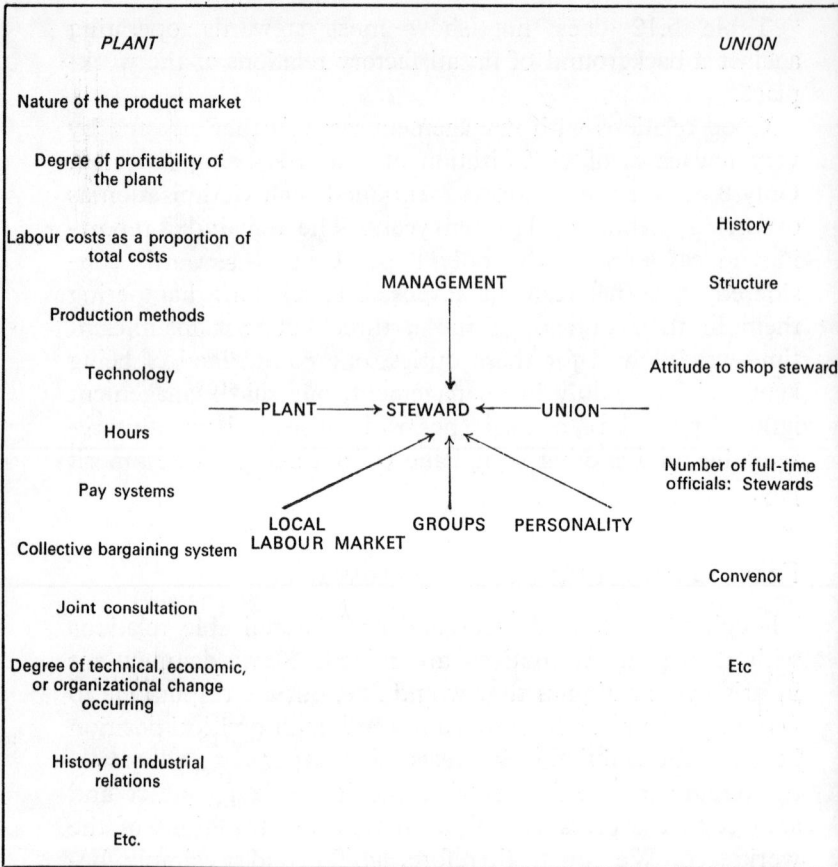

Fig. 5.1. A summary of the major behavioural factors affecting shop stewards

Company information

The questionnaire included queries on whether stewards would like more company information, it being thought from our discussions with individuals that they would value the information on which management based its arguments. They felt that managements could use it to push a policy the stewards might disagree with, but on which they had no facts. In such situations, it is easy to accuse stewards of 'irresponsibility'. The response to our questions was as set out in Table 5.13.

Table 5.13. Shop stewards and company information

Scale: How often is management quoted company information accepted?	Percentage response
Every case	0
Most cases	32
Few cases	30
Very few cases	28
Never	10

This supports the contention that stewards are often unwilling to accept management's presentation of company information and, answering a further question, showed interest in having such information as that of companies' financial performance, overtime working and allocation, merit rating, etc.

Replying to Questions 27 and 28 on company information, respondents replied overwhelmingly they would like it as support in collective bargaining in that it would allay their suspicion and their constituents'. Discussion with the nineteen stewards in the first survey revealed that fourteen felt the use of sanctions a good insurance against being confused by biased presentation of facts by management. While knowledge of confidential information could present problems, it may be useful in allaying the suspicions of unionists. Some managements distinguished different situations in which full information was or was not to be given. Managers thought this a viable exercise in times of intense competition or poor trade, feeling that full information would be conclusive in 'taking the wind out of the stewards' sails'. There was less interest in periods of prosperity.

Table 5.14. Shop stewards and company information

Stewards who would like to see more company information (%)	
YES	NO
86	14

Shop stewards and joint consultation

A point of friction between stewards and managements may be joint consultation, individual stewards revealing that some felt that managements attempted to use a formal joint consultative system to prevent stewards drawing topics into collective bargaining. In fact, worker representatives on joint consultative bodies rather than the stewards were getting results, managements seeming to favour the regulation of relationships by this means. Where there is informal consultation, by excluding some stewards from the process, their effectiveness can perhaps be seriously impaired in lacking the information to help them to do their job competently. Our questions on joint consultation were, however, meant to refer to formal rather than informal consultation, answers being tabulated in Table 5.15.

Table 5.15. Shop stewards and joint consultation

Number of shop stewards who have joint consultation at the workplace	Number of stewards who sit on joint consultative committees	Number of cases in which joint consultative committees are considered to interfere with stewards in collective bargaining
77%	35%	35%

Where stewards themselves sit as 'councillors', possibly the lines between joint consultation and collective bargaining become blurred. No steward with a place on joint consultative bodies thought consultation interfered with his collective bargaining activities.

Relations with the trade union

Since union communication channels are often criticized, stewards being accused of acting outside the official framework without consultation with full time officials, respondents were asked about the frequency of contact with full time officers. The response is analysed in Table 5.16. Average meetings with union groups is set out numerically in Table 5.17.

Table 5.16. Steward contacts with full time officials.
Incidence of meetings with full time officials

All respondents	Average percentage
Ad hoc	20
Every day	1
Once a week	6
Once every two weeks	1
Once a month	43
Once every three months	10
Once every six months	15
Once a year	1
Less than once a year	1
Never	2

Table 5.17. Average incidence of meetings with full time officials

Skilled	Once every 3 months
Ex-craft	Once every 4 months
General	Once every 5 months
Single industry	Once every 1 month
White collar	Once every 2 months

This does not picture most stewards as being out of touch with full time officials, although meetings can be very infrequent. Of the 19 per cent meeting full time officials less than once in three months, only two felt it would be useful or necessary to do so more often suggesting only once in six and nine months, respectively, to exchange general information. Twenty four per cent of all respondents wished to meet the official more often, 20 per cent suggesting once a month to exchange information.

A further question was asked about attendance at branch meetings to ascertain, *inter alia*, how often respondents used this union channel of communication. The information summarized in Table 5.18 was obtained.

This reveals a high level of branch attendance, and only for skilled groups and white collar unions are there appreciable numbers of low attendances. Among the latter, respondents from DATA stated that a representative was appointed from

Table. 5.18. Shop stewards' attendance at branch meetings (Percentage)

Union Group	All	1/2	1/3	1/4	1/5	1/6	1/7	1/8	1/9	1/10	Less than 1/10
All respondents	88	2	3	1	3	1	—	—	—	—	2
Skilled	50	25	—	8	—	17	—	—	—	—	—
Ex-craft	50	20	25	5	—	—	—	—	—	—	—
General	80	—	—	—	6	—	—	—	—	—	14
Single industry	90	5	—	—	5	—	—	—	—	—	—
White collar	50	17	12	—	—	12	—	—	—	—	9

the office committee to attend branch meetings; they themselves, therefore, did not.

With low attendances at meetings, probably most stewards attend fairly regularly, the rank and file attending less frequently, if at all. Answers to Question 36 on the importance of branch meetings, suggest that stewards consider them a useful vehicle for two way communication in the union, a source of information about practices in other firms, and an opportunity to discuss tactics and ideas with other stewards and union officers.

Shop stewards and education

Since the TUC/BEC joint statement in 1962, interest in the education and training of stewards has grown. We therefore asked about the educational experience and wishes of stewards. We asked about classes in which stewards had participated, their replies being collected in Table 5.19.

University adult education classes and WEA classes being often run in conjunction in the Nottingham area, these sets of figures could be read as one. This body provided most courses attended by stewards, with the unions second, and evening institutes third.

We also asked which subjects stewards themselves had found most useful. The only two subjects receiving considerable support were industrial relations, mentioned by half the respondents, and economics, by one fifth. Of subjects stewards

Table 5.19. Educational experiences of shop stewards

Type of course	Number of students who have attended or were attending
Union day schools	15
Union weekend schools	21
Union summer schools	13
TUC schools	9
University extra-mural classes	9
University extra-mural weekend schools	6
University extra-mural summer schools	2
WEA classes	16
WEA weekend schools	15
WEA summer schools	4
NCLC classes	7
NCLC day schools	4
Ruskin College	1
London School of Economics	—
Fircroft College	—
Correspondence courses	5
Evening Institute classes	16
Other classes	5

would like to study (as a help to them as shop stewards), industrial relations claimed 40 per cent of respondents and economics 15 per cent. Only one subject, industrial law, received more than 10 per cent support, the only other topic mentioned more than once being work study (5 per cent).

It appears that courses run by the university adult education departments and WEA districts, which are usually based on industrial relations and economics, are regarded by students not only as providing a liberal education, as is their aim, but also a groundwork of knowledge for their jobs as stewards.

Conclusions from the questionnaire

Our results confirm that stewards deal widely with important matters of job regulation such as pay, policing agreements, union membership, etc., and also underline the breadth of stewards' duties and activities in the workplace. A serious problem is the paucity of education and training opportunities for most stewards.[3] Most must learn the job through experience or from advice from fellow stewards. Though long tenure of the job gives much scope for learning in this *ad hoc* fashion, scope for error must also be great. With little education and training, and conceding the nature of the steward's position as being subject to multiple pressures, we are inclined to emphasize the difficulties of his task and to solicit the sympathy of critics and commentators.

There appears no justification for not revealing to union negotiators more company information during collective bargaining and, appreciating the difficulties of stewards' tasks, it would seem a necessary aid to them. For example, pressure from militant constituents, with whom the steward does not agree, could often be easily quelled by presenting the facts. At present, he may need to argue that management *says* the constituents cannot be satisfied because the facts of the situation are against it.

Further findings from the detailed survey

Though these findings are admittedly based on inadequate statistical material, and definitive statements are not possible, it is useful to compare the results of analysis of work diaries and personal investigations into individual plants with those of the general survey. Some results of this study of nineteen stewards have been outlined in Chapter 6.

As against our survey, pay or hours seldom appeared important. Probably this is because the general unions dominated this sample, fifteen of the nineteen being general union stewards. Their duties are probably confined to the less contentious matters of meetings, welfare, shift work, etc. It is useful to recall that not all stewards can negotiate on pay problems. Table 5.20 illustrates the variety of issues covered by different stewards.

The average time spent on duties per week by stewards was 3 hours 55 minutes, considerably less than the survey indicated. This, again, is probably due to the preponderance of general union stewards, with relatively closely confined duties.

Table 5.20. The range of duties of the nineteen shop stewards

	STEWARD																		
	1	2	3	4	5	6	7	8	9	10	11	12	13	14	15	16	17	18	19
Time spent on duties in eight week period (hours)	32·4	28·6	30·2	1·3	5·0	6·1	52·8	102·3	105·2	25·9	35·3	24·7	30·4	25·8	28·7	29·0	26·3	24·0	6·2
Pay	×	×			×	×	×	×	×	×	×			×					
Hours	×				×			×	×								×		
Safety			×													×			
Demarcation				×															×
Hygiene							×						×	×					×
Overtime							×		×	×	×	×	×			×	×		
Union membership											×							×	
Observance of agreements									×	×	×					×	×		×
Branch meetings	×	×	×	×			×	×	×	×	×	×	×	×	×	×	×		
Steward meetings *	×	×	×	×			×	×	×		×	×							
Job performance		×	×	×							×	×			×				
Victimization									×						×				
Shifts										×					×	×			
Production queries					×			×											
New works agreements																			
Holidays		×	×		×		×	×	×			×				×	×	×	×
Complaints about management					×		×									×			
Staffing	×	×			×		×		×			×						×	
Apprentices		×					×		×										
Welfare of constituents							×		×	×	×					×	×	×	
Dues†	×							×					×	×	×				
Discipline		×	×			×		×										×	
Work study						×												×	
Redundancy					×			×										×	
Suggestions scheme						×		×										×	

* These meetings were concerned with other topics in the list, but the topics also arose outside the meetings.

† Including collecting dues and problems arising from non-payment.

Table 5.21. Analysis of time spent on duties (percentage)

STEWARD

	1	2	3	4	5	6	7	8	9	10	11	12	13	14	15	16	17	18	19
Time spent on duties in eight week period (hours)	32·4	28·6	30·2	1·3	5·0	6·1	52·8	102·3	105·2	25·9	35·3	24·7	30·4	25·8	28·7	29·0	26·3	24·0	6·2
Pay	20	15	10		37	63	3	8	10	37	9			20		12	32		
Hours	12			22	11				9		4	13	16	8					
Safety							1	27					23						
Demarcation																			
Hygiene											6								
Overtime							12		4	3	8						15	15	15
Union membership											5							15	23
Observance of agreements															26				
Branch meetings	30	11	15	12			14	11	12		15	40				27			45
Steward meetings	33	32	30	66			27	20	18	42	34	43	47	42	43				
Job performance																			
Victimization		3														7	22		
Shifts			25							13									
Production queries					20			7	9						11	7	8		
New works agreements					17		32	5											17
Holidays		16			13		6		17									12	
Complaints about management		8	30				5												
Staffing	5										19	4				40		21	
Apprentices									21	5									
Welfare of constituents									10					30					
Dues								17					14		20			23	
Discipline		15			12			5									33	29	
Work study																			
Redundancy						29													
Suggestions scheme						8													

Relations with the supervisor

Most stewards bypassed the foreman on the grievance procedure. For example, H. (Photography) went straight to the manager with 50 per cent of his problems. At Precision Engineering, both N. and P. had no departmental problems during the period, being busy with factory-wide issues, but interviews with the foremen demonstrated that only in minor matters of heat, light, etc., did stewards do anything but inform the foreman that they wished to leave the job to take up a matter at a higher level. At Refining and Wharfage, management tacitly encouraged circumvention of the supervisor, though the grievance procedure specified an initial approach to him. Consequently, at Refining, A. and D. took only 50 per cent of their problems to the supervisor, and C. only one out of seven. C. felt the supervisor lacked enough knowledge to help, and an approach was useless. He justified this, 'for fear of embarrassing him with problems he knows nothing about'. At Wharfage, E. did not approach the supervisor, again for much the same reasons. F. and G. at Wharfage did, as the grievance procedure demanded, approach the supervisor although for neither was a solution usual at this level.

To sum up, at all six plants only twice did supervisors appear sufficiently knowledgeable about issues commonly raised by the steward to suggest that they had regular contact with him. Both supervisors dealt with maintenance craftsmen, B. at Refining and M. at Synthetic Fibres. Otherwise, supervisors knew little about the stewards or their duties seeing them, through the grievance procedure, on average only once or twice a month. Thus, as shown in our main findings, the tendency to circumvent the supervisor appears widespread.

POSTSCRIPT: The results of the Royal Commission's survey

The research reported above has demonstrated the wide range of steward's duties and responsibilities, but it is based on a limited sample of 119 shop stewards. It is therefore interesting to compare this with the principal findings of the Royal

Commission's inquiry into workplace relations, conducted by the Government Social Survey and published as a Research Paper by W. E. J. McCarthy and S. R. Parker.[4] In the course of this inquiry, 1,600 shop stewards, 200 full time local trade union officials, 500 foremen, 300 works managers, 150 personnel officers, 500 trade unionists, 400 non-unionists, and about 150 representatives of employers' associations were interviewed. The major findings and conclusions of this inquiry, as they relate to shop stewards, are given below.

Thirty per cent of stewards appear to have had some training for the job, and over 50 per cent were not interested in promotion within their firm. The 'typical shop steward' had not been through a contested form of election, was responsible for about 60 members, and spent about six hours a week on his duties as a steward. The authors felt that usually shop stewards have good facilities for contacting members and meeting fellow stewards in the workplace. Stewards covered by the survey had held the position for six years on average, and 62 per cent had worked for their present firm for 10 or more years. Using an average constituency size of 55 the authors suggest that there may be as many as 175,000 stewards in Great Britain, an increase of 14 per cent in ten years.

The range of their bargaining activities is demonstrated in the following tables:

Table 5.22. Broad topics of shop steward negotiation

Groups of issues	% of stewards who negotiated on each topic
Wages	83
Working conditions	89
Hours of work	75
Discipline	67
Employment issues	67

About one sixth of stewards did not settle any issues at all with management, and those stewards with a wide range of bargaining were usually senior stewards in large, multi-union plants.

On the question of shop stewards' negotiations with foremen, 59 per cent of the latter said that all or most grievances

Table 5.23. Stewards' range of bargaining

Type of issue	Discussed and settled:			
	As standard practice	Rarely	*Ever (grouped)	As standard *practice (grouped)
	Per cent	Per cent	Per cent	Per cent
(a) *Wage issues*				
Piece work prices	20	8		
Other forms of bonus payments	25	18		
Plus payments for dirty work, etc.	19	20	83	56
Job evaluation	20	13		
Allowances of any other kind	20	16		
Merit money	17	16		
Up grading	24	21		
(b) *Working conditions*				
Distribution of work	25	18		
Pace of work	22	16		
Quality of work	27	12		
Safety questions	54	18		
Health questions	40	20		
Manning of machines	21	12	89	73
Transfer from one job to another	33	23		
General conditions in the workplace	56	18		
Introduction of new machinery/jobs	23	16		
(c) *Hours of work*				
Level of overtime	34	13		
Distribution of overtime	34	14	75	49
Breaks in working hours	23	16		
Stopping and starting time	24	20		
(d) *Discipline*				
Reprimands by the foreman	26	28		
Suspensions	22	20	67	34
Dismissals	23	26		
(e) *Employment issues*				
Taking on new labour	24	16		
Number of apprentices	10	8		
Acceptance of up grading	21	14	67	43
Short time	15	9		
Redundancy questions	20	16		

* i.e. those who discussed and settled at least one of the issues within each group.

Note: A small number of stewards said they also discussed and settled holidays or annual leave and a few other issues, but since these points were not put to all stewards no figures are shown.

and claims raised by stewards were settled without reference to a higher level of management. Forty per cent stated that their permission was not necessary before stewards were allowed to contact higher levels of management. Seventy per cent of foremen admitted that there were ways in which stewards could short-circuit them, and most of these foremen disapproved of such short-circuiting. Ninety-five per cent of managers claimed that they kept their foremen fully informed of issues which they had decided with stewards, and 80 per cent of foremen agreed this was the case. About 12 per cent of foremen said that they usually heard about such decisions from stewards.

Over half the stewards covered by the survey had regular meetings with their officials. A third of the sample wanted their officer to play a bigger part in local negotiations but two thirds felt that he already played an extremely important part. Only a quarter of the officers wanted to play a bigger part in local negotiations. Stewards' attendance at branch meetings appears from the survey to be much greater than that of members. Forty-four per cent of stewards said that they were present at nearly all branch meetings.

Over two thirds of management would prefer to deal with stewards rather than full time officials. Only 15 per cent of works managers and 26 per cent of personnel officers felt that full time officers should become more important in their system of industrial relations.

Thirteen per cent of stewards said that they had been victimized by management although very few cases appear to have resulted in dismissal. Managers in the sample felt that stewards were, if anything, treated more leniently than other workers. The vast majority of stewards and members thought that management was very fair in matters of discipline. Fifty per cent of stewards were in favour of changing their system of payment from a payment by results system to another type.

Evaluation of the system of workplace relations

Stewards have widely varied influence and functions, but there is little evidence from the survey that stewards are more militant than their members, nor are they more likely to resort to unconstitutional action. They are more typically seen, and see themselves, as reasonable and even moderating influences—'more of a lubricant than an irritant'. Stewards emerge as the crucial point of contact between members, full time officials, and the union, and this applies equally where there are workplace branches. Their leadership of their members is based on persuasion and consent, rather than on compulsion. Relationships between stewards and their union full time officials are both 'complex and interdependent', but essentially they share certain objectives and assumptions.

The surveys gave the overwhelming impression that most people are fairly satisfied with the present state of affairs. In some aspects of the system a minority expressed dissatisfaction—as for instance over discipline and dismissals. Eleven per cent of trade unionists and 10 per cent of non-unionists said that they felt that there was a risk of unfair treatment on dismissal. Twenty five per cent of stewards said that they knew of cases in which their members had been victimized, in addition to the 13 per cent who claimed to have been victimized themselves. Nevertheless, the survey revealed overwhelming support amongst participants for the system as it is. This, the authors comment, could be the result of complacency and self-satisfaction. It might also reflect the fact that participants have little experience outside their present working environment to make realistic comparisons which would lead to a critical evaluation of their present position. The point that the industrial relations system is of concern to external parties, notably the public, is also made.

The results of the surveys suggest that those involved in the system of industrial relations in the United Kingdom are not clamouring for sweeping changes. They do not suggest that there is any urgent need for changes in 'formal rules'.

Conclusions

Stewards are 'essentially shop floor workers, using all the opportunities presented to them to satisfy their members' grievances and claims'. They are prepared to 'use every avenue of access to management' and, if necessary 'circumvent established rules and procedures to get what their members want'.

Stewards also appear prepared to use industrial action in pursuit of their objectives, as had been the experience of one third of those interviewed. Yet, alongside this managers and stewards negotiate together and appear to have reached a level of mutual tolerance and acceptance. The surveys show that the amount of intra-plant activity is very great indeed and appears to be growing. Mutual interdependence between managers and stewards appears to be the norm. Dr McCarthy sums up by saying that 'in workshop relations in Britain there can apparently be role conflict without conflicting role expectations; objectively there are clashes in interest and function, but subjectively the participants often accommodate themselves to this situation and as a result they do not expect the position to be otherwise'.

Several practical proposals for the reform of workplace relations are examined in the light of the surveys. It is concluded that attempts to enforce procedural rules by legal methods are not likely to be very successful, and suggested that, since attitudes towards procedural and other rules are pragmatic and flexible, the parties should be encouraged to engage in a general review and revision of the internal rule-making process.

It is also felt that trade union officers are not likely to support legal intervention to 'assist' trade union control over members and shop stewards. It is suggested that the surveys indicate that statutory props to union control might reduce the influence of trade union officers over members, and the idea bristles with practical problems. The authors of the Research Paper discuss the advisability of introducing more formal procedural and substantive agreements at plant level, and suggest that this change would not involve totally new ways of behaving. The surveys showed that currently 'formal procedures are ignored, supplemented and short-circuited in various ways'. However, many firms appear to have added their own formal plant procedures to national procedures and most of them have formed plant-wide negotiating committees 'if only on an informal basis'.

It is concluded that the need to integrate shop stewards into the union structure can most easily be met by basing the branch on the place of work, in which case 'no great change is involved in many unions'. However, unless workshop-based branches can meet at the place of work and, if possible, during working hours, then they are not likely to prove an effective substitute for an informal shop meeting where stewards can meet their members and discuss workshop policy.

References

1. *Trade Union Officers, op. cit.*
2. Thurley, K. E. and Hamblin, A. C., *The Supervisor and His Job*, DSIR. Problems of Progress in Industry, HMSO 1963, pp. 14–15.
3. Some of the problems associated with the education and training of shop stewards are outlined in Appendix B.
4. Royal Commission on Trade Unions and Employers' Associations, Research Paper No. 10., *Shop Stewards and Workplace Relations*, HMSO, 1968.

6

Shop Steward Organizations and Hierarchies

Earlier, we examined the influence of both union rule books and constituents on stewards' activities. To this must be added the nature of relationships *between* stewards, and the influence of the organizations they have formed. Again, the picture is that of an unstructured and uneven proliferation of *ad hoc* arrangements being indicative of the inadequate response of traditional systems to recent developments. The inadequacy is that they largely failed to anticipate or incorporate new forms of workplace organization. Consequently, workplace bodies have emerged meeting indisputable needs while being beyond external regulation. Perhaps most stewards' organizations emerged to augment services provided by unions, but many now challenge and may undermine union functions. They illustrate the challenge from below to the nature of both unions and collective bargaining arrangements, also showing that these are no longer structures with single sources of authority and decisiveness.

Certainly, the activities of stewards' committees may not be complementary to the unions' nor to their agreements with employers' associations centrally, although some unions have attempted to integrate internal and external union action. However, even where this link exists, the connection appears more systematic on paper than in reality. In practice, preserving the union 'chain of command' currently relies on appeals to loyalty as much as on processes valued by stewards on utilitarian grounds. The increasingly internalized regulatory pro-

116

cess produces workplace arrangements between stewards, which possess their own institutional interests, to be defended against membership as against management and unions. They are almost embryonic company unions, though drawing strength from access to the larger 'parent' bodies outside. Availability is everything, though usage may be minimal. Consequently, the role of external unions and joint machinery has declined in relative if not in absolute importance.

The need for workplace organization, as distinct from workplace representation, has emerged with increased numbers of stewards and their experience of common problems. Stewards, usually either lacking or explicitly denied permission by unions, have formalized inter-union relationships in the workplace. Their formality varies, much informal interaction between stewards takes place, reaching high levels during crises over issues affecting all stewards and members, reverting otherwise to regular though infrequent meetings. Sometimes there is no stated basis, contact being informal; at others inter-union and inter-work group rivalry may inhibit co-operation.

A close analogy exists between inter-union organizations and the TUC. Membership is voluntary, and some representatives, e.g. of white collar workers, stay outside. Secondly, individual freedom of action is little regulated by the centre, whose disciplinary powers are slight. The leadership of officials of the joint organization may be accepted or rejected, their policies being subject to approval by other stewards who can opt out. Yet the convenors' influence can be considerable, particularly on plant-wide topics where all unions have similar interests and where convenors have good 'records'. Finally, management, like the government, may often negotiate successfully with the joint organization's officials, but occasionally exaggerate the sway these officials have. So, the danger exists of the leading stewards' interests being different on occasions from those of the workgroups.

Pressures have led to works based organizations, often incorporating seniority and precedence, many being unacknowledged by the unions. Although co-operation between stewards does not always take committee form, particularly in small establishments, they are found throughout manufacturing industry, especially in large metal working sections.

Variations are legion, so we must begin our analysis by classifying the committees.

Types of shop steward committees

(1) Single union, single department, or plant

This type, with membership restricted to those in a single union, is the simplest, involving fewest problems for a union. The committee may consist only of stewards, meeting to exchange information and to co-ordinate their activities. They may elect a senior steward or union convenor. Stewards of one union in a large factory may form their own departmental committees as well as a factory-wide single union committee, this being unnecessary in smaller works. In other cases, the shop committee may not contain only accredited shop stewards, but also rank and file members who act as a check on those representatives. Alternatively, the whole committee may negotiate with management, rather than leaving it to individuals.

Some unions, e.g. the Hosiery Workers, do not base their workplace structures on representatives, but rely on shop or factory committees. Other unions regard workplace organization of stewards as secondary to workplace representation; indeed few union rule books allow for such organization. Among the few, the ETU encourages steward committees, while the AEF rules have recognized shop committees since 1930. In both, the committees can elect a convenor, thus strengthening their stewards against those of other unions, and emphasizing membership of a union as the basis of organiztion and the focus for loyalty. Other variations in organization can be found. For example, the Foundry Workers, the Tailors and Garment Workers, and others initially allow for individual representatives, but stress shop committtees which include those representatives and rank and file members.

The incidence of intra-union workplace committees has been estimated in the AEF, Marsh and Coker finding about one steward in ten a convenor,[1] i.e. a senior steward among AEF stewards. This ratio suggests about 3,000 convenors among all AEF stewards. It is not known how far employers accept this role, though informally it seems widespread.

Perhaps the best example of workplace, single union *organization* is in printing, an orderly system of single union chapels having long been established. Each union chapel, i.e. all members, elects chapel officials including a FOC to act as senior representative in the department or establishment. This structure is closely integrated into each union in the industry.

(2) Multi-union, single department

These committees are found formally in relatively large establishments. Stewards of different unions from the same department form a joint shop committee to co-ordinate activity, face management, or act jointly in the plant-wide committee if departmental loyalties occasionally supersede union affiliation. The joint departmental committee may elect a convenor as representative at convenors' meetings.

(3) Multi-union, whole plant

This inter-union joint committee is perhaps the most usual form of steward organization, being known as the *The* Joint Shop Stewards' Committee (JSSC) within a factory. Membership derives simply from being a shop steward. A committee of all union representatives is thus formed irrespective of union affiliation. When an overlarge committee hampers the conduct of business, the JSSC may elect a convenor and an inner committee as the executive body. In smaller plants, the necessity for a further committee between the total body of stewards and the convenor, normally secretary of the JSSC, is less likely. However, other officers, e.g. treasurer or representatives on management/employee committees, are still necessary. For example, the employee side of Joint Works Committees at Ford's consists of stewards elected by and from the stewards in each plant.

Variations in nomenclature make identification and understanding of function difficult. For example, Works Committees were established in federated engineering establishments under the 1919 agreements, still being found today. They were joint management/employee bodies with a specific but optional part in disputes procedure, to settle issues unresolved at shop manager level, and avoid getting to works conference stage.

They were not originally part of internal steward organization, though consisting invariably of stewards. Stewards who are members of the Works Committee in federated establishments can meet in works time and usually form the executive of the JSSC. The secretary of the JSSC, the convenor, is normally secretary of the workers' side of the Works Committee, and is normally[2] responsible to the JSSC. Other worker representatives on the Works Committee may also be responsible to the JSSC and/or steward committees based on union affiliation or on a departmental basis.

Inter-union JSSCs focus union activity within a plant, especially if it is small. Here the whole committee negotiates on inter-departmental interests. Otherwise, an inner executive headed by a convenor acts on inter-departmental issues or in formal meetings with management. Electoral rules may allow the convenor powers to negotiate on behalf of all members, irrespective of union, and this practice may be tacitly acknowledged by management. Tactically, however, the convenor often prefers at least one other steward to accompany him.

Thus, the common multi-union stewards' committee seeks to overcome some disadvantages of union structure, and their failure to adapt internal organization to the needs of workplace activity. Though performing a function, formal recognition by union and management is minimal. Management particularly may recognize a convenor *de facto*, but neither has been anxious to stimulate powerful JSSCs. Both sides may attempt to ignore their existence.

(4) Company-wide combine committees

A shop stewards' combine committee is one of stewards from different establishments of a multi-plant firm. A common employer creates such committees, which frequently run counter to the district basis of union organization. Where branch factories are close geographically, the committees are more cohesive, those at Rootes, Morris Engines, and Standard Triumph International factories near Coventry being good examples. If organized in multi-product firms, the committee also cuts across different 'industries', and possibly industry-wide bargaining institutions. Usually such a committee comprises a few stewards from each plant, depending on size, normally including the works convenor. Organization of stewards within the same company but at different locations grows to meet the situation, e.g. a dispute, where a convenor at one plant contacts another at a different plant. This contact may evolve through correspondence to informal meetings, and to a loose framework. It may remain *ad hoc*, or develop into a company-wide combine committee with its own, usually part time, officers, funds, a written constitution, and regular minuted meetings.[3]

Such combine committees are most easily found in large firms, e.g. BMC where formal meetings take place in different towns every two months. The Rootes Group Stewards' National Committee meets monthly in London, the directors having occasionally met the full committee. In Ford's, meetings were once secretive, but the committee has been acknowledged by senior management who now meet the plant convenors twice a year. Such committees exist in most large companies, and are not restricted to the 'engineering' industry. For example, shop stewards at ICI have links through the so-called ICI National Joint Committee, but this body is not recognized by the company. Meetings are usually supplemented by correspondence where distance inhibits regular contact. As stewards at different plants of one firm exchange information for mutual advantage, so do combine committees, particularly those from firms in competition. For example, the Ford and BMC combine committees exchange information with other committees in the motor industry, while stewards from the new motor plants on Merseyside have had informal meetings. Despite this, there seems little contact between stewards' organizations in different firms in one area. A shared employer constitutes a stronger link than a local labour market.

(5) Industry-wide committees

National industry-wide committees are generally regarded as a challenge by existing unions and encounter more definite opposition, in contrast with the somewhat equivocal reaction to workplace and combine committees. Industry-wide committees of stewards occur in several industries, notably in electricity supply, engineering, building, exhibition contracting, and, until recently, in the motor industry. Similar industry-wide organization of workplace leaders is found in the docks, through the Portworkers Liaison committees. However, their formality, influence, and degree of representativeness varies widely. Some committees are industry-wide, but are more accurately described as 'industry based', their influence varying considerably by region. For example, unofficial site organization in building is stronger in London, through the London Building Workers Joint Sites Committee, than elsewhere. During the last war, the Shop Stewards National Council was influential in the aircraft industry, and subsequently throughout engineering. In the 'fifties, the BMC joint stewards combine committee created an industry-wide Shop Stewards Committee, holding meetings attended by stewards from all major car manufacturing companies. This Committee had a formal constitution, and met regularly, but since the late 1950s it has disintegrated, though informal contacts are maintained.

The Engineering and Allied Trades Shop Stewards' National Council has long existed and was particularly influential during the last war. Its present significance is arguable, but it was condemned by the TUC in 1960. The unofficial stewards organization in the electricity supply industry seems stronger in London than elsewhere, emerging during national wage negotiations to put pressure on official negotiators. During negotiations in 1963, its call for a 'go-slow' was followed in some power stations. Though its leading spokesman was expelled from his union, the committee still exists and publishes a periodic newsheet, *The Power Worker*.

The titles of some bodies claiming to be national stewards organizations are much more grandiose than realistic. Most lead a shadowy existence, spasmodically emerging during crises. During wage negotiations in July 1963, London stewards claimed that they had organized stoppages on building sites in London, Liverpool, and Manchester. Most cannot be regarded as permanent, national bodies. More accurately, they are groups of militants, frequently dominated by members and sympathizers of extremist political bodies. Attendance at meetings is left to individual choice, though workplace stewards' committees may pay the expenses of attendance.

122

Officially, most unions dislike or prohibit participation; this may inhibit their development, but does not stop the flow of literature.

(6) National and other committees, irrespective of industry

Industry-wide stewards committees retain at least an ostensibly advantageous organizational form, in their 'rational' industrial basis. However, other, less theoretically justifible, committees exist, e.g. attempts to call national conferences or to form a national organization of stewards to challenge individual unions and the TUC in national policy. The TUC condemned 'the abortive conference in December 1959 convened in the name of the Firth Brown stewards'.[4] Others attempt organization by region, e.g. the London Shop Stewards Defence Committee. These bodies are less significant even than industry-wide committees, their purposes and sponsors being perhaps more suspect.

There is little evidence of formal organization between stewards of firms using the other's product. Where contact exists it has seldom evolved, in the absence of geographical proximity, beyond correspondence and exchanged information. Lerner and Bescoby[5] quote an example of a loose liaison between the joint stewards committee of a Sheffield crankshaft firm and the BMC Combine Committee. Before the merger of Briggs Motor Bodies and Ford's, links between their stewards were close, because of geography, competition in the same labour market, and the dependence of one plant on the other.

The reasons for shop steward committees

The emergence of steward committees has been encouraged by many factors, some closely associated with the advent of stewards themselves. Bargaining opportunities in the plant, the divorce of branches from the workplace, low branch attendance, and union structure are examples. However, other reasons explain the need for co-ordination between workplace representatives.

The size of manufacturing establishments and of companies has increased generally. In June, 1961 over 48 per cent of employees in manufacturing worked in establishments employing more than 500 people, over a third in establishments of over 1,000.[6] Work in large plants obviously demands formal contact between stewards. Moreover, the distribution of stewards, in engineering at least, is disproportionately concentrated in large establishments,[7] and over recent decades representation has deepened. Increasingly large-scale manufacturing units, and more stewards per member, simultaneously make committees desirable, on numerical grounds alone.[8]

Tactically, there is an obvious logic for joint steward committees. The stewards of different unions face a single employer, whose policies affect them all. They have similar working conditions, consultative machinery, wages structure, personnel policies, and general practices. Unionism is steeped in ideals of fraternity and unity, the latter having repeatedly been of enormous strategic value. The unions recognize the need to meet employers collectively in industry-wide bargaining, either through a federation or an *ad hoc* negotiating committee. The effectiveness of united activities and policies is similarly apparent to stewards. Joint organization facilitates a concerted response to management, offsetting the often weakening effects of separate working policies.

Autonomous JSSCs may act on policies not uniformly supported by each union in the plant. However, it is more likely that such committees will take decisions on issues on which their unions have no predetermined policy, or formally offer no guidance. Thus, joint committees may not so much clash with union policies, as determine supplementary ones, though these may subsequently be repudiated officially.

Inter-union contact at workplace level is not only of tactical value, but is perhaps primarily induced by the search for information and the pooling of knowledge about the employer. It supplements information from branch meetings about conditions in other firms. Managements are sensitive to the activities of firms in the same labour market, privately exchanging information on such labour matters as earnings, holiday arrangements, shifts, discipline, etc. Management is also aware of dissimilarities between departments of the same plant and between plants. For the unions, the locality is covered by residence based branches, but the absence of a union mechanism to exchange information about factory practices has led stewards to create their own organizations.

Sometimes, this latent organization has been impelled towards formality by various joint management–employee committees. Committees forming part of the procedural chain, or general consultative, production, safety, and other internal committees including employees bring together workplace representatives. Agendas must be formulated, and the secretary and members elected. If they discuss relatively significant problems, stewards endeavour to obtain seats on them. As consultative and other committees discuss topics of specific union interest, as is the trend, management will require authoritative union representatives.

The difficulties of co-operation at branch level between different unions may be exacerbated by inter-union competition, which may extend to their workplace representatives. The numbers of unions and representatives in a plant also complicates workplace organization, however desirable to stewards. Despite this, the number of unions claiming representatives in a plant is often exaggerated by reference only to very large industrial firms. Marsh and Coker found that workplace union structure in engineering was relatively simple, e.g. in establishments with fewer than 1,000 manual workers, on average less than four unions had stewards. The average figure for establishments in the 1,000–5,000 range was only six.[9] In the industry most frequently quoted to illustrate union structural inefficiencies, the organizational problem therefore appears manageable, in terms of the number of stewards to be brought together.

The interdependence of workgroups resulting from modern technology further stimulates joint organization within a firm. Action in one section has immediate repercussions on employment elsewhere. Joint organization does not prevent sectional action, but it aids support action or at least forewarning. This information centre may similarly mitigate undesirable repercussions, or reveal new means for settlement. Certainly, realization of interdependence has promoted the development of co-ordinating committees in firms.

The functions of joint shop steward committees

The activities of joint stewards committees could all be classified as co-ordination. Enquiring of the value of such a committee, the most frequent justification was as a source of information about events in the plant. Details of current problems and of practice in different departments predominated at JSSC meetings, respondents emphasizing the up-to-date nature of the information, as against that from branch meetings. Our respondents indicated that some committees met regularly each week, others quarterly, but most were 'monthly, plus, as and when necessary'. Pooling of information about current problems and practice was highly valued, presenting a more coherent picture of managerial policy than was otherwise available to individual stewards. For example, one steward said, 'Every steward is in the picture about management'.

The committees were also considered important in uniting aims, in allowing common policies to be developed, and as one respondent put it, enable 'One approach to management instead of four separate ones'. Others mentioned that they revealed the consensus of opinion, and that they promoted unity among union members. Thus, inter-union committees do more than provide information; they develop common policies for stewards of different unions. These policies were related to all the workshop problems which stewards encounter, respondents specifically mentioning discussions on pay, job rates, differentials, machine speeds, redundancy, grading, holidays, shiftworking, safety, welfare, JWC agenda, demarcation, union membership, overtime, and work study. After similar investigation in engineering, Dr Lerner concluded that 'These committees have provided most of the initiative for extending the scope of factory agreements.[10] Clearly, plant committees provide a forum for discussion of stewards' current problems, and a mechanism promoting common lines of approach. Such policy making is, in the strict union view, outside the scope of stewards, taking place in a body beyond union control.

Most inter-union committees elect officials and possibly a smaller executive committee to be concerned with plant-wide issues. This executive, e.g. a works committee, is regarded as senior, assisting stewards in their union or their area who have registered 'failure to agree' in early stages of procedure. They, in turn, often pass problems to the works convenor. Respondents noted, for example, 'The weekly meeting gets fairly rapid results through the convenor'. The committee may nominate candidates for management/worker committees and, as from its own officers, will receive periodic reports. One respondent stressed that 'the formation of sub-committees to look into particular questions is useful', another mentioning that the work load could be shared. This division of labour suggests that policy formation has achieved some degree of refinement.

The JSSC also has an educational function. Many respondents mentioned that the committee enabled them to 'air problems and get good advice'. Others stressed the help of experienced stewards in advising their younger colleagues. The meetings gave stewards an opportunity to raise problems, and they valued the advice they received. Again, the committees fill a gap left by the unions, this time in 'training'. This has important implications, practices tending to be perpetuated, the stewards' functions being subject to equalizing pressures irrespective of union. The influence of more experienced stewards is probably extended at the expense of full time officials. Some senior stewards mentioned the committee as a valuable communications system for passing information to constituents. Some committees published newsletters for factory circulation, financed from JSSC funds. Some managements provided facilities, in other cases it was done less openly.

Committees raise funds through raffles, sweepstakes, and levies. These funds have many uses, e.g. administration and secretarial assistance, publication of bulletins, compensating stewards for loss of earnings when not otherwise provided for, expenses of such committee officials as delegates, such welfare benefits as funeral wreaths and donations, and other activities.

While their functions vary, one major activity is providing information before bargaining, discussing bargaining priorities, consolidating aims, and co-ordinating action. Committees widely attempt to standardize practices among departments, and management is made to feel vulnerable if its policies are applied inconsistently. Even slight variations over small issues, e.g. the number of times late before a warning, provoke claims for uniformity of treatment. More significant are similar equalization claims on such topics as piecework and bonus rates, overtime distribution, etc. There are, almost inevitably, inconsistencies in piecework prices to be used as a lever, and the joint committee can reveal them. These are exploited by appeals that, in fairness, similar jobs should receive similar rewards, the equity of sharing overtime equally, 'why aren't maintenance men warned for bad timekeeping', etc. As one steward put it, 'anomalies arising on the shop floor can be ironed out'. The use of comparability, and managements' sensitivity to it, enables concessions in one department to be transmitted throughout the plant, and regenerated by appeal to customary differentials. Pressure is exerted in vulnerable departments or plants for improvements, and the gains spread across the plant by intra-plant whipsaw tactics. Management in large plants faces an enormous communications problem if it is to contain this form of advance, as do multi-plant companies in face of a combine committee, for their techniques are essentially similar. The building industry affords another variation on this form of pressure. Organization between stewards on large sites is often better than that between different subcontractors on the site. Here the comparisons bargaining technique is applied to each employer in turn, 'original' pressure being directed against the most vulnerable subcontractor from time to time. Firms whose contracts contain penalty clauses may be especially open to workplace pressures and, with no co-ordination between the firms, this ratchet advance can be perpetuated. Similarly, strong workplace organization prevents management transferring work held up by a dispute, outside officials having difficulty in discovering the truth.

Company-wide combine committees

Company-wide combine committees' opportunities for fruitful comparison are largely limited to those afforded by management. Owing to difficulties, their principal communication concern is with major conditions, e.g. earnings, manning production schedules, discipline, hours, grading, etc. In engineering, where the national agreement makes no provision for fringe benefits such as retirement pensions, sickness benefits, redundancy payments, etc., some combine committees have been preoccupied with this topic, although others are also frequently discussed. Transfers of work to new plants in Development Areas have caused anxieties in the older motor factories, and have been discussed by the Combine Committees.

Companies whose wage structure is relatively simple, e.g. those based on time rates for few grades in a job evaluation scheme, as at Ford's, or in the chemical industry, or where there is centralized control, plainly limit their scope. In contrast, companies with complicated payment systems, with large incentive components, and a high degree of decentralization, provide endless opportunities for plant pressure on the grounds of 'fair comparison'. Conversely, regular contact between stewards from different plants probably inhibits management from attempting to take advantages. Managements do not oppose variations in principle, e.g. in earnings, as in different locations this may be consistent with an adequate labour force. Their acceptance of standardization is partly the result of union, and partly steward pressure.

Having studied earnings for six categories of workers in several branches of engineering, Lerner and Marquand[11] concluded that combine committees equalize earnings upwards through multi-plant firms. This hypothesis explains the absence of correlation in most regions between high or low earnings, and high or low labour demand. The strength of the committees is a factor in transferring earnings improvements, in time, from high labour demand areas to others. Moreover, companies with interests in several branches of engineering, e.g. Rolls Royce, Vickers, English Electric, AEI/GEC, etc., also facilitate the transfer of improvements between factories and between different 'industries'. Thus, increases justified by productivity improvement in the motor industry are transmitted by coercive comparison to workers of similar skills, and union membership, in other sections of the firm. This transfer has very wide implications. Both 'industry'

129

and 'district' earnings statistics figure prominently in union and steward arguments for improvements locally, and so the committees' activities stimulate reactions outside the firm concerned.

Employers also undertake wage surveys, noting conditions provided by competitors in the industry, and in the same locality. This criterion for granting or rejecting claims for improvements is often used by employers in negotiations, inducing stewards to obtain similar information. On the local criterion, stewards are often informed through their branches or district committees. AEF stewards complete a detailed report on workshop conditions and rates every quarter, to be discussed at the quarterly district meetings of stewards. The gap in information about their company left by union organization regionally is partially remedied by combine committees, while communication between stewards in competing firms further supplements bargaining material. Some unions, e.g. the T & GWU and NUVB in the Midlands motor industry, have sought to recover this function by organizing meetings of stewards from one large firm, and from competing firms.

Combine committees are seldom recognized by unions or management, but Ford's has sought to associate the committee with its internal communications system. Periodic meetings between convenors and company (as opposed to plant) management are conducted 'consultatively', giving convenors accurate information and management opportunities to clarify policies and kill rumours. Other companies tacitly acknowledge combine committees by listening to points raised by stewards known to be influential on them, or by providing them individually with information.

Company-wide combine committees thus occupy an anomalous and necessarily unofficial position, but their proliferation has not thrown up as many problems for the unions as might be expected. They co-ordinate JSSCs, gather and disseminate information, and act as pressure groups on both management and official union negotiators. Their activities, methods, and perhaps policies stem from the failure of multi-plant firms to develop comprehensive, company-wide machinery, although many provide such channels on a plant basis.

Convenors and senior stewards

The variety of stewards' workplace organizations is reflected in the different bases for the election of convenors and chief or senior stewards. For example:

(a) In large plants, workplace organization may be based on a hierarchy of shop committees, each electing a shop convenor, he in turn representing them on a plant-wide convenors committee which forms the executive body of the JSSC. This shop committee may have a multi-union composition.

(b) Stewards of one union may elect a senior steward or convenor from amongst themselves, to represent their union in plant-wide discussions.

(c) Collectively, the stewards in a plant (or shop convenors or single union convenors) may elect a works convenor, who will represent stewards across the whole plant. Always, the convenor is answerable to the body electing him, either within one or across several unions. He is normally subject to re-election, but many convenors continue in office as long as they retain the stewards' confidence.

The formality of procedures for the election of convenors can be exaggerated, but it tends to be more regularized than is management's attitude to the hierarchy of stewards. The Engineering Employers Federation has not recognized convenors, though many federated companies do. The Confederation of unions formally acknowledged them in 1947, and has endeavoured to draw works convenors into its structure. Managements usually recognize convenors or senior stewards informally, but some avoid these terms. They acknowledge that a certain steward, e.g. the convenor, is influential and has a wider brief than others, but will not acknowledge the role as such. Thus, recognition *de facto* is common, but *de jure* definition of the office avoided. Some firms accept the convenor *de jure*, though understating the extent of his officially acknowledged functions. Other firms fully accept the situation and provide such facilities as office, telephone, and possibly clerical help for the works convenor. Fairfields, Jaguar, and Vauxhall[12] do this.

Thus, management wavers between grudging recognition and enthusiastic assistance. Many purposely leave the position flexible for fear the present convenor may be replaced by someone less acceptable. Thus, liberal facilities afforded one convenor, freedom of access throughout the plant and to senior management, can it is thought, be limited if his successor shows signs of abusing them. For this reason, most firms insist that convenors retain some connection with the job they nominally hold, by working the start of their shift, or by clocking in as if for their nominal job.

In large plants, a works convenor may come to spend most or all his working time on his representative duties. Clegg *et al.* (1961) note that in Birmingham 'local employers and trade union officers seem prepared to agree that about fifty convenors (or other representatives) spend more than half their time on union business, and that most but by no means all are in the engineering industry'.[13] The question of payment is handled in various ways. Management may agree to pay the convenor an agreed salary as a convenor, though more usually he is paid the average earnings for his work group, or rarely the basic rate. Whatever the practice, the joint stewards committee usually makes up any loss of earnings from their own funds. It is not unknown for members' contributions to make up a convenor's entire earnings.

The degree to which management recognizes a works convenor will influence his role. Some withhold recognition totally, restricting him to internal administration among the stewards. Much more often, however, management acknowledges his influential position, and attempts to utilize it. The convenor enables management to discuss problems common to many unions within the factory, reducing the number of occasions when solutions wait on external officials not readily available. His presence allows more problems to be kept domestic, if both sides desire this. Also, managements may dislike local union officials, therefore channelling negotiations through convenors and stewards. The reverse can also apply, management sometimes seeking to restrict the role of workplace representatives in favour of district or national officers,

132

or to maintain management prerogatives. A T & GWU national officer has claimed that at Ford's '. . . nearly every matter which was likely to become a dispute was within the field in which shop stewards were not allowed to negotiate. They were not allowed to discuss merit pay, line speeds or labour content, work standards and movement of labour.'[14]

Often the works convenor is an experienced unionist, and is regarded by both sides as an elder statesman. In our experience, senior positions in steward organizations, convenor or works committeeman, are often held by one person for long periods. A convenor's ability to influence his fellow stewards is valuable to managers, permitting ready consultation on plant-wide topics, avoiding duplication and saving time. Such topics are frequently raised by management, and the presence of a convenor facilitates a quick and convenient reference for management if the interests of workpeople are affected by a change. In a case study of one factory, Alan Fox notes that the 'convenor', who was branch secretary of the workplace based branch, was '. . . a pivotal figure in the whole pattern of management-union relations. . . . Nominally he was a leading hand in the warehouse and received the rate for the job, but came to spend the whole of his time on union business. In negotiation and discussion, his complete authority over the men meant that if a matter was cleared with the convenor it was cleared with them all. His behaviour was not only that of the redoubtable fighter for the workers' rights and interests, it also carried some of the flavour of an auxiliary to management. This was an outcome not of sympathy with management or Company, but of identification with Milton as a working community.'[15]

In large plants, there are difficulties of contact between stewards and management. A convenor, trusted by his committee, will facilitate frequent contact and the growth of confidence between the senior steward and management. Many managements labour to establish cordial personal relationships, emphasizing their availability to the convenor, who is rightly thought important in determining the attitude of stewards. An established convenor adds continuity to the conduct of labour relations, especially where turnover of shop stewards is high.

However, the works convenor is not always universally accepted by work groups, which limits his influence and the unity of the factory labour force. Working solidarity may be achieved only if the convenor is accompanied by a deputy works convenor of a different union. If a convenor is generally accepted by other stewards, he is asked to advise them individually on problems, tactics, and possibly policy. A long established convenor is particularly useful for his knowledge of plant practices and precedents, for these are seldom written into agreements. Additionally, he is expected to protect the interests of members temporarily without a steward, and often supervises elections. Thus, he is generally thought of as advancing the interests of *all* employees, being free of sectional bias, almost in forgetting to which union he belongs. The works convenor's position is like that of a steward adviser, a day to day co-ordinator on issues referred to him by stewards. He may take a part in the progression of grievances depending how far an individual steward has gone, procedural practice within the firm, the importance of the issue, etc. He may limit himself to issues which run across union membership or departments, or problems with policy implications, or new issues. Management may regard him as a trouble shooter, and expect him to influence other stewards in observing procedure, and to use his expertise and experience to calm troubled waters and prevent hasty action.

The research reported by Clegg, Killick, and Adams included twenty eight completed questionnaires from convenors, though not distinguishing shop, union, and works positions. Consequently, there are limitations to the conclusions which can be drawn. For example, average size of constituencies was 978, but excluding those convenors responsible for less than 100 members, the average constituency becomes 1,648. One respondent said he was personally responsible for 18,000 members. The results showed that the convenors spent, on average, eighteen hours of working time, and five hours of their own time on union business per week. They spent much more time in negotiations with management above foreman level than at that level, time spent with senior management being five times greater than with shop floor supervision. Such negotiations took just over one third of all the time spent, while 'discussions with members and stewards', presumably strongly weighted by the latter, accounted for another third.

These averages obscure individual variations, and certainly hide the convenor who is concerned with industrial relations nearly full time. It is difficult to say how many convenors fall into this category, for the informality of practice leads to underestimation. Rigid interpretation of 'full time' leads to similar understatement. Thus, Clegg *et al.* guess at more than 500 full time convenors, or their equivalent, in this country. Not all are in manufacturing industry, and of these by no means all in engineering. 'The number giving half their time or more to work of this kind might be as high as two thousand.'[16] This is little less than the 2,500 given for ordinary full time union officers and is certainly rising more rapidly, indicating their importance and potential as works based 'full time' union representatives.

Convenors and the unions

In contrast with salaried union officers, shop and works convenors elected by multi-union committees are not accountable as convenors to any union executive. Integration is possible only where the unions are linked through federation or, less likely, where all unions accept the primacy of a works convenor over other stewards, allowing his union to exercise supervision. It is extremely unlikely that this will be accepted by other unions or stewards, as it implies subordination of interests to one union, perhaps a union without the majority of members. The best contemporary arrangement is found in the building industry. The National Federation of Building Trades Operatives has wide powers over its member unions. A federation steward is appointed on each site, being responsible to the Federation. He is normally accepted as senior by stewards of other unions, and can convene meetings to decide issues affecting members of more than one union. Also, the Federation has monthly meetings of stewards of affiliated unions, attended by federation stewards. The NFBTO comes closest to formal integration of 'chief stewards', being allowed by member unions to exercise some co-ordinated control.

In large printing establishments, an Imperial Father is

135

sometimes elected to co-ordinate issues affecting members of several chapels. However, traditions of craft differentiation, separate union organization, and the weakness of the Printing and Kindred Trades Federation at workplace level have limited the development of this office.

The Confederation of Shipbuilding and Engineering Unions adopted a link with convenors in 1947, recognizing Joint Shop Stewards Works Committees and giving Confederation credentials to the chairman and secretary of these committees. These confederation stewards 'shall act on behalf of and be responsible to the Confederation District Committee'[17] with direct access to the Confederation's district secretary, a full time official of one union. In addition, the forty eight district committees hold quarterly meetings of the chairmen and secretaries of stewards' works committees. Thus, the framework for communication and control exists, but the authority of the Confederation has not developed, the term 'confederation steward' being little used. As stated, the Engineering Employers Federation has not recognized these offices. Secondly, the Confederation has minimal autonomy from its constituent unions locally, and the machinery for control remains largely on paper. Unions within the Confederation have not altered their rule books to allow for this provision, and such rule books are still the primary reference for stewards.

Limitations on steward committees

So far, we have discussed both intra-plant and inter-plant joint steward committees, emphasizing the reasons for their existence and the value stewards attach to them. However, there are contrary pressures militating against them, currently perhaps being a greater check than any formalized system outside a powerful federation.

At plant level, the unions may be in sharp conflict, e.g. over membership or work allocation, which inhibits co-operation between stewards. Certain sections may advance their own interests while ignoring others', and may positively injure the interests of members of other unions. At BMC's Coventry plant in 1966, production workers of one union struck in protest against the unofficial activities of internal transport workers organized by another union, because the latter's protracted action limited their piecework earnings.[18] One union's members may be harmed by the advance of others, particularly over demarcation and manning, as during the introduction of the web offset process in printing. Certain groups of workers may not feel they have much except information to gain from co-operation, e.g. maintenance workers in relation to production workers, staff union representatives and manual workers. Small unions fear their interests would be submerged in any association, independence being preferable, although stewards' committees seldom infringe the freedom of action by 'affiliated' stewards. This view is commonly held by skilled maintenance men, who seldom fully accept non-craftsmen as convenors. As noted, unions often refuse to allow convenors from other unions to negotiate for their members.

Personalities and politics also enter the undercurrent of stress dividing stewards. Local full time officials may take a strong line over participation in inter-union committees. Certain sections may be considered to be benefiting disproportionately from joint organization. Shift working makes meetings difficult, and infrequent contact leads to suspicion. This infrequency is especially important in inhibiting combine committees between remote plants. Further, the interests of different plants are not identical. For example, the location of extensions may be influenced by the labour relations in various branches. In difficult times, work allocation between units makes some more vulnerable to short time working and redundancies. Further, there may be suspicion that the convenor is utilizing his position to advance the interests of members of his union, while neglecting those of others. Thus, inter-union competition, over membership, composition of joint stewards committee, and other problems limits the cohesiveness of workplace committees. Combine committees may be particularly hampered by lack of funds, lack of data implied by the absence of full time assistance, changes in personnel, and the difficulties of attendance. Indeed, having recently surveyed the motor industry, Turner, Clack, and Roberts concluded that national firm-wide committees had

had little effect, and that 'the effectiveness of the stewards' associations seems roughly in inverse proportion to their distance from the workplace'.[19]

Committees, unions, and bargaining

Joint shop stewards committees are patently considered useful by stewards, but they have created opportunities for independent action. They may challenge existing union policies and the established machinery for regulating relationships. Despite this, their relationship with the unions and management has not, in the main, presented major difficulties. Some notorious, but exceptional combine committees or JSSCs have ignored established trade unions and collective agreements, interposing themselves between the rank and file and union officials. Examples were those at Briggs Motor Bodies, London Airport, and Ford's in the late 'fifties and early 'sixties. Court of Inquiry Reports documented the financial strength, independence, and extremism of these committees, indicating the attractions of these powerful 'private unions' to men dedicated to industrial disruption for political reasons.[20]

The unions are aware, as the TUC put it, that 'some joint arrangements between stewards have been harmful', to unions as to employers. Further, 'cases of muddle, duplication and even conflict have arisen through these bodies acting as though they were independent of union obligations'.[21] The *potential* freedom of action within contemporary union workplace organization is well attested by the TUC's view. Union coolness to joint steward committees has not prevented their appearance. The unions must now live with them, and find ways to influence them.

Certainly, present trends suggest the continued growth of stewards' committees, highlighting the problem of lack of a mechanism for drawing these bodies into official union organizations. The rules do not allow for their development and so they grow through expediency to meet day to day requirements. The dynamic of modern manufacturing and the urgency of many problems demand rapid decision taking. Reference to external union bodies is time consuming, and it is likely that the periodic meetings specified in federation rule books are devoted to previous events, rather than to determining new policies for the future.

If the unions are to increase their influence over joint committees they must radically reorganize their structure, shifting its base into the workplace. Full formal control, however, is impossible without single unionism, or of federations, or *ad hoc* inter-union arrangements with vastly greater powers than the present multi-union organizations. Adaptation within existing structures may help to strengthen communications, e.g. meetings between representatives of joint shop stewards or combine committees in a company, and the national union negotiators. The ETU, in its evidence to the Royal Commission, suggested that union officials on national joint negotiating councils should be able to communicate directly with the joint membership down to workplace level.[22] In 1962, the Ford NJNC agreed to such meetings between factory convenors and the union side of the NJNC on a six-monthly basis. Clearly, such links are easily established where bargaining is with a single company, but more urgent, and difficult, in the large multi-company negotiations more characteristic in Britain. Such steps are mere stopgaps; their achievements may be slight, but they do represent an advance.

Inter-departmental and inter-factory comparisons stimulate claims, but the information stewards gain is not subject to verification by unions or management. It may be inaccurate, but once believed on the shop floor it affords opportunities for exploitation by any interested group. Thus, management may recognize the JSSC or combine committee as the only way to increase the flow of information, and to combat misinformation. If such recognition and consultation within a company became widespread, and embraced negotiating functions, established collective bargaining machinery and employers' associations would be severely challenged. Many recent productivity agreements have pointed in this direction, associating stewards and their committees systematically with bargaining at company and plant levels. Indeed, one basic principle of plant based productivity bargaining has been the acknowledgement of two-tier unionism, emphasizing the position of stewards, and, the impracticality of relying on external union officials. However, Turner, Clack, and Roberts felt that, in the motor industry at least, stewards' organizations. like full time officials, operated as a 'buffer' between employers and operatives.[23] As this implies the balancing of immediate sectional interests against the broader factory and longer term interests of the stewards and their organizations, they could themselves begin to experience the difficulties of control faced by any 'establishment' in the unions.

References

1. Marsh, A. I. and Coker, E. E., *op. cit.*, p. 177.
2. The name 'works committee' is a source of confusion. It is now more commonly applied to a committee of senior stewards with explicit and preferential negotiating arrangements with managements, rather than to the joint seven-a-side management/steward committees of the 1919 Agreement.
3. See Lerner, Shirley W. and Bescoby, John., 'Shop Steward Committees in the British Engineering Industry', *British Journal of Industrial Relations*, July, 1966.
4. *TUC Annual Report, 1960*, p. 129.
5. Lerner and Bescoby, *op. cit.*, p. 163.
6. *Annual Abstract of Statistics.*, No. 102, 1965, Table 139.
7. Marsh and Coker, *op. cit.*, p. 189. Their sample showed that two thirds of AEF stewards in federated engineering firms were in establishments employing over 500 manual workers.
8. *Report of the Joint Labour Council for the Motor Industry* into disputes at the Rover Company's assembly plant at Solihull, December 1965. This Report showed that with a total labour force of 5,204 there were 240 shop stewards, i.e. an average constituency size of 22. Of the unions involved, the NUVB had 121 stewards, the T & GWU 80, and the AEF 21.
9. Marsh and Coker, *op. cit.*, p. 187.
10. Lerner, Shirley W., 'Factory Agreements and National Bargaining in the British Engineering Industry', *International Labour Review*, January 1964, p. 6.
11. Lerner, Shirley W. and Marquand, Judith, 'Regional Variations in Earnings, Demand for Labour and Shop Stewards Combine Committees in the British Engineering Industry', *Manchester School*, September 1963.
12. Marsh and Coker, *op. cit.*, state that the AEU District Returns for 1961 showed only 40 full time AEU convenors, but they considered that this figure referred to those provided with office facilities by management.
13. Clegg, Killick, and Adams, *op. cit.*, p. 179.
14. Report of Court of Inquiry, HMSO Cmnd 1999, 1963, para. 78.
15. Fox, Alan, *The Milton Plan*, Institute of Personnel Management, 1965, p. 19–22.

16. Clegg, Killick, and Adams, *op. cit.*, p. 180.
17. Confederation Minute, Quarterly Meeting, 19th February, 1947.
18. The *Financial Times*, 15th April, 1966.
19. Turner, H. A., Clack, Garfield, and Roberts, Geoffrey, *Labour Relations in the Motor Industry*, George Allen and Unwin, 1967, p. 22.
20. HMSO Cmnds, 131, 608 and 1999.
21. *TUC Annual Report, 1960*, pp. 129–130.
22. As reported in the *Financial Times*, 7th November, 1966.
23. Turner, Clack, and Roberts, *op cit.*, p. 222.

7
Workplace Bargaining and Shop Stewards

Collective bargaining between employers and unions has evolved through several stages. In the late nineteenth century, agreements between unions and employers were characteristically by district, but in this century increasingly gave way to industry-wide settlement, applicable by all employers in an industry who belonged to the employers' association. This change was deliberate, but recent developments have been less so.

During and since the Second World War, bargaining activities have shifted, for though the traditional machinery remains the 'centre of gravity' has moved away from industry-wide committees. Such bodies retain former functions; they no longer represent all bargaining, and in many industries their importance has been considerably undermined. This movement has not been conscious decentralization, but unplanned and until recently unannounced. As industry-wide bargaining is characteristic rather than universal, so there are variations in the extent of workplace bargaining. Perhaps its greatest development is in engineering, but similar trends appear in most manufacturing and to a lesser extent in the service sector. Workplace bargaining has altered the role of the steward; he is no longer a guardian of national agreements, but is concerned to improve them, now widely exercising influence on the conditions of employment of his constituents. He is a rule maker and a negotiator as well as a custodian and rule enforcer. The changing scope of industrial relations has broadened the issues regulated jointly in the workplace. While many are small, detailed and complex, cumulatively they influence both earnings and costs. Their multiplicity taxes, if not exhausts, the capacity of traditional machinery and its union officials.

Workplace bargaining was not designed, but just happened. Its scope is obscured by its informality, and its recently recognized importance has not yet provoked adequate institutional response. Indeed, this delay in adjusting the existing structure, which emphasizes external regulation of employment relationships, is responsible for many problems of present concern.

The value of industry-wide negotiating procedures

Traditionally, unions, employers, and governments support a voluntary system of industrial relations, the two sides regulating their relationship as they wish. Government intervention has intended to stimulate growth of voluntary joint negotiating machinery, to protect unorganized workers, or provide further means of reaching peaceful solutions after the exhaustion of voluntary procedures. More recently, government intervention has reflected a different view, that settlements are no longer of purely private interest, but also affect those of both the public and the government. Indeed, in the House of Commons in November, 1966, the then Minister of Labour said that the public interest was of overriding importance. Recent government policy has repeatedly reflected this tripartite view of collective bargaining.

Historically, the unions stressed the equity of workers of similar ability performing similar jobs being paid similarly. They were concerned with the 'rate for the job', seeking to equalize it throughout industries and occupations. Industry-wide rates also promoted union solidarity and the development of common interest amongst union members. It prevented competition between workers unfavourably affecting the wage paid, being particularly valuable in periods and areas of high unemployment, a national standard being more easily defended than numerous district rates. The standard rate increased members' dependence on the union, while centralized bargaining facilitated the extension of union organization throughout an industry or occupation. Moreover, it conserved union resorces, and enabled the unions' experienced officials to conduct negotiations.

The employers also felt it offered strategic benefits, notably in restraining undercutting wages and 'unfair' competition. Individual employers were protected from special claims, nationally organized unions could be matched, and some balance of power achieved. Industry-wide bargaining reduced the risk of a firm being strikebound while its competitors still produced, thus protecting its share of the market. Simultaneous wage increases similarly preserved the relative position of firms. If increased wage rates resulted in higher unit costs, all firms could raise prices in co-ordination.

The organization of bargaining over *major* conditions on an industry-wide basis inhibits disputes over these issues in individual firms. The time consuming negotiations involved can be left to specialists in the employers' association, and being remote from any one firm, do not jeopardize relationships within it. Moreover, negotiations being external, collective, and centralized, employers are free from 'inspection' by outside union officials not subject to the company's sanctions. Inevitably, negotiations are generalized, and the individual firm is shielded.

However, multi-employer collective agreements generally allow employers to supplement their terms locally if necessary. Employers may want their own wages structure, they may want a direct incentive, for example, and generally prefer flexible rather than rigid national agreements. Industry-wide negotiations allow unions to obtain improvements for some members which might not be possible in local labour conditions. But, with labour scarcity, or other favourable conditions, members can supplement the standard rate taking 'two bites at the cherry'. Thus, in new employment conditions since 1945, centralized wage bargaining has not inhibited unions' bargaining opportunities elsewhere. National bargaining is a valued part of a dual system, particularly in unevenly organized industries, in 'marginal' firms, and in safeguarding the position of senior union officials.

Reasons for the development of workplace bargaining

(1) Full employment

The growth of workplace bargaining cannot be wholly explained by the state of the labour market, but undoubtedly
full employment since 1945 has been crucial. Scarcity is no
longer exclusive to skilled labour, but applies generally, thus
enhancing labour's bargaining power. This emerges in national
negotiations, but more profoundly in the extension of bargaining to the workplace. Stewards have secured improvements
on national agreements, employers usually passing on higher
costs in higher prices. Employers have had to pay more to
recruit and retain labour, and to maintain industrial peace.
A tight labour market has induced regular comparisons and
competitive bidding between employers, while buoyant
product markets, greater process interdependence, etc., have
increased the force of stewards' sanctions. Similarly, employers' sanctions have lost much of their edge. In short, the
balance of power is now with labour, and this greater bargaining power has been channelled into the workplace and into
the components of earnings determined there, e.g. bonuses,
merit rates, over-time, etc. Greater pressure is also applied to
non-financial issues.

(2) Procedural facilities

Procedural means for passing on complaints and claims in
the workplace are provided for in collective agreements,
which allow representatives to progress issues by recording
failure to agree at successive internal stages. This process
makes issues collective, and its impersonal nature prevents
managements from handling issues individually, as they might
for unorganized workers. Thus, an open-ended avenue is
provided for workplace representatives. Procedural machinery
may be used without limit, although managements occasionally refuse to discuss certain topics as non-negotiable, but
evidence suggests it is increasingly used. Marsh and Jones[1]
found a doubling of hearings at works conference level in
the Engineering Procedure between 1956 and 1963. This is

surprising when workplace parties evidently desire to keep issues domestic, and when many firms operate informal procedures supplementing those in national agreements in order to encourage it. However, Marsh and Jones quoted an 80 per cent chance of settlement at this semi-domestic level.

(3) Collective agreements

Industry-wide collective agreements are not usually accepted as providing terms which cannot be supplemented. They are more typically regarded as minimum guarantees to be improved upon, though conventions in some employers' associations have discouraged this from being done openly and directly on basic wage rates, length of the working week, length of holidays, etc. Secondly, collective agreements often omit subjects of joint interest, and often fail to define the rights of the two parties comprehensively. For example, basic wage rates, premium rates for overtime, public holiday rates, shiftworking allowances, the length of the nominal working week, and holidays are normally specified, but do not regulate shift rotation, discipline, engagement and dismissal, distribution of working hours, spacing of breaks, redundancy, pay methods, supervision, etc. If these topics are mentioned it is for guidance only, most national agreements being totally silent. These gaps leave scope for workplace regulation, assuring workplace representatives an influential role. Moreover, the standardization of industry-wide terms does not reflect company variations in productivity, profits, labour supply, orders, etc., all these being exploitable at company or workplace level. District officials having wide responsibilities may be preoccupied with problems elsewhere; but stewards are ever present, have a narrower brief, and often form inter-union committees to overcome structural handicaps.

(4) Fixed period agreements and government intervention

The time span of national agreements is seldom specified, but recently fixed period agreements have become customary. In October 1965, 27 per cent of employees were covered by such agreements.[2] By restricting national claims for several years, these agreements transfer attention to the workplace. Future national improvements are assured, and national officials' hands are tied, but stewards can exploit local opportunities. The tendency for improvements to be more easily achieved locally also reflects coercive government interest in national agreements. Workplace improvements are less publicized, being small and numerous, and thus are not susceptible to the same scrutiny, particularly in small firms.

(5) Payment by results

Payment by results systems are significant in local improvements. While national agreements customarily stipulate an incentive rate at a level enabling a worker of average ability to earn a minimum ratio of the basic rate, the schemes are usually supervised at workshop level. This is not invariable, e.g. the cotton textile and some sections of the boot and shoe industries have district price lists, but even here workplace representatives can exercise influence over their constituents' earnings. Changes in production, in layout, working conditions, quality standards, etc., stimulate renegotiations, usually resulting in higher earnings. Work measurement techniques are insufficiently accurate to prevent discrepancies. exploitable by stewards. In April 1961, 42 per cent of manual workers in manufacturing worked under incentive schemes, a figure exceeded in several industries in which stewards are active. They covered 62 per cent of wage earners in shipbuilding and marine engineering, 52 per cent in vehicles, 47 per cent in general engineering and electrical goods.[3]

(6) Consultative procedures

During and after the Second World War many companies established joint consultative machinery, generally to aid efficiency and co-operation through improving management–employee communications. In the workplace, these committees dealt with domestic problems such as production, safety, and welfare. Although negotiations were explicitly prohibited, management often failed to maintain fine distinctions between consultative and negotiable topics. Many accepted the change in function of joint consultation, others resisted it. Practice varies, but the evidence suggests that pure joint consultation is declining.

(7) Management's preference for shop stewards

Some managements prefer to deal with stewards, resisting the participation of full time officials, of both unions and their employers' association, in workplace problems. Many consider it a failure, as well as a loss of control, to call in outside officials. Stewards may be similarly inclined to restrict the access of full time officials. Unlike officials of an employers' association, company managements must live with the solution obtained from external machinery, and suspect that the association's officials will allow precedent and their wider concern with other members to influence settlement of a problem. Moreover, it is common sense to solve a problem as low and as early as possible. Stewards are subject to the firm's sanctions, are readily available, better informed of facts, views, and members' probable reactions. Personal relationships between managers and stewards may be better than those with outside officials, and may be enhanced by keeping topics domestic. Moreover, the volume of issues may make it expedient for management to deal with stewards rather than the officials of several unions.

(8) Personnel specialists

Another development in workplace bargaining is the introduction of specialists by management, e.g. work study officers, labour relations and personnel officers. The largest post war growth in members of the Institute of Personnel Management, absolutely and in percentage terms, is found in engineering including vehicles and aircraft.[4] And here, stewards have perhaps reached their highest density and development. The expertise of some firms in labour relations exceeds that of employers' associations, while their knowledge of the intricacies of a problem, and of management policy, means they are often better equipped to handle the management case. A similar comparison holds between experienced stewards or convenors and full time officials. The emergence of company-wide steward combine committees also reflects the trend for increasingly domestic industrial relations activity, committees defining the company as a bargaining unit. It may be suggested that active workplace bargaining will increase the importance

148

of labour relations specialists within management and they may promote an 'internal' policy.

(9) Informality

Most workplace agreements are informal and unwritten, which affords both sides some advantage in flexibility of operation. Management may prefer this uncodified system, thinking it will allow downward reinterpretation in better circumstances. However it is arguable whether 'custom and practice' is more vulnerable than a written agreement, or whether purposely bad memories are less provocative than overt bad faith, on either side.

The influence of stewards on the pay, working conditions, and terms of employment of union members is widespread, substantial, and increasing. Modification of this generalization is progressively less necessary. The absence of incentive schemes no longer precludes workplace bargaining on financial issues. For example, Dr McCarthy found that 'stewards in such trades as confectionery, or in services like gas, electricity and local government, can base an effective system of workplace bargaining on obtaining local improvements in the rates of work'.[5] One rota representative in a municipal bus undertaking felt that the rigidity of the national agreement prevented local negotiations on wages and earnings. He therefore acted to protect members' working conditions, making life (as he said) 'cushier' by resisting reductions in services and in running and journey times, etc.

Workplace bargaining, or at least regulation, of the many components of earnings is often loosely assessed by reference to the gap between earnings and wage rates. Thus, before examining other aspects of workplace bargaining, wage drift must be examined.

Wage drift

The concept of wage drift is often confused with its measurement. Wage drift has been authoritatively defined by Professor Phelps Brown, who states 'the essence of drift is that the effective rate of pay per unit of labour input is raised by arrangements that lie outside the control of the recognized procedures for scheduling rates',[6] i.e. negotiated agreements, awards, or statutory orders. Dr Lerner adds that 'drift can occur in two ways: a worker's earnings may increase outside the terms of the recognized collective agreement, but no change occurs in the degree of utilization of his labour; a worker's earnings may remain constant between scheduled rises, but his labour is underutilised as compared with the period when the recognized collective agreement was negotiated.'[7] Thus because of variations in labour inputs it cannot be said whether increases in earnings under payment by results schemes are or are not drift. Similarly, overtime earnings cannot be automatically classified as drift. Loose piecework rates, unadjusted to improved techniques, increase earnings per unit of labour input and constitute drift. Conversely, greater application of labour inputs by workers in speed and effort in unchanged conditions, resulting in higher earnings, is not drift. Thus, changed labour inputs and occupational movements bedevil the accurate measurement of wage drift.

It is comparatively easy to measure an 'earnings gap' statistically, but it is not drift. Moreover, Ministry of Labour classifications do not coincide with bargaining units, but a few examples illustrate the widening gap between basic weekly wage rates and average weekly earnings. In June 1967, the consolidated national time rate in engineering was 221s 8d for skilled fitters and 187s 4d for labourers. Average weekly earnings for fitters on timework ranged from 417s in marine engineering to 515s 6d in motor vehicles, and for fitters on piecework from 456s 1d in electrical engineering to 540s in motor vehicles. Labourers' earnings on timework ranged from 309s 10d in electrical engineering to 360s in motor vehicles, and on piecework from 331s 9d in mechanical engineering to 365s 9d in marine engineering.[8] In April 1967, the minimum weekly wage rate for adult male workers in the tobacco industry was 235s 6d, but average earnings of all adult male manual workers were 444s 7d.[9] In the municipal bus industry, the NJIC basic weekly rate for drivers in July 1967 was 257s and average weekly earnings 446s 5d.[10] Figure 7.1 provides a more general impression.

Essentially, wage drift is associated with two forces in the workplace:

Fig. 7.1. Weekly rates of wages, average weekly earnings for manual workers, average salary earnings, and retail prices, 1955–67

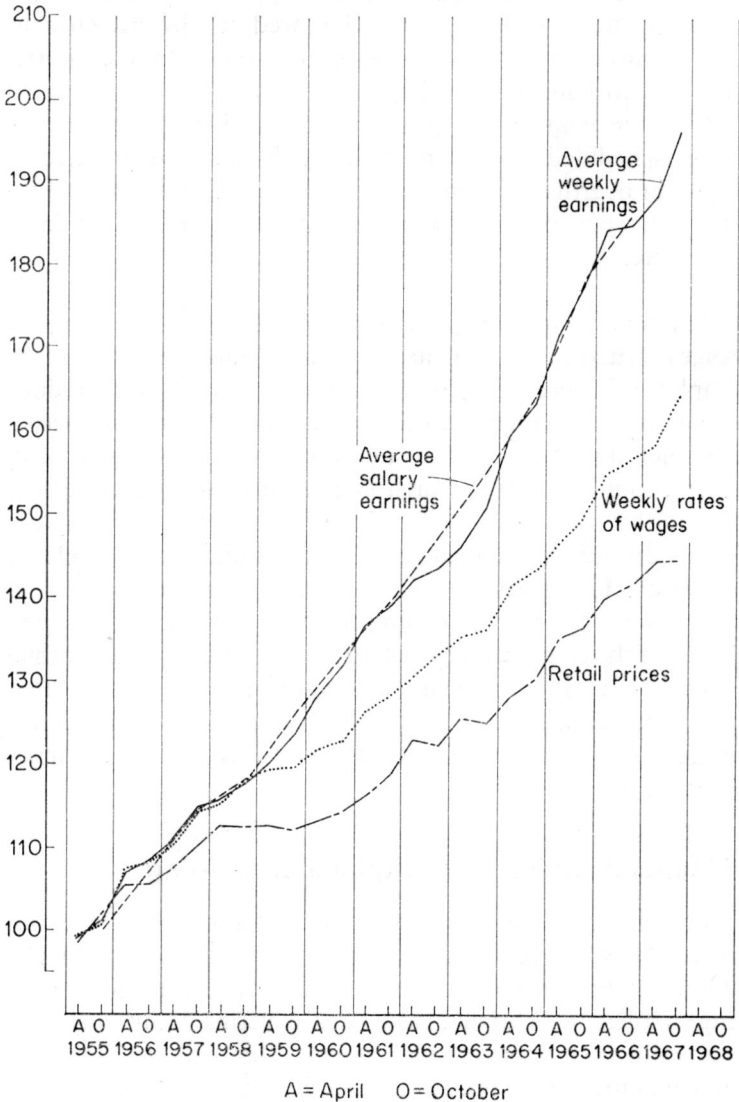

A = April   O = October

(Source: Department of Employment and Productivity Statistics on Incomes, Prices, Employment, and Production.)

(*a*) Stewards or their equivalent press management to increase earnings above the scheduled rate. This pressure may be applied initially at strategic points, or be associated with gradual improvements by pieceworkers (primary drift). This is followed up by pressure to reorder the wages structure in response to these initial disturbances (secondary drift).

(*b*) Management may grant higher earnings by raising the scheduled rate or, more likely, by contriving increases in overtime, failing to revise piecework rates, introducing or improving bonuses, artificially regrading jobs, etc.

Ultimately, management is responsible for arranging its wages structure to fulfil its policies, within the limits of its employees' ideas of fairness. A company wanting to reduce wage drift has primarily to accept that some loss of production does not always exceed the alternative prospective increase in unit labour costs. Wage drift is generally less, the closer the control by management of daily administration of the agreement. In this way, management can influence the role of stewards, for wages systems, structures, and controls help determine stewards' bargaining activities. Drift is also likely to be less if the company negotiates its own agreement rather than participating in multi-employer agreements. It seems that avoidance of payment by results reduces opportunities for wage drift, as these schemes often undermine management control.

Financial topics in workplace bargaining

Bargaining over issues of payment is a vital activity of stewards in industry, movements in earnings beyond rates nationally agreed giving *some* indication of this. Normally, such bargaining supplements national basic rates, covering many workplace determined components of earnings. Stewards are, however, active in improving occupational or job rates, especially where multi-employer agreements only loosely categorize jobs. For instance, the engineering agreement is concluded for adult men principally in terms of skilled fitters and unskilled labourers, and though mentioning *some* sub-groups among the skilled, it does not contain even minimum rates for semi-skilled grades. Thus, it fails to outline differentials between many occupational groups found in the industry. They are, thus, left to workplace agreements. Specific occupational groups, e.g. sheet metal workers, submit claims at works level, which *may* be settled early and internally by stewards. Different groups of semi-skilled workers, e.g. inspectors, may seek to restore their position, similar sectional claims being presented by their stewards with external officials only asked for ratification. Periodic 'domestic' claims by sub-groups constitute open bargaining at works level, and management eager to settle them may do so without directly involving external union officials.

A claim for a domestic sectional increase is perhaps the most obvious example of a steward's bargaining role, but stewards do bargain on other money topics. Indeed, wage rate bargaining may be precluded by the nature of the agreement, and the conventions of union and occupational organization in the workplace. However, such factors are a lesser obstacle when incentive payment schemes apply.

(1) Payment by results

With full employment, a major vehicle of wage drift is payment by results schemes. It is no accident that 'in the engineering, metals and vehicle industries . . . shop stewards devote more time to negotiating incentive rates than to any other function of industrial relations'.[11] Opportunities for wage drift under such schemes are numerous. Continuous repetition makes an operator more proficient; he can thus earn more for the same effort. Small but cumulatively important changes in layout, handling methods, etc. are introduced constantly, though each by itself may not warrant a restudy of the job. The inconsistencies of work measurement, as well as small method improvements, lead stewards to complain of the tight rates—while defending loose ones. Cohesive work groups, where restrictive group norms influence individual earnings, hide slackly rated jobs. Changes and discontinuities in production permit new negotiations, e.g. between different jobs in a jobbing factory, over the introduction of new machinery

153

which increases output without increasing labour inputs or over movements of labour to new jobs. Loss of earnings militates against labour mobility, and so management often provides compensatory allowances or favourable retraining rates. Changes in materials have similar effects, and understandings need to be reached on the quality of materials, on quality control standards, and arrangements for reworking faulty pieces. Agreements also are necessary on shortages of materials, the condition of equipment, procedure during breakdowns, and the size and composition of groups on group incentive schemes. Almost any change initially induces defensiveness in shop floor workers, though also affording bargaining opportunities. Innovation is a topic on which stewards seek consultation, and on which their duty to advance their members' interests is well developed.

Concessions in one section of a plant provoke restorative action elsewhere. For example, existing relativities between pieceworkers' and timeworkers' earnings will be upset unless the latter are safeguarded by having a built in ratio to pieceworkers' earnings. Failing this, timeworkers' representatives claim, on grounds of equity, increases in lieu of bonuses, which management may concede to avoid trouble. While primary and secondary drift can be isolated in theory, in a complex factory with different work groups and frequent work changes it is difficult to specify which claim starts the cycle. A wage structure may always appear anomalous to *one* group, and differentiation of the labour force leads to multilateral bargaining.

Stewards in factories with incentive payment schemes can help determine the rates *ab initio*. Stewards' books of rates, extending back over long periods, are known to pass from a steward to his successor. The steward's knowledge of prices, times, and precedents, may exceed management's. Not all jobs can be referred to previous standards. Work study is not universal and can be challenged in any case, while new jobs may run without timing and guesswork is still widespread among shop floor supervision. A recent investigation into a piecework dispute in a large motor plant revealed '. . . that supervision at the company has to rely considerably upon shop stewards for its facts and figures in relation to the booking of new and untimed work. At the same time the information so provided is a major factor in determining a piece-work time to stand perhaps for many years'.[12]

(2) The effort bargain

Unlike payment by results, timework offers fewer opportunities for stewards to influence directly their members' pay. However, as the price per unit of input is the basis of negotiations under incentive schemes, so it is on timework, though the process is different. The process is described as an 'effort bargain', as against the 'money bargain' on incentive schemes. A man's earnings may not be threatened by changes, but job content and effort may alter. Generally, this issue is less immediate and less easily measured than a piecework price, but timeworkers' stewards are no less conscious of its importance. The problem here is manning, or labour content. Stewards in timeworking motor plants keep logs of assembly line speeds, existing manning quotas are defended, and attempts to speed up the track or reduce manning are resisted. If management successfully reallocates or reduces labour, then unless the technology prohibits it, the remainder may induce overtime. Overmanning is pervasive in British industry, being particularly acknowledged in the steel and printing industries.

(3) Overtime

Where incentive schemes are not applied, overtime is the principal way of raising short term earnings. Only 40 per cent of wage earners are paid by results, but for them, overtime is an additional opportunity to supplement weekly earnings at premium rates. Traditionally, these premia were applied to discourage employers asking workers to work outside normal hours. It was accepted that the exigencies of production, seasonal fluctuations, urgent orders, increased output, etc., might occasionally demand overtime working, but employers were to pay premium rates to offset the inconvenience. This original concept does not reflect contemporary attitudes to overtime, though it may apply to individual cases. Overtime has become systematic in many industries and firms, being relied on by management to achieve production schedules,

155

and by employees as a regularly source of income. With labour scarce, and if employers adhere to their association's conventions to respect established wage rates, and overtime is a method of adjusting rewards to meet the market. Indeed, the length rather than the brevity of working hours is frequently used by firms in recruiting. Retention of overtime is induced by other firms adopting the same policy.

A prospering firm short of labour will extend labour supply by lengthening working hours, both to increase production and attract new workers. However, if the latter is more important, the atmosphere during overtime hours may not lead to much extra production. Men may simply be marking time. One effect of systematic overtime, commonly complained of by management, is that it induces absenteeism on normal working days. Further, if men prefer increased income to leisure, the availability of overtime may affect their job performance in working hours—a job may be spun out to create overtime. Briefly, premium rates provide an incentive to maximize overtime, particularly as overtime working is not compulsory, and can be accepted or refused by the individual. Spinning the work out may be deliberate, or induced by an atmosphere that accepts the availability of overtime.

In 1938, actual hours worked in industry were less than the usual standard working week, i.e. 47·8 compared with 48. After the Second World War, actual hours worked did not fall much despite cuts in the nominal working week, though they have markedly declined recently. Obviously, overtime hours, at premium rates, have increased as a proportion of weekly earnings.

Table 7.1. Average weekly hours worked by men operatives in manufacturing industries

1938 October	47·7	1955 October	48·7
1943 July	53·1	1957 October	48·0
1945 July	49·4	1959 October	48·2
1947 October	46·2	1961 October	46·8
1949 October	46·6	1963 October	46·8
1951 October	47·6	1965 October	46·1
1953 October	47·9	1967 October	44·3

Source: Department of Employment and Productivity

Overtime worked varies, but reaches very important levels in certain industries. For example, in 1966 the average hours worked in road haulage were 57; for production workers in bakeries average hours were $51\frac{1}{2}$, though there was nominally a 40 hour week.[13] Overtime working has widely become customary; attitudes towards it vary, but the impression is that it is sought rather than avoided, and in certain industries relied upon. Professor Turner concluded that 'variation in average hours seems more closely, and of course inversely, connected with the wage levels of particular trades than with their activity. Overtime has clearly become a systematic method of raising lower male wage rates'.[14] Of the twenty one manufacturing industries where average hours worked by adult males in October 1967 exceeded forty seven, only two equalled the manufacturing industry average hourly rate of pay, despite their heavy loading with overtime premiums.

While premium rates paid for overtime, usually a proportion of the wage rate, are included in national agreements, its level and distribution is regulated in the factory, stewards rather than full time officials protecting members' interests. Customarily, stewards are most concerned with the distribution of overtime opportunities, striving towards fair shares, often by means of a rota system. However, in the writers' experience, they may also seek agreements guaranteeing overtime working. Such pressure reveals both the gulf between long term official union policy and the short run views of members, and the uncertainty induced by large but inevitably unreliable overtime earnings.

The *upward* consolidation of overtime working by stewards is described by Flanders, in his analysis of the Fawley productivity agreements.[15] He notes that initially overtime was increased to deal with specific circumstances in different departments at different times, but that the level was maintained by a ratchet effect. That is, 'the almost automatic adjustment in work habits and behaviour. Everyone comes to count on it for the completion of tasks.' Then 'notions of equity' came into play, accusations of favouritism were made, and stewards demanded fair shares in overtime distribution. 'To meet such charges management began to collect statistics and broadly accepted the principle of equal opportunities. In

157

consequence, although decisions about the working of overtime nominally remained with supervision, the stewards,
acting as guardians of the principle, came effectively to control
its distribution. Moreover the application of the principle was
pressed to increasingly fine limits . . . equalisation reached the
point where the stewards, on a week by week basis, wanted to
see their men working within an hour or two of each other'.
This situation is widespread in British industry. The fair
shares principle has, in our experience, been applied by
stewards to different shifts, within and between departments, and between different crafts. Stewards apply it less to
different local factories, but loss of labour may obviate the
necessity.

Systematic overtime remains discretionary for the individual, but employers cannot shed the burden so easily. Considerable overtime working has its own momentum. To the
worker, overtime is lucrative, to the steward it is an area of
joint regulation, over which management has lost unilateral
control. This may not apply when management wants to
increase overtime, though some collective agreements restrict
this,[16] but a downward revision is usually resisted. The
elimination of high levels of overtime is accepted as a negotiable topic, for which compensation must be paid.

Stewards also try to regulate the incidence of overtime, in
stating when it will be worked, for how long, what notice
shall be given, etc. They may favour at least one hour a night,
no overtime on Fridays, and try to substitute Sunday for
Saturdays. As management normally require the concurrence
of stewards, and as overtime is voluntary, management's
bargaining power is relatively small. Overtime affects internal
wages structures, particularly if opportunities to work vary
between different groups. This stimulates restorative claims,
not necessarily for overtime, by those who feel aggrieved.
Professor Robertson found that 'unskilled workers quite
generally appear to restore some of the gap in their relative
earnings levels as against more skilled groups by working
longer hours'.[17] Conversely, not all workers seek overtime.
This is especially true of women and the usual obligation to
work a 'reasonable' amount of overtime contained in national
agreements is for them a dead letter.

(4) Other financial topics

Multi-employer bargaining units imply that the results arrived at will not suit equally all the firms concerned. The terms are necessarily broad, being possibly appropriate to only less prosperous firms in relatively favourable labour markets. Firms may want to adapt their wage structure for such purposes as rewarding long service, special responsibility, or skill, and compensating for unpleasant working conditions, marking status, building in a promotional element or progressive scale, adopting their own incentive scheme, etc. Generally, a federated firm trying to apply individual policies increases the amount of bargaining within the company, and thus almost necessarily involves its stewards in workplace bargaining.

Over the past decade or more, many firms have introduced job evaluation, by which jobs are graded into a few categories according to their content, thus reducing the number of different pay rates. Often stewards, particularly convenors, are actively involved in implementing job evaluation, sitting on appeals committees, etc. Clearly, disputes arise over job gradings, particularly with production changes, and stewards may advance complaints. However, if it replaces payment by results, job evaluation reduces the scope for workplace bargaining. It often produces individual rather than collective complaints, for claims on behalf of one grade automatically imply changes in all. Day to day haggling is generally much reduced. Job evaluation is found most extensively in the chemical industry, being applied in the national agreement. It does not eliminate disputes, but once introduced involves less debate. However, it does not eliminate wage drift, for specious grading, e.g. raising the pay of scarce categories of skill beyond that indicated by the principles of the scheme, is essentially the same as purposely loose piece rates, or 'manufactured' overtime.

Many companies, particularly those paying on a time rate and/or job evaluation basis, have built merit payments into the structure. The principle theoretically applied is to assess the operator rather than evaluate the job. Factors which can be objectively measured, e.g. timekeeping, attendance, and length of service may receive special payments but are often included in merit schemes, together with such 'personal qualities' as reliability, job performance, co-operativeness, etc. The subjective nature of these assessments is the antithesis of trade union principle of 'the rate for the job', and inevitably provokes accusations of favouritism. Stewards frequently oppose such schemes, press for equality of 'merit money' once introduced, and challenge the allocations. In turn, management may use merit money to reward the occupation rather than individual performance, particularly where the grading structure is too rigid for adequate recruitment.

The list of workplace company determined supplements is a long one. Many engineering firms pay a 'company bonus', and 'house rates' are commonly negotiated by FOCs in the printing industry. Christmas bonuses are widespread in building and other industries, all supplementing nationally negotiated rates. Some payments are provided unilaterally by employers, others are the result of negotiations. Stewards help secure, defend, and apply special allowances. Some national agreements provide for them, with special payments for dirt, heat, danger, height, fumes, etc. Allowances are made for tools, walking, and washing time, etc., and many outlive their justification. One large firm found itself still paying a few men 'shutter money' fifteen years after the end of the Second World War. Many companies have schemes for sickness and pensions, and stewards seek more favourable principles in their administration, even if they cannot directly negotiate over the level of benefits. The provision of clothing by a firm, across the plant or to specific jobs, frequently involves stewards, while they and the labour market may partly account for the stability of canteen prices. The list is virtually endless. The national agreement may be silent, employers' associations may advise resistance, but inroads are made gradually by stewards in the workplace.

The range of shop steward bargaining

So far, we have discussed aspects of workplace bargaining directly affecting the price of labour, but stewards also help regulate its utilization within a factory. Some rule books, particularly those of the craft unions, charge stewards with 'defending the interests of the trade'. This gives them scope on topics such as job demarcation, labour mobility, discipline, manning, union membership, supervision, apprentices, dilutees, etc. Many assume such responsibilities without instruction. Some employers find this joint regulation within the wage/price bargain alarming, for there is little acceptance of the legitimacy of the workers' desire to protect their interests on the work side of the employment contract.

Some unions with craft traditions have determined some aspects of entry, work performance, and content unilaterally, but these working rules are subject to pressures with technological and economic change, and the steward may find himself essentially on the defensive. However, the notion of property rights to and within a job is spreading among all workers, and attempts to extend it explain much non-financial bargaining in industry. The defence of protective working practices is appropriate to workplace representatives, as they are well placed to understand these often informal practices and to detect attempts to undermine them. Such privileges being often peculiar to one plant and not codified in union rule books or collective agreements, stresses the importance of stewards, helping to account for the decentralized nature of 'productivity bargaining'. Clearly, the steward is able to build up and defend the customs protecting members from capricious change, and may be able not only to reduce members' vulnerability to sudden management decisions, but also gain acknowledgement that certain decisions are to be made jointly. Whether day to day pressures on aspects of work regulation are bargaining is debatable, for the processes by which workers gain more influence over their work environment can be both dramatic or scarcely perceptible. Marsh thus describes the general position: 'Stewards are prepared to bargain about anything which appears to affect the interests of their members in the workplace, and all situations appear to offer some opportunities for this'.[18]

While stewards cannot bargain on every issue they would like, they have nevertheless secured agreements on various topics. After an inquiry covering forty five works agreements in engineering in five cities, Dr Lerner made this list of subjects covered.[19]

Trade Union and Shop Steward Status. Employers recognition of unions, stewards, and (sometimes) works convenor; 100 per cent union membership; the obligations and rights of stewards; payment to stewards for working time devoted to negotiations; works dispute or grievance procedure; stewards' meetings on works premises; use of bulletin board and other facilities.

Hours of Work. Starting and finishing times, meal breaks, teabreaks; distribution of overtime; guaranteed overtime; restrictions on overtime; choice of shifts, rotation of shifts.

Redundancy. Consultation with shop stewards; measures to keep dismissals to the minimum, e.g. limit recruitment, work sharing, transfers, etc.; length of notice; selection of employees to be dismissed; appeals; aids in securing other employment; severance payments; re-engagement.

Miscellaneous Provisions. Works rules; personnel records; physical examination; safety provisions; collections; leave of absence; promotions and transfers; joint productivity committees; joint consultative committees. These were the subject of workplace agreements, and would involve local full time officials and stewards, though the latter would obviously raise the issues initially and supervise any agreements.

Dr Lerner emphasizes that the list is a summary, and can certainly be extended within and outside engineering. Moreover, it lists positive *agreements*, excluding topics on which stewards make representations but do not record agreements. For example, in our experience, stewards play an active role in works discipline, challenging specific cases of warning, suspension, or dismissal, and also reaching agreements over the general procedure.

There are, in time working production departments, agreements over labour content and production pace; workplace interpretations of what is meant by national agreement terminology, especially such indefinite adjectives as 'suitable', 'reasonable', and 'appropriate'. Stewards are concerned in the transfer of members, job rotation, and mobility of labour generally. Holiday arrangements, ballots over dates, distribution of holiday period working, and staggering of holidays, *all* particularly involve maintenance workers' stewards. They are also concerned in demarcation issues, in such industries as shipbuilding devoting much time to this topic. Our questionnaire showed that stewards spent considerable time on factory hygiene and in discussions about improvements in physical working conditions.

It is not always clear whether an agreement exists. For example, an individual case may be resolved, but a management anxious to avoid setting precedents emphasizes its *ad hoc* nature. Failure to resolve a problem, particularly one in an area regarded as a management prerogative, still allows stewards to attempt attrition on the issue, thus gradually increasing their influence. Management may publicly proclaim its prerogative, but opposition by stewards may constrain its exercise in practice. Examples include sub-contracting work, appointing supervisors, introducing new labour, and employing consultants, etc.

Our questionnaire and our experience suggest that stewards bargain with supervisors and rate fixers on the shopfloor, but spend considerable time negotiating with higher management such as departmental, plant, and personnel managers. In many factories, the reference of major issues to foremen may be perfunctory. The supervisor cannot assess claims by stewards, and both will be aware that he must refer upwards. In these instances, stewards are anxious to reach the decision maker, and in time may bypass the supervisor.[20] Similarly, line management at departmental level may forego time consuming negotiations, particularly on plant-wide issues, passing the problem to higher levels or to specialist personnel departments. All this enhances the status of stewards, creating problems in the relationship between them and supervisors. Stewards as workers accept the foreman's authority, but as stewards, may have contacts with higher management not readily available to foremen. The latter may resent their ambiguous situation, particularly if they are not informed about the progress of issues, and if their views are not canvassed by management about daily working and discipline. Access to management may, independently, enhance the importance of topics raised by stewards. Conversely, stewards frequently serve as channels of information down from management. If management intends to 'tighten up' discipline, stewards often receive forewarning. Similarly, they may assist management, especially supervision, in handling difficult individual cases, in placing 'convalescent' employees, etc.

Most procedures, and unions, expect workplace representatives to handle complaints initially, to the stage when external officials must take over. Whether, in fact, the full time officials can always do this depends on several factors, not least their availability and the willingness of management or stewards to involve them. District officials may place embargoes on stewards discussing certain problems with management, yet the dynamics of a problem and simple expediency make implementation of this rule difficult. Moreover, some stewards resent the implication of lack of competence. If stewards decide to reject such limitations, e.g. by a joint stewards committee decision, the practical redress of full time officials is limited. More topics are discussed, joint regulation of employment is extended, stewards can secure acceptance of new principles in the relationship, members' interests being advanced. The official limiting stewards to the traditional areas will be suspected of bureaucratic behaviour if he is unable to secure improvements more effectively than his stewards. On the other hand, if his bargaining skills are superior, his participation will be more frequently sought.

Bargaining techniques

The right of stewards to progress grievances is widely accepted, though not invariably protected by industry-wide agreements. Given this procedural channel, the steward's bargaining strength revolves around the support of his members, his ability to gain acceptance of new agreements, and to lead them collectively. The vulnerability of employers to these sanctions varies. A factory assembling components into one product is susceptible to any sectional stoppage. Conversely, firms can continue for long periods despite strikes in certain sections, e.g. among draughtsmen. Firms dependent on overtime for normal production provide stewards with another weapon. Capital intensive industries, with labour co-operation crucial, again exemplify technological and other influences on bargaining. Management, too, has its sanctions, though the classical lockout is now largely precluded by public opinion. Management can change its policies, apply positive and negative sanctions; it can redistribute labour, making life difficult for stewards by adhering to the letter of agreements, refusing very minor changes, and attacking informally acquired 'privileges'. In one case, management responded to an overtime ban in one section by cancelling it across the entire plant.

Stewards do not simply present demands threatening action if they are not fully accepted, though this does happen. Experienced stewards pride themselves on their negotiating skill, and few persistently take precipitate action. Workplace bargaining, like all bargaining, involves tactics. Indeed, success depends on tactics, and however good relations are, both sides need to exercise skill to be sure of obtaining the best agreement. Honour has to be satisfied, usually by hard bargaining. Neither steward nor manager could feel he is adequately carrying out his duties if he depends merely on the goodwill of the other.

As negotiators, stewards employ various negotiating techniques, but particularly arguments of equity. Often, they appeal to ethical values, evaluating management by these standards; stewards, and their members, assess a firm and especially to its managers personally. They examine the motives, integrity, and personality of managers they negotiate with, and frequently stewards and managers come to respect each other. Both appreciate the other's problems, but acknowledge the man as well as his role. Thus, mutual trust and the anticipation of reasonable treatment largely prevent the breakdown of relations. Such relations are established gradually, but can disappear rapidly if the expectations of one side are not reasonably fulfilled.

Among the criteria of fairness are those of equality of treatment, consistency, and comparability. Comparisons of conditions and terms are made between crafts, grades, departments, shifts, different plants of the same firm, local firms, and within the industry. Notably, the Engineering Industry three year agreement of 1964, trying to restrain workplace bargaining for that period, provided that, 'As regards domestic claims there shall not be any of a general character covering all or substantially all of the manual workers in an establishment. Claims on behalf of individuals or groups of workpeople within an establishment shall be permitted provided they are based on alleged anomalies or inequities.' Once a disturbance occurs in a quasi-static situation, reference to comparability will spread its repercussions throughout and possibly beyond a factory. On wage and bonus issues, the reaction may be immediate; one group has 'got out of line' and regaining the *status quo* involves many adjustments. This argument of 'fair comparisons', especially referring to the immediate past, is accepted almost as much by managements as rough justice as on the shop floor. Inconsistency of treatment in similar cases, at different times or departments provides stewards with bargaining opportunities, largely acknowledged as just by management. Thus, bargaining often proceeds by appeal to values both sides acknowledge, though to differing degrees. The degree of management acceptance of 'fairness', e.g. comparability and consistency, helps determine the shop floor view of management's 'reasonableness'.

Another standard used by stewards is that of custom and practice. This argument is used to challenge any changes management introduces which are not favourably received on the shopfloor. Existing arrangements are greatly valued and change is resisted, for anticipated opposition may deter management from making proposals. The use made of 'custom and practice' by stewards illustrates the fear many of their members have of change, not only for security of employment. It also involves earnings, a particular job, and more broadly the security stemming from the routine of work and one's known workmates. However, defending old practices assists stewards in obtaining compensation for more permissive patterns of work.

Closely associated with 'custom and practice' is the use of precedent by stewards in bargaining. Actions by management are subjected to the criterion of previous practice, 'unfavourable' departures being challenged, e.g. the degree of consultation taking place before changes. This technique particularly applies to discipline, where case law is often accepted by management as overriding the letter of works rules. Stewards

166

are not constrained by the infrequency of negotiating meetings, being ever present. Agreements they reach are not as limited as those in most national agreements. Workplace problems are continuous, receiving daily attention. Managers, unlike national negotiators, cannot restrict negotiations to quarterly meetings on a previously determined agenda. Lengthy intervals to fix attitudes and consider claims are not available, though either side occasionally uses delay tactically.

Workplace bargaining is also influenced by the stewards' conception of their own position in relation to management. Both are concerned with power in the workplace, and tend to view the other competitively. Stewards seek to extend their scope and, however good their relations, do not allow their influence to rest simply on the goodwill of management. To define topics on which consultation is required is to define areas of joint regulation, reasserting the steward's importance in being strategic and 'non-bypassable'. Management may seek to restrict its dealings with stewards, or may elevate stewards to a position of interchangeability with outside officials. Stewards may exploit the differences between their constituents and the union. All this is part of a power game, as real when the rules are observed as when the weapons chosen breach the traditional morality. Briefly, stewards have become powerful, and often skilled negotiators—a position which management has on the whole fostered, and which the unions have been unable to prevent.

Workplace bargaining is diffuse, has evolved spontaneously, its processes being relatively unchronicled. It is pragmatic, continuous, and often intensive. Workplace bargaining is partly revealed by wage drift, which continues even in unfavourable conditions, implying it now has its own institutional momentum. The stage of development varies between and within industries. In some firms, workplace representatives have actually challenged basic rates while in others, bargaining is confined to non-monetary topics, though both have implications for production costs. Similarly, management finds its independent pursuit of policy objectives progressively limited, its behaviour modified, and its prerogatives eroded by the presence of powerful union representatives in the workplace.

References

1. Marsh, A. I. and Jones, R. S., 'Engineering Procedure and Central Conference at York in 1959: A Factual Analysis', *British Journal of Industrial Relations*, July 1964.
2. Banks, R. F., 'Long Term Agreements and Package Deals', *Industrial Welfare*, Vol. XLVII, October 1965.
3. Ministry of Labour *Gazette*, September 1961.
4. Chrichton, Anne, 'The IPM in 1950 and 1960', *Personnel Management*, December 1961.
5. McCarthy, W. E. J., 'Shop Stewards at Work', *Aspect*, April 1963, p. 31.
6. Phelps Brown, E. H., 'Wage Drift', *Economics*, November 1962.
7. Lerner, Shirley W., 'Wage Drift, Wage Fixing and Drift Statistics', *Manchester School*, May 1965.
8. National Board for Prices and Incomes, Report 49, *Pay and Conditions of Service of Engineering Workers*, HMSO, 1967.
9. HMSO Statistics on Incomes, Prices, Employment and Production, March 1968.
10. National Board for Prices and Incomes, Report 50, *Productivity Agreements in the Bus Industry*, HMSO 1967.
11. Lerner, Shirley W., 'Strikes', *District Bank Review*, June 1963.
12. *Report of the Joint Labour Council for the Motor Industry*, Dispute at Standard Triumph International, Coventry, August 1966.
13. National Board for Prices and Incomes, Report 17, *Wages in the Bakery Industry*, HMSO 1966.
14. Turner, H. A., 'Wages: Industry Rates, Workplace Rates and Wage Drift', *Manchester School*, 1956, p. 113.
15. Flanders, Allan, *op. cit.*, pp. 57–64.
16. The Engineering Agreement limits this to 20 hours in any four weeks, but the qualifications provide sufficient loopholes in practice.
17. Robertson, D. J., *Factory Wage Structures and National Agreements*, Cambridge University Press, 1960, p. 151.
18. Marsh, A. I., *Managers and Shop Stewards, op. cit.*, p. 12.
19. Lerner, Shirley W., *International Labour Review, op. cit.*, p. 14.
20. See Thurley, K. E. and Hamblin, A. C., *op. cit.*

8

Shop Stewards and Industrial Conflict

The implicit basis of collective bargaining is a conflict of interest between the parties. Bargaining, in which shop stewards are increasingly involved, is concerned with reconciling divergent interests. However, it is clear that this is not always achieved peacefully. The very term 'bargaining' implies the availability of sanctions, and so the association between stewards as bargainers and the use of sanctions implicit in that role must now be examined. However, expressions of conflict in industry stimulate largely emotional reactions, making it necessary to digress, temporarily, to look at the system which provokes one of the few manifestations of organized social conflict in this country.

The bases of industrial conflict

Despite areas where the interests of management and employees often appear compatible, and where co-operation commends itself to both in order to achieve their objectives, plainly the employment relationship involves many divergent interests. Thus, representatives of each group are concerned to manage this conflict, as far as possible preventing it from being damaging. The extent to which the conflict of interest is constructively regulated and peacefully channelled depends broadly on how well the values and behaviour of both sides conform to a mutually acceptable standard. It also depends on the skill and alacrity of the representatives in handling problems.

Conflict of interest exists most openly over payment, or more broadly over the distribution of rewards arising from the working relationship. There is no accepted formula for allocating a firm's profits between the various claimants. If labour persistently obtains a disproportionate return it may eventually destroy that employer. High costs mean uncompetitiveness, lack of business, and jeopardized employment. Thus, even of wages, it might be argued that in the long run interests are not incompatible, assuming labour is concerned with job security, acceptable alternative jobs being few. However, in the short run and in buoyant market conditions, management can pass on cost increases in price rises, or otherwise offset wage increases. Thus, limiting earnings rarely appears to employees as self-interest. Labour, then, seeks both higher earnings and a larger share of total returns, seldom regarding this as jeopardizing future employment.

There are other, less obvious, features of the work situation which are equally divisive. The division of authority, stemming from the primacy of managerial objectives, creates authority relationships, suggesting in sociological terms that some conflict is inevitable. The authority may be challenged, particularly on topics debatably within management's prerogative over which employees wish to exert some formal influence. Authority also creates real and perceived differences in status, causing conflict both within and between management and shop floor groups. Examples of conflict stemming from the authority structure are commonplace, e.g. discipline, but there are other less evident manifestations. For instance, management aims at an internal structure and production methods considered most appropriate. However, this formal system is subject to the reaction of employees, and their attempts to protect their interests. Management tends to regard labour as a necessary factor but also as a cost to be minimized, as against labour's view of the nature and purpose of employment. Clashes between the firm's impersonal objectives and the employees' personal values appear inevitable.

In employment, workpeople give up some freedom, implicitly undertaking to obey the management. Instructions emanate from managerial decisions intended to realize company objectives, e.g. cost reduction, profit or production maximization, etc. However, the contractual element in the relationship is vague or even silent on the degree to which management can command. The national collective agreements or works rules seldom specify when management can act unilaterally, and the exercise of managerial authority becomes subject to traditions and expectations in the workplace. Thus, in fact, it is subject to joint regulation, formal or otherwise.

Employees try to reduce their vulnerability to unwelcome managerial decisions, and to extend their influence over their work environment. Probably, their attempts at such regulation, as well as attempts to limit managerial freedom of action, will run counter to management's view of its own interests. They may well inhibit the achievement of management's prime objective, efficiency. They may seem attacks on management's right to manage, and thus on management's status, to which many contemporary managements are sensitive.

Other evidence supports the hypothesis of industrial employment as a conflict situation in which co-operation may be achieved, rather than as a basically harmonious system occasionally breaking down. In certain industries, the technology, i.e. the types of jobs, production organization, and control systems, engender conflict. The motor vehicle assembly line is frequently quoted to illustrate a managerial philosophy giving precedence to mechanical efficiency, to the exclusion of the social and other needs of employees. Possibly, here, the mechanically imposed discipline and repetitive short job cycles contribute to endemic disputes. Certainly, this technology appears likely to create frustrations, with concomitant aggression or resignation.[1]

As both manufacturing establishments and companies become larger, human relations problems increase, for the individual worker's remoteness from the employer leads to impersonality. Often, the individual worker feels insignificant, and that the firm is indifferent to his personal employment. The identification with and personal commitment to a firm is usually less in large firms than in small, where there is frequent contact between employer and employee. Problems of communications between shopfloor and management are frequently cited as major background causes of industrial conflict. These shortcomings exacerbate problems, but their improvement alleviates rather than removes more fundamental causes of conflict.

The employment relationship is obviously one of interdependence, but it is also one of expediency. It is an economic relationship, the result of bargaining, in which both parties attempt to optimize what they derive from it. One writer[2] has summarized the conflict between employees and management as that between the efficiency centred outlook of management and the security orientated values of employees. In that these interests are incompatible, conflict can be anticipated. However, in many ways, the interests of the two parties are not inconsistent, i.e. where providing security facilitates the achievement of efficiency. Perhaps the relationship may be usefully summarized as one of antagonistic interdependence.

To argue that conflict is inherent in contemporary industry does not imply that it is necessarily damaging. Its expression in established negotiating procedures is not generally considered harmful, compared with, say, unofficial strikes. Indeed, arguably, the conflict is constructive. When grievances on either side find a remedy, the relationship is adjusted to ensure continued co-operation. Attention centres on either party's dissatisfactions, and acceptance of the constraints on the other allows agreement. The problem is then revealed as one of identifying areas of conflict, and of regulating the expression of conflict. It does not mean suppression or denial of conflict, but rather its relief through accepted machinery. Thus, the relationship of unionists and employers proceeds by identifying areas of conflict, and regularizing their expression procedurally, together with advancing the aims of both through co-operation where interests overlap.

A strike is an interruption in the flow of consent, an overt expression of conflict; as such it attracts attention. However, conflict may be less dramatically expressed, in restrictive practices, unco-operativeness, limiting production, overtime bans, go-slow, work to rule, and through labour turnover and absenteeism. The method of venting dissatisfaction varies with the situation, and with what is considered legitimate, or effective, or customary. The possibilities quoted reveal the myopia of the obsession with strikes, and the dangers of assessing industrial relations by reference to the strike record. In industry, a cold war can be more damaging than a hot one. Moreover, some evidence suggests that considerable organized conflict is not inconsistent with high morale,[3] and that certain strikes benefit work performance.[4]

The importance of unofficial strikes

The Department of Employment and Productivity has estimated that 90 to 95 per cent of all strikes in the UK are unofficial. It also estimates that, in 1960–64, unofficial strikes accounted for nearly 60 per cent of days lost, though if the 'unusual' national one day token stoppages are excluded the proportion is over 75 per cent.[5] Definitions, however, are crucial. Perhaps, the most succinct is given by Knowles,[6] that 'an unofficial strike is one which is not recognized by the Executive Committee of a union'. Ambiguity arises, however, in a strike being official to one union but unofficial to another, and the position changes over time. Some begin unofficially, i.e. not being called by a trade union, but subsequently receive recognition, as indicated by the payment of strike benefit. The Department combines these criteria in the figures given above, defining unofficial strikes as those 'not called or recognized by a trade union'.[7] A further distinction exists between unconstitutional and unofficial strikes, the former contravening an agreed disputes procedure. Most unofficial strikes are also unconstitutional, but not all, e.g. action taken after the exhaustion of the procedure, but remaining unrecognized by the union. The Department of Employment and Productivity notes that official strikes seldom occur before the procedure is exhausted.

Many initially unofficial strikes gain union support when the facts become known. In a survey of 445 strikes during 1956–59, the TUC reported that 'in about half the cases reported to the General Council where strikes began without official sanction, the unions paid dispute benefit. The other half were less spontaneous and included instances where strike action was taken or prolonged contrary to general policy and specific advice.'[8]

Unofficial strikes are often regarded as a post war pheno-
menon, but while more frequent in the post war decades, they
are not novel. For example, Professor Phelps Brown, writing
broadly about the later nineteenth century, observes that
sudden outbreaks of strife surprised union officials who
condemned members for breaking agreements, the public
blaming the leaders for being out of touch with the rank and
file.[9] Before the Second World War, the Ministry of Labour
estimated that only a third of stoppages in 1936–37 received
union approval as evidenced by payment of strike benefit.[10]
Further perspective on the importance of strikes is given by
comparisons of days lost recently as against earlier years, and
by contemporary international comparison.[11]

Unofficial strikes are frequently condemned for damaging
the economy, exports, and individual firms. The usual
criterion is 'working days lost', though this indiscriminating
measure is, as Knowles observed, 'not unlike estimating
air-raid damage by reference to the bomb tonnage dropped,
irrespective of target or type of bomb'. This crude measure
may distort the *real* loss of production. For example, to equate
'days lost' and 'output lost' may apply passably in service
industries, but less so in manufacturing. In manufacturing,
'lost' production may be rapidly regained, though involving
such extra costs as overtime. Employers do not *always* regret
the loss of output, e.g. if they are producing for stocks. In the
motor industry, the number of working days lost directly in
the 'fifties varied almost inversely with the number of strikes,
strikes being commonest in high demand periods and least frequent during recessions.[12] Again, not all stoppages are reported
to the Department of Employment and Productivity, and
figures exclude days lost at establishments other than that in
dispute. This can reach important proportions. For example, it
has been estimated that from 1960 to 1964, over 260,000 working days were lost per year in the motor industry at establishments other than where each stoppage took place, compared
with 480,000 days lost *directly* through stoppages.[13] The
figures may also understate the real loss of production from
recurrent unofficial strikes in one firm. These may deter
customers, suggesting unreliability to foreign buyers. Domes-
tically, strikes may transfer demand to other companies or

other goods and services. Further, the 'days lost' standard ignores the ability to continue operations without the strikers, or the delay before a strike has any effect. The effects of *threats* of strike action also count. These may not directly affect production, but may produce important management concessions. The presence of these sanctions forms the background to workplace negotiations, being a 'deterrent' to some management behaviour.

The number of days lost through strikes in this country is extremely small. For example, the then Minister of Labour indicated that, in the first six months of 1963, only one of every 5,000 working days was lost through strikes. In the three industries where days lost per thousand workers in 1965 were highest, the loss of working days due to all stoppages was less than one third of 1 per cent in shipbuilding, and coalmining and slightly over two thirds of one per cent in the motor industry. Nevertheless, recently the *number* of strikes has increased. The annual average of 2,458 for 1955–66 was an increase of almost 40 per cent on the 1945–54 figure.

Increased numbers of unofficial strikes provoke objections on ethical as well as economic grounds, and has also drawn the suitability of traditional procedures and institutions into question. Unofficial strikers are condemned for breaking formal agreements when they feel it advantageous, and for selfishly exploiting local conditions. Certainly, workers often press claims when the situation strengthens their bargaining power.

On the other hand, employers know that procedures allow them to change the *status quo* and then listen to objections from employees which can then be lengthily resisted owing to the delay in exhausting the procedure. Demand conditions may tempt employers to 'reinterpret' national or plant agreements and customs with this intention. Unhappily, moralizing criticism of unconstitutional strikes concentrates attention on their impropriety rather than on the circumstances of the dispute or the suitability of procedures.

Increasing unofficial strikes may reflect a changing moral and social climate, in which to breach traditional machinery is not regarded as seriously as formerly. But it also reflects changed collective bargaining, the different nature of unionists' understanding of 'joint regulation of employment', and the declining relevance of some procedures to contemporary problems.

The background of unofficial action

Unofficial action, characteristically taken by workers in a firm under the nominal leadership of a shop steward, has many facets, and is attributable to various 'causes'. It may be seen as a strategic weapon employed consciously by workplace leaders who assume the mantle of generals or conspirators. Unofficial stoppages have the military virtue of surprise. Another view is that unofficial action is a necessary explosion of pent up frustration, released often by a trivial incident. Again, on other issues, immediate reaction may be necessary if the issue is not to be lost by the tardiness of negotiating machinery, e.g. questions of conditions, allowances, closed shop, etc. Further, unofficial strikes may be seen as a rational exercise by unionists, from which benefits gained outweigh costs incurred. At one level, they may be a response to a specific incident, at another an outburst of unrest associated with social conditions at large. The great variety of unofficial strikes, their circumstances, and their causes may make any one of these descriptions accurate in a given situation.

As, usually, unofficial action is also unconstitutional, the question arises whether lengthy, industry-wide grievance procedures remain acceptable, particularly to rank and file members. Confidence in them on the shopfloor may be minimal. Secondly, they may be impractical for some disputes, e.g. the so-called 'perishable' issues needing immediate solution, or those on questions previously excluded from union influence, i.e. management's refusal to negotiate on a particular topic. Thirdly, the procedure may be inappropriate to the changing nature of workplace disputes. Though successful in such traditional issues as wage claims, it may be inappropriate to changes in working arrangements, job content, or the treatment of individuals. Fourthly, the procedure may be insufficiently adaptable to new requirements, becoming inappropriate for the industries it covers, e.g. the engineering industry procedure (1922) is applied to much of the motor industry.

One criticism of existing procedures is that they are too slow. Marsh and Jones[14] found, accepting wide variations, that on average in 1959 it took about thirteen weeks to progress issues in the engineering industry procedure from the first works conference to central conference. However, they suggested that unions rather than employers were mainly responsible. Delay in using the external machinery can give tactical advantage to either side, while increased use of procedure overburdens union officials, thus involving delay.

Not all procedural delay stems from traditional machinery outside the firm. Procrastination by middle management causes discontent among workplace representatives, but may stem from the emphasis stewards place on precedent and uniformity of treatment. However, there are limitations to the view that small issues blow over, or that a 'cooling off' period is required. Postponement often exaggerates small issues into major problems, precipitating action. If this causes many disputes, the provision of speedier procedures should not be difficult. Some agreements already make provision for 'express routes', e.g. in the tobacco industry, while others, e.g. coal industry, limit the time for a problem to pass from stage to stage.

Unofficial strikes are occasionally described as 'strikes against the union'. The rank and file may feel that their officers are unable to interpret their problems, or to secure concessions. This is partly internal to the union, becoming more difficult as union size increases. Large unions have co-ordination problems dwarfing those of our largest companies. However, it may also uncover very *real* differences in outlook, for the district officer has to look beyond the short term interests of a few members.

Unofficial action is occasionally used by the rank and file to draw the attention, usually of union officials, to problems at shopfloor level. It is thus designed to modify the behaviour of officials, making up for deficiencies in union communications. It may indicate a declining reliance on full time officials. The official may be unavailable for an urgent problem, or his anticipated moderation and support of constitutional machinery may be discounted. He, personally, may fear repudiation by his members, or feel a strike justified, and be deliberately unavailable to management. Over a period, unofficial action may represent a desire by union members to reorder the balance of authority between them and the union. The power structure of a union, particularly in full employment, more closely resembles an inverted pyramid than an orthodox one, yet the formal structure does not acknowledge the transfer of bargaining opportunities. Increased unofficial action within the membership is predictable in that the formation of breakaway unions is extremely unlikely, given the hostility of established unions, employers, and the TUC disputes committee.[15] In certain sectors, disaffection with the established union and its organization is serious, e.g. in the docks, but though less developed elsewhere, its causes are by no means absent.

Full employment and the general economic environment in post war years have reduced the identification between members and their union. Some improvements in conditions are more closely associated with stewards than with outside officials and remote negotiating bodies. This reduced dependence, externally, appears particularly true of non-skilled men, against whom union sanctions are less powerful. Also, the constitutions of most basically craft unions provide for greater local autonomy. The Welfare State has reduced members' reliance on union friendly society-type benefits. Earnings are such that the loss of a few days' pay is not so strongly felt as formerly.

However, a basic change in post war years has been increased bargaining at workshop level. The growing number of strikes has taken place beside a redistribution of union functions in favour of the workplace representative. Outside the coal industry strikes 'caused' by claims for wage increases have increased as a proportion of all stoppages in recent years.[16] That shop stewards lead unofficial action is probability rather than an invariable truth, for the degree and direction of stewards' influence on members varies. However, unions have little effective redress against the steward who occasionally exceeds his authority, and assumes the powers to extend his role. If members do better under the leadership of stewards than the union, then the stewards will be most influential.

Managements could seek to contain pressure in the workplace by avoiding haphazard concessions, or by refusing to concede to stewards something formerly denied to external officials. This is influential in determining the actual, as well as formal, attitude of the union to unofficial action. If managements create the impression that more will be achieved by surprise strikes than by negotiations, they invite employees to take such action as the only way to secure change. For example, 'BOAC admitted that over a long series of unconstitutional incidents the shop stewards had produced a run of successes as a result of which they had no doubt come to be regarded by the workers as astute leaders . . .'.[17]

Union claims to discuss topics previously held by employers to be non-negotiable are generally resisted more firmly nationally than at plant level. As on earnings issues, progress here is often faster in the plant than nationally. Management may view such pressure as a battle over the principle of who is to control the factory, believing success necessary to preserve its control. The costs of an increase in piecework prices is easily calculable, and can perhaps be passed on to the customer. But an issue over, say, management's right to discipline unilaterally or to subcontract work involves deep principles. Management may question such challenges *a priori*, regarding them as part of the 'insatiable' demands of employees with only harmful effects on efficiency. Yet, the real ability of management to discipline employees is much modified by what its employees will accept. Consent cannot be ascertained, as the expectations of both sides are imperfectly known, but some companies have successfully clarified the position by acknowledging joint regulation where it already existed in practice.

Traditional procedures may be well attuned to usual grievances, e.g. pay complaints, yet not sufficiently sensitive to new issues of importance on the shopfloor. Lines of communication are a problem, but the *content* of information flowing upwards is also important. Selection at intermediate levels may distort information concerning 'new' problems. The responsiveness of the system to expected complaints, e.g. on wages, hours, etc., may lead to frustrations being translated into an 'accepted' topic. This may yield agreement, without solving the real problem.

The behaviour of management may also lead to unofficial

action. Delay in dealing with grievances, haphazard concessions, *ad hoc* solutions, hurried decisions, and failure to consult all contribute to unofficial action. On the other hand, individual employers are vulnerable to workplace pressure, for a stoppage at certain times affects their ability to meet delivery dates and obtain subsequent orders. Small strikes allow competitors to benefit, and make decisions to resist or concede extremely delicate. Often, managements rigidly emphasize the sanctity of agreements, valuing constitutionalism rather than examining the causes of a dispute. Managers thus obscure any doubts they may have of the morality of their behaviour on the issue itself.

The role of shop stewards

Strikes in the UK are characteristically small, short, local, unconstitutional, and unofficial. They are usually against a single employer, and frequently restricted to one establishment or even one group of workers. The obvious implication is that they are led by workplace leaders, though not necessarily by acknowledged representatives, who have no union authority to initiate such action. This often reveals the disparity between formal authority and actual power, but does not necessarily mean that the unions are out of touch with their members, or opposed to the action. It may help officials in negotiations, and accelerate a favourable agreement. H. A. Clegg observes that 'Union officials may sometimes inform employers that unless a certain concession is granted they cannot be responsible for the actions of their members. On occasion, officers have been known to suggest to shop stewards that a demonstration of the validity of this kind of statement by their members would be of assistance in negotiations.'[18]

To presume that stewards *lead* unofficial action is to oversimplify though, in the main, probably valid. However, often, a steward is forced to defend unofficial action he has not instigated, and members reject his 'constitutional' advice, accepting the leadership of men with no union position. Similarly, men may strike without reference to their representatives, who may attempt to reduce stoppages as a long term policy.[19] If, in conflicts, stewards cannot influence their members, their

180

validity as representatives is undermined—and management is not blind to it. Potentially, however, the steward has unique opportunities to influence his union members. He may, if he is accepted, be regarded as a leader of opinion in labour–management relations. His position, contact with management, knowledge of union affairs, experience of negotiations, and access to information not available to his constituents all foster his leadership. The present position allows a steward to take action if he considers it justified. Assessing the justification is an individual matter. For example, the issue itself, the need for prestige, an enjoyment of power, the pressure for success exerted by members, and his experience of previous unofficial action are influential factors.

In the long term, the steward's behaviour appears likely to reflect the values of his constituents. In contested elections, the steward elected and his subsequent behaviour are circumscribed by his constituents' expectations, and views of the management. An elected representative is occasionally unable to lead effectively in changed circumstances. If he does not respond to a different situation, or the changed feelings of his members, his advice is likely to be ignored and he is, in practice, replaced as leader. Gouldner[20] describes how conciliatory union leaders, in a plant with deteriorating labour–management relations, were replaced in practice, though not formally, by more extreme leaders when members felt a strike necessary. Such examples are common on the shopfloor, but are more publicized nationally when moderate leaders come under pressure from militant groups, amending their behaviour to retain actual as well as formal leadership.

This analysis of the steward's position suggests his leadership is subject to the discretion of his constituents. Failure to carry out his often ill defined 'job description' to their satisfaction renders him ineffective or leads to his replacement. However, there are limitations to this. It assumes, for example, that there are individuals of different types, with different views, prepared to accept the position. This is not always so. Secondly, it assumes that constituents can express their feelings and opinions to the steward; this is seldom easy in the workplace, and mass meetings are not conducive to reasoned debate. Indeed, most members may be apathetic, making little effort to influence the steward. Thirdly, members may think it the steward's function to gain the most benefits, not being concerned if his tactics and style in so doing do not reflect their own views. Approval of the end may justify the means. A 'proved' steward, with a good record for improving the conditions of his members, may carry them with him repeatedly in unconstitutional action. This may well become accepted, especially if it is thought to be the only thing management understands. It is reinforced by union strategy of solidarity, and threats of social or other sanctions against non-conformists. Men often follow stewards in unofficial strikes in ignorance of the issues. Also, the rank and file often have a very hazy impression of the minutiae of procedure, their outrage at an evident injustice overriding their understanding of their obligation to follow established procedural methods.[21]

Thus, though the steward must have his members' confidence to retain his position, the pressures they apply on him may be weak and infrequent. An established steward can exercise his discretion. A militant steward can play on the fears of his members, and a political zealot may well extend overt action. Unconstitutional methods, once accepted as justified may become habitual, and be difficult to remove. This is perhaps the greatest danger indicated by the upward trend of the strike statistics, corresponding to the experience of several large firms in which a strike has become a first rather than a last resort.

Leadership of unofficial strikes, and the threat to use them, is usually the principal objection to the activities of shop stewards. However, unofficial action is not confined to the unofficial strike. The impression is that, recently, such 'cut price' weapons as the overtime ban or work to rule have been used more frequently, the strike being simply one of many sanctions. They suggest the leadership of men, presumably stewards, with some knowledge of tactics and the position of the firm, and discredit the 'spontaneous outburst' explanation of unofficial action. To estimate how much considerations of strategy are present in unofficial strikes is difficult. Statistical support for stewards viewed as tacticians planning campaigns against management is largely limited to wages and related topics, *in which the discretion over timing is in the hands of stewards*. For example, in an examination of the north east shipbuilding industry, G. C. Cameron observed that, 'Thus whilst insecurity provides the basic cause of such (wage) disputes, their timing is largely dictated by the state of the market for labour... Fifty-six of the eighty-one (wage) disputes started when the level of unemployment was either at the lowest annual point or not greatly in excess of that point'.[22]

Professor Turner considered that 'most strikes are not initiated in support of some new demand on the employees' part, but in immediate protest against some act of the management concerned—or against the terms on which it intends to implement a change'.[23] It is difficult to classify the principal cause of a strike as either aggressive or defensive, as the chain of causation is so involved, but many strikes appear to be responsive.

There is a danger of condemning all stewards for the behaviour of a few, but stewards do sometimes persistently disregard established procedures, perpetuating strike activity as an end in itself in seeking to disrupt working relations, employment, and production. There is evidence of political groups committed to disruption establishing themselves among stewards, but little evidence of their success. There have been few well documented situations where stewards might justly be accused of manufacturing grievances rather than managing them. Sometimes, stewards have pressed members unwilling to participate in recurrent unofficial strikes, in some areas fines being paid to stewards' committees. Abuse of the position of the shop steward undoubtedly occurs, but evidence is slight in relation to the large numbers of stewards, and despite the consequent widespread possibilities of abuse. Some unions, notably the Boilermakers Society, have very liberally recognized strikes called by stewards, not regarding them as usurping the authority of the union.[24]

The normal position permits stewards to initiate action in breach of union rules and procedure agreements, and contrary to union policies. A few unions have occasionally disciplined stewards for so doing. BISAKTA has repeatedly asserted its formal authority in this way, while the T & GWU, the NUGMW, and other unions have taken similar action, less consistently. Competition between unions for members, often with militancy as the cutting edge, has limited the application of this sanction, despite the advice of the TUC. Many union officials consider that expulsion not only creates martyrs and hostility to the union, but also removes offenders from the union's influence, while not preventing them influencing union members.

Persistent use of strikes by stewards contrary to union advice is commonplace, e.g. Briggs Motor Bodies 1957, Ford's 1962, BMC 1965, London and Hull docks in 1965 and 1966. Here, union officials appear unable, or unwilling, to assert themselves. The onus for breaking the cycle is often left by management to the unions. Managements fear the consequences of imposing their own discipline, though feeling aggrieved at the open disregard of legitimately constituted agreements. Reliance on procedural rules may be justified, but it is often false to portray an injured management with no responsibility for the situation, or for correcting it. Appeals for unilateral union action have not generally been successful. Such situations have usually been relieved by management action, e.g. at Ford, Rootes, and BMC, and/or by joint action to improve relationships by examining the fundamental issues.

Another important factor in the behaviour of stewards is their relationship with full time officials. This could appear competitive, both seeking to restrict the functions and information of the other. Certainly, a steward is well able to harass branch officers and district officials, particularly if management prefers to deal with stewards. District officials subject to periodic re-election may also find it difficult to oppose influential stewards in plants with a large membership. However, generally relations between the officials and stewards are good, each regarding the other as complementary, informal limitations on freedom of action thus being accepted voluntarily. Certainly, stewards value their contacts with the union, most are regular attenders at branch meetings. Many branch positions are filled by stewards.

The role of stewards in controlling rather than creating conflict is often obscured by publicity given to the few who attract the headlines. However, this view is changing. The absence of accredited union representatives in certain industries, notably the docks, is now acknowledged as a weakness, for both union control and orderly workplace relations. The T & GWU experimented in introducing stewards into the docks at Hull in 1966, a court of inquiry into a dock strike at Bristol in 1966 similarly recommending their introduction. This has proceeded rapidly since decasualization.

The availability of sanctions is now accepted in day to day employment relationships. Both sides are aware of how their interests can be threatened. For example, stewards may support output limitations, sponsor an 'unco-ordinated' disinclination to work customary overtime, or an open overtime ban. They may not attend normal meetings with management, for joint consultation, insist on the letter of previous agreements, or progress every issue raised by members with time consuming conscientiousness, etc. Briefly, they can make changes in their co-operativeness very difficult for management to combat. As individuals, they may withdraw from what Kuhn calls the 'helper functions', in which stewards assist foremen in daily labour management, e.g. absenteeism, poor performance, timekeeping, etc. 'A shop steward can talk to an offending worker as a fellow worker and defender, while the foreman is always suspect.'[25]

Moreover, McCarthy notes wide divergences in the value attached to established procedures by management and shop stewards.[26] He observed that management regards facilities for the progression of grievances as a concession, for which stewards should be grateful. Their gratitude should be demonstrated by invariably abiding by the 'no collective action before the exhaustion of procedure' clause commonly found in these procedures. Stewards regard the procedural and substantive contents of agreements as guaranteeing only minimal rights, which are to be improved upon. As such improvements are gained, they are assimilated into 'custom and practice' to be defended as stoutly as a written agreement. Moreover, management attempting to 'tighten up' is regarded as breaking plant agreements, and stewards feel free to respond similarly. Quite simply, the primacy of 'peace clauses' is not accepted equally by both sides. Moreover, situations arise where managers challenge representations made by stewards, as being beyond the stewards' brief. Such behaviour may be regarded by stewards as unreasonable, justifying the application of pressure irrespective of agreed procedure. Clearly, the evaluation of the 'morality' of managers' behaviour on a given issue often outweighs obligations to follow procedure.

If management fails, in stewards' eyes, to honour agreements, stewards may regard this as more grave than their own repudiation of procedure they themselves did not negotiate. As workplace agreements proliferate, the parties acquire many obligations, and agreements made at one level *need* not be consistent with those at another. Unfavourable revision provokes accusations of bad faith with possibly immediate effects and long term deterioration in relationships.

This emphasizes the leadership of stewards in defending understandings developed through the daily regulation of relationships. Stewards who have personal loyalties among their constituents have wide discretion in reacting to managerial behaviour, in being predisposed towards immediate action or caution. However, such strong leadership is not universal, stewards' advice may be rejected, and sometimes stewards find themselves following their members in actions they think inappropriate. Thus, it is impossible to define the role of stewards in conflict in generally applicable terms; different case studies demonstrate variations in the part they play. One recent strike, of which the writers had first hand experience, illustrates this. A large multi-plant industrial company proposed to reallocate work among its factories, causing some redundancy at the factory in question. Manual workers' stewards, through the JSSC, announced, without calling a meeting of members, a one day protest strike, which took place. White collar stewards convened members to consider similar action, which was firmly rejected. After the stoppage, criticism of the manual workers' stewards by their members reached such a level that the long serving factory convenor resigned, serious divisions appeared in the JSSC, and between its leaders and the rank and file, threatening to break up inter-union organization at the factory. It also weakened the stewards' hand in subsequent negotiations over transfers and redeployment. Clearly, stewards must 'beware marching too far in front of their army' if individuals are to retain their positions, and if management is not to exploit both their failure to represent their members and divisions within their organizations.

The increase in unofficial strikes and other workplace sanctions reflect the changes in the location and subject matter of employment regulation. In view of this structural change, challenging the framework of traditional institutions, it is perhaps not surprising that the present pattern of overt conflict does not fit into the traditional mould. Its causes are deeper than mere personalities, more complicated than advocates of punitive solutions suggest, and, as has been recently observed, more likely the result of local democracy than of local autocracy. However, the immediate impact of unofficial action is upon management. These effects and other repercussions of the internal representational system must now be examined.

References

1. Goodman, J. F. B. and Samuel, P. J., 'The Motor Industry in a Development District', *British Journal of Industrial Relations*, November 1966.
2. Flanders, Allan, 'The Internal Social Responsibilities of Industry', *British Journal of Industrial Relations*, March 1966.
3. Scott, W. H., *et. al.*, *Coal and Conflict*, Liverpool University Press, 1960.
4. Paterson, T. T., *Glasgow Ltd.*, Cambridge University Press, 1960.
5. Ministry of Labour, Written Evidence to the Royal Commission on Trade Unions and Employers' Associations, HMSO, 1965, para. 127.
6. Knowles, KGJC, *Strikes*, Basil Blackwell, 1954, p. 30.
7. Ministry of Labour, *op. cit.*
8. TUC Annual Report, 1960, para 60.
9. Phelps Brown, E. H., *The Growth of British Industrial Relations*, Macmillan, 1960, pp. 231–32.
10. Quoted in Turner, H. A., *The Trend of Strikes*, Leeds University Press, 1962.
11. See Appendix A.
12. Turner, H. A. and Bescoby, J., 'Strikes, Redundancy and the Demand Cycle in the Motor Industry', *Bulletin of the Oxford Institute of Statistics*, May 1961.
13. Ministry of Labour, *op. cit.*
14. Marsh, A. I. and Jones, R. S., *op. cit.*
15. See Lerner, Shirley W. *Breakaway Unions and the Small Trade Union*, George Allen and Unwin, 1961.
16. Goodman, J. F. B., 'Strikes in the United Kingdom: Recent Statistics and Trends', *International Labour Review*, May 1967.

17. Report of the Court of Inquiry at London Airport, HMSO, Cmnd, 608, 1958, para. 62.
18. Clegg, H. A., *General Union*, Blackwell, 1954, p. 133.
19. See Turner, H. A., Clack, G. and Roberts G., *op. cit.*, pp. 224–229.
20. Gouldner, A. W., *Wildcat Strike*, Routledge and Kegan Paul, 1955.
21. See Scott, W. H. *et. al.*, *The Dockworker*, Liverpool University Press.
22. Cameron, G. C., 'Post-War Strikes in the North East Shipbuilding and Ship Repairing Industry', *British Journal of Industrial Relations*, March, 1964.
23. Turner, H. A., *The Trend of Strikes, op. cit.*
24. Cameron, G. C., *op. cit.*
25. Kuhn, J. W., *op. cit.*, p. 31.
26. McCarthy, W. E. J., *The Role of Shop Stewards in British Industrial Relations, op. cit.*, paras. 36–45.

9
Implications for Management

The rise of stewards presents a challenge to individual managements, as well as to the existing institutions of industrial relations. Managerial behaviour is increasingly subject to close scrutiny by powerful, internal union representatives. This position has often inhibited managements from initiating changes they think desirable, but which are not carried out through fear of their unsettling effects. While some managements are faced with obstructionism, post war change in the location of union activity has not made management's task impossible. It is our thesis that management is best placed to affect the quality of human and industrial relations in its plants, and the emergence of stewards makes management's attention here even more pressing. Stewards may, in one sense, increasingly constrain managers, but they also enable management to manage, in another sense, with greater certainty.

The importance of shop stewards to management

Until recently, it was widely held by students of industrial relations that managers prefer to bargain with full time officials rather than stewards. The reasoning was that management prefer the periodic attention of the stereotype 'knowledgeable, reasonable, and responsible' full time officials rather than the continuous and 'irrational' approach of stewards. Additionally, it was felt that management would resent encroachments on its prerogatives, i.e. the right to decide unilaterally, by stewards anxious to enlarge their spheres of influence. For managements, logically it seemed best to bargain with officials rather than their own employees, pressure from the latter having 'dangerous' implications of increasing industrial democracy, with all the ideological over-tones this concept has in British industry. Arguments ran, therefore, that the duties of stewards needed confining and defining precisely to keep the majority of collective bargaining activities for the attention of full time officials.

Recent evidence has, however, challenged this belief, showing the attitudes of management afresh. Research by Clegg, Killick, and Adams[1] on the attitudes of personnel officers to stewards shows they prefer dealing with stewards in collective bargaining. Returns from their questionnaire show that 69 per cent of those officers in the survey preferred to bargain with stewards as against 17 per cent with officials, both being equally competent. The reasons given by the majority included stewards' intimate knowledge of the circumstances (expressed by half the 69 per cent), preference for keeping issues within the factory, better contact of stewards with members (or control over them), and the beneficial effect on relationships within the factory. While these were the expressed reasons, possibly others also apply. Managers, no doubt, know that stewards may have less freedom of action than officials, being subject to the firm's sanctions whereas the latter are not. In practice, stewards wear two hats, one as a union representative and the other as an employee of the firm. The two roles become confused since a steward is unlikely to forget that he is employed by those he is bargaining with. This encourages more mildness, possibly making him less effective than he would like, or indeed has opportunity for in bargaining. The management's preference for dealing with stewards is hardly surprising. Negative sanctions are available, i.e. the steward may fear losing his job or his privileges within a firm. Positive sanctions also exist in that stewards are interested in promotion. Our survey of a hundred stewards revealed that no less than 79 per cent were interested in promotion, clearly an influence on them during bargaining. Therefore, management's attitudes towards their stewards are attempts to gain the benefits of company unionism by conducting most negotiations with lay union officials who are on their own staff, excluding officials with an independent status outside. The latter can bring outside pressure to bear upon management, supporting sanctions materially with official strike pay. A shop steward's threat does not have these advantages and is frequently countered by managers calling in the full time official, utilizing the trade union outside as a 'fire brigade'. This is not to say that *all* managements prefer to deal with shop stewards. As policy, or where they dislike a steward, they can always deal with officials as often as possible, trying to exclude the steward from the bargaining. Dr McCarthy quotes an example of a paint firm which dealt directly with the local official even over piece work prices, the steward having little to do.[2]

Personnel managers may feel that the more they discuss and negotiate with stewards, the more their own status is enhanced. Their work load is increased and they have opportunities to participate in bargaining as line management seek their aid by passing stewards on to them. Personnel specialists then have means of preventing disputes from breaking out, their own roles being necessarily enhanced. Certainly, by negotiating together, both stewards and personnel managers are more likely to make a mark on industrial relations within a factory than negotiating with officials probably unknown to management and able to spend only a short time with one personnel manager. Another factor motivating personnel managers in dealing with stewards is that matters so settled are confined to the plant, presenting them favourably as able to settle with their own employees without relying on outside intervention. Many personnel managers we met commented on this ability, as proud of not calling for external assistance from either employers' association or union.

The managerial approach to collective bargaining

A major implication for managerial policy arising from relations with unions in general and stewards in particular is the need for objectives to be clearly thought out and policy goals firmly stated. Also, that there should be greater willingness by managements to bargain with specific proposals. It has been aptly remarked that 'Management, accustomed to consider the initiation of new schemes as an essential part, indeed the very core of its job, in all other aspects of industrial life, has been curiously slow to innovate in the field of labour relations. Traditionally, managements have waited for an approach to be taken by the unions rather than themselves assuming the lead.'[3] This state of affairs is due to a variety of factors. Firstly, traditions in collective bargaining are against such processes, as the quotation suggests, and since in bargaining as in industrial relations in general, traditions are so important in determining behaviour, quick changes cannot realistically be expected. Secondly, the application of the line and staff principle to personnel departments means that they are largely advisory. Most important decisions in labour relations are taken by line managers concerned with production, and whose time for labour matters precludes deeply conceived policies.

Thirdly, decisions about labour relations are often taken by employers' associations following negotiations with union associations. Minimum wages and working conditions emerge for large sections of an industry. Individual firms within the associations are not encouraged to be radical, innovations at one workplace being used by unions in attempts to spread them at others throughout the industry. Many marginally profitable firms could not afford to implement such a policy and, therefore, unless nationally agreed, innovations are unlikely to reach these firms at all. This situation enables unions to make the running in labour relations, the changes being made often originating with the union. Innovating employers are usually outside the associations, where they are 'free' to be radical without involving other firms. Employers' associations appear to militate against widespread changes in relations through collective bargaining procedures. Some recent research in the neglected field of employers' associations suggests, however, that this point should not be overemphasized. A Royal Commission Research Paper by V. G. Munns and W. E. J. McCarthy notes how difficult it is for employers' associations to maintain control over member firms, both in the sphere of wages and working conditions and over more general industrial relations questions. Their survey showed that 72 per cent of national association officials and 42 per cent of national federation officials considered that they made little or no attempt to influence the industrial relations activities and decisions of member firms. Only 14 per cent of all national officials said they tried to influence their members 'a lot'. Nevertheless, non-federated firms with formal responsibilities only to themselves have much more scope to innovate than federated firms. This supports the view that more formal bargaining should occur at plant level. Fourthly, implementing big changes at plant level involves large sums of money, available only to firms with large resources. This is shown in productivity agreements achieved in the UK, the companies involved being usually large, the *quid pro quos* given to unions being also large. Consequently, small firms cannot usually participate in such comprehensive innovations. Finally, in some plants managements face many unions, and are made to act defensively as unions quarrel over such subjects as demarcation lines or wages differentials. Continually, management meets individual demands, giving little opportunities to present clear policies.

In general, managements are defensive in collective bargaining, the unions usually taking the initiative. This is to be deplored, it being the job of management to manage. Here, this means presenting viable policies to the unions, getting consent for them, and administering them. Failure to do this places real responsibility for changes with the unions. This is unsatisfactory, their negotiators are not inclined, not knowing the company's economic position, to make realistic proposals based on these facts. As one shop steward commented, 'I neither have the knowledge nor the desire to make policy for this company, and I have to constantly remind management that it is their job to manage'. Not surprisingly, therefore, accusations of irresponsibility by managements against union negotiators state that demands exceed what the company can afford. More fairly, perhaps, the complaining managers are irresponsible in surrendering their responsibilities for managing and innovating. Continually and purely defensive management is inadequate management.

A clear evaluation of their interests might lead managers to conclude that a responsible attitude amongst their employees could best be accomplished by giving them fuller knowledge of the situation. This would mean revealing such matters as the firms' financial record, profits, etc. to union inspection. Then, representatives would be more closely involved in the firm's performance, and better informed bargainers. Possibly, union leaders would be against such collaboration with management. They would feel that the information inhibited them, by putting them on both sides of the bargaining table. Seeing problems from both management and union view-points might interfere with their success, at least in the short run, in collective bargaining. It is not axiomatic that unions cannot operate with representatives on both sides, for in West Germany unionists sit on a supervisory board with powers over the board of directors and access to economic and tech-nical information and this does not preclude collective bargaining at shop level, where other union representatives can function. Even sharing information with management does not necessarily obviate opposition, it being possible to claim wage increases or better conditions with reference to profitability as with reference to such factors as comparability and differentials. Sometimes, information makes the situation very plain. Then, unionists may find their hands tied, but in this case it is unlikely in any case that the union will get what it wants. The reasons for this are better shown in black and white than unionists taking management's word for it.

Our questionnaire survey of a hundred stewards revealed that 83 per cent of them wished to see information about profits and other financial matters, 57 per cent wanted information on management's evaluation of individual con-stituents, and 38 per cent would like information on overtime distribution and its availability to individuals. There is, then, considerable interest among stewards in having managerial information, principally to strengthen their knowledge in bargaining.

Thus, attempts to innovate through the bargaining system usually involve stewards with little knowledge. These attempts become, therefore, questionable and likely to be resisted, thus militating against the welfare of the firm. Yet, traditionally, employers reluctantly retail knowledge to employees, partly in insisting on the 'prerogatives of management'. This problem was summarized by a leading lay official who said, 'The more management insist on their prerogatives the more we must insist on challenging them. This is vital if we are to remain a strongly unionised factory.' One commentator has observed,[4] 'employers may well be reluctant to supply the detailed and hitherto mainly confidential information necessary to make a reasoned assessment of the firm's position and prospects. To refuse however would imply rejection by employers of the notion that wage rates should be determined by reference to factual and objective considerations and would certainly render impossible any real attempt to relate changes in wage rates to changes in productivity.' In addition, management should pay more attention to innovation and to formulating long term plans. These need to be sufficiently detailed to commit departments, and even work groups, to defined procedures. Without clearly stating goals and priorities, bargaining cannot be particularly fruitful for management. Commitment to a positive labour policy should include all management, especially production, not just personnel specialists. The personnel function should apply to all managers, all having a personnel function to perform. If given responsibility through bargaining for personnel decisions, they are more attentive in implementing them than if excluded from decision making. In practice, departmental personnel policies should be decided with line management, the latter sitting at the bargaining table when wages and conditions of employment are discussed. This includes departmental foremen who are often found on the front line of administration of factors under the title of 'personnel'. Thus, one steward remarked, 'The foreman is regarded as a sort of assistant personnel officer by the employees here'.

Probably, these suggestions would be acceptable if present bargaining structures were altered, since present agreements are widely reached at district or national level. It is possible, thus, to frame a broad approach, yet in each workplace more specific policies must apply. Innovations in the workplace might awaken an employers' association's fears of precedent. The most impressive innovation locally is in non-federated firms.

Positive management

The need for management definition of objectives demands action to achieve them; nowhere is this more necessary than in labour utilization. Disguised unemployment is pervasive in the British economy and excessive overtime is another manifestation of the misuse of labour. Thus, Mr A. Flanders states,[5] 'No one denies that part of this sustained postwar overtime in Britain has been deliberately contrived for no other purpose than to produce an adequate weekly pay packet. Employers provide such "policy overtime", as it is called, to attract or to keep workers whose earnings cannot be supplemented sufficiently or at all through payments by result systems or plus rates and bonuses of various kinds.' Professor Clegg notes how this undermines attempts to increase efficiency, writing that,[6] 'Large sections of British workers are taught by their system of payments to waste time at work. Quite apart from the unfortunate results (of overtime) on their own lives of not being able to use their own leisure time as they might wish, this has unfortunate consequences within industry. What is the point of telling workers that machine time is valuable, that wastage of material must be avoided at all costs, that the aim of the firm is to make efficient use of its resources, if their own time is being wasted in this way.'

The need to utilize labour fully faces all managements, it being their responsibility to alter the situation. To quote Flanders again,[7] 'When managements blame trade unions for standing in the way of change what they are really objecting to in most cases is the challenging task that confronts all democratic governments of having to win the consent of the governed.' This is possible, despite those who accuse unions of obstructionism. The following case study shows how one management set out, and succeeded, to win consent for radical innovations.

Refining Ltd: A case study

It was decided at Refining Limited[8] in 1963 that overtime should be reduced, demarcation lines broken down, some workers absorbed into more productive work, and craft shiftwork introduced to secure higher productivity and 'to provide a framework for the future within which change will be more acceptable'.

Ideas of change originated in 1960, when consultants suggested changes involving reduction of both hourly rated and staff employees. Therefore, changes were made, managers and office staffs becoming redundant. Redundancy among the hourly paid staff did not materialize, the eleven trade unions refusing to discuss redundancies and threatening sanctions.

Further management changes were made in 1962, with the appointment of a new Refinery Manager and a new Employee Relations Manager. Changes on the lines of the Fawley Blue Book were suggested, and the two newcomers were instrumental in getting them accepted. Both, being tolerant and humane, quickly became popular among employees, which was important in improving relations with the stewards, suspicious after the actual and threatened redundancies of 1960.

In 1962, the company conceded a forty hour week after a few sporadic stoppages. Union officials, both local full time and lay, were then told that the company wished soon to negotiate a productivity plan for the refinery. This did not surprise the unions, management hints of change and the presence of consultants for about two years indicating coming changes.

Management did not, however, move until October, 1963, and meanwhile an addition to the labour relations staff had been made. A new officer was appointed to help in negotiation of the plan. Previously he had been a T & GWU branch secretary in South Wales. Together with the Employee Relations Manager, he undertook most of the detailed discussions with stewards and union officials, and he acted as a bridge between the two cultures.[13] Performing most day to day detailed consultation with the stewards, his personality helped win their trust.

The first official meeting was held in November, 1963. The company presented the maintenance stewards and their full time officials with outline proposals to provide a stable salary, a 'genuine' forty hour week, to maintain working, and to improve refinery productivity. The unions allowed the stewards to discuss the details, calling in officials for negotiation. Management stressed that all the discussions assumed that the unions would be involved in negotiating the package. There were to be no redundancies under the plan, while the company was willing to add 25 per cent to the basic rate to compensate for overtime and condition money lost. This was to be a weekly salary, not hourly pay, being calculated from the average take home pay, which was 25 per cent above basic rates.

For months, discussion took place between the stewards and management, and stewards and their constituents. Meetings with full time union officials covered matters of union policy, as well as progress. The convenor and deputy convenor acted almost full time as plant union representative, and as matters affecting each trade group arose, the appropriate steward was called in.

The negotiations were difficult, certain groups opposing the plan at times. As agreement was voluntary, these groups could have compromised the whole plan. The civil trades group at first refused to grant 'flexibility', i.e. to break down demarcation lines, but were eventually persuaded by management increasing the compensation rate to 32·5 per cent of the basic rate. The CEU and the pipefitters, HDEU, opposed next, also being worried about dilution of their skills; again, they eventually accepted. Those reluctant, then, were members of unions where the skill gap was narrow. They felt more vulnerable to broken demarcation lines than other groups. In the latter case, the skill necessary for the job obviated the fear that the supply of labour could be quickly increased. Flanders notes that every craft union member guards against any breach of demarcation lines because 'the fences (of demarcation) are not fixed and unalterable; they would be more secure if they were. As it is, much depends on the vigilance and militancy shown in their defence at the place of work. And almost every craftsman knows, with the instinctive knowledge that embodies the historical lessons of his social group, that it is his duty to the union and to his fellows to prevent trespass and, if possible, to gain more ground. Anything deliberately done to reduce even slightly the existing territory is suspect because it might eventually lead to destruction of the craft. One can never tell for sure where it will end; where one step on this slippery slope may lead.'[9]

The ETU were also worried over upgradings, a special agreement being made providing that the upgraded personnel should not do more hazardous skilled jobs for a period. Eventually, all groups accepted the proposals, only individuals with special reasons for not transferring being allowed to stay. For instance, those close to retirement remained as shop helpers but not as craftsmen's mates.

After fourteen months, both sides agreed to a documented plan which came into operation in January, 1965. In certain respects, the plan surpassed the suggested outline. More flexibilities were obtained than had been bargained for, employees worked some overtime without pay in the first six months, and overtime was reduced from an average of 20·5 per cent to 5 per cent within a month. On the other hand, the company increased its offer from 25 per cent to 32·5 per cent (addition to the basic rate), plus £50 per annum per man after six months. This £50 was partly to satisfy those unions asking more than 32·5 per cent before implementation of the plan and partly to encourage employees to co-operate during the vital first six months of the plan, when craftsmen's mates were upgraded to craftsmen and employees worked up to 16 extra hours per quarter without pay. Also, of course, these months were psychologically important in winning employees' acceptance of the plan.

The negotiation of this plan was extremely smooth and successful. Since such positive action by management is increasingly essential, to analyse its success is appropriate.

The reasons for success at Refining Ltd.

(1) The success of the Esso Blue Book

The success of the Blue Book experiment set a precedent, allowing the stewards to feel they were not first to intrude into the demarcation preserves of craft groups. There was greater readiness to accept the plan at the outset than at Fawley.[10] In addition, before discussions, the convenor had attended a course run by the Industrial Welfare Society which was centred on the Esso Blue Book, and the reasons for its success. He was, therefore, well informed about the case for 'productivity bargaining' and how far management had succeeded, and how much the unions had conceded, at Fawley.

Also, of course, management could use the Blue Book as a challenge. Both sides determined to do at least as well as Fawley. Being a smaller unit of 880 employees with only eighteen shop stewards, Refining Ltd. was more compact in organization, and therefore had a better chance of success. The plan came into operation immediately, except for the time necessary to retrain staff, though at Esso it was phased over two years. Overtime dropped from an average of 20·5 per cent in the six months before the plan to a 5 per cent average in the two months after. Shortly after this, it was eliminated. The union obtained 32·5 per cent, in real terms representing a wage increase of, on average, 5·5 per cent per man per week. At Fawley, a supplementary settlement was necessary in 1962 to give some craftsmen an income gain in real terms at all.[11]

(2) The voluntary nature of the agreement

The fact that agreement was voluntary reassured the stewards that their wishes would be respected since, obviously, management wanted everyone to participate. Also, it enabled those stewards in favour of the plan, fourteen out of the total of eighteen, to pressurize those against. If groups remained outside, dissension among employees could compromise any acceptance. As the company introductory letter to the final agreement states: 'If the plan is finally accepted, the spirit in which it is implemented will determine its success or failure'.

(3) The size of the wage agreement

The real increase in wages for those employees in the plan was a sufficiently large inducement for co-operation. As from July, 1965, the new weekly salary was 10·4 per cent higher than average earnings during January–November, 1964. No steward wanted his constituents left outside, earning about 10 per cent less than other maintenance workers. Also, psychologically, it demonstrated management's determination that employees should not suffer from the change but that their interests were important.

(4) The role of the stewards

Success was facilitated by the willingness of management and unions to let the stewards help determine the final plan. Thus, those responsible for implementing the plan also participated in its construction. The stewards felt that it was their plan as well as management's, they were interested in it, as well as showing a general determination to see it through. The chief opponents were the two T & GWU stewards who felt that, since the craft unions supported it, they must oppose it. Representing such semi- and unskilled T & GWU maintenance staff as drivers, labourers, and canteen workers, they resented the strong position of the craft unions. Yet their *constituents* were almost wholly in favour, forcing them to accept it!

If the stewards had not participated so fully, negotiations having taken place over their heads, they might have felt that the plan had been imposed upon them. Their resentfulness might have reduced their willingness to implement it.

Indeed, in some instances, this involvement has gone even further. At Petrochemicals Limited, stewards presented proposals for a flexible approach to the operation and maintenance of the chemical plant. Some skilled tasks were listed for trained craftsmen, but others were to be done by staff immediately available. Management invited the approach, allowing stewards to widen the proposals which were then put into practice.[12]

Certainly, the participation of stewards in productivity bargaining is necessary if those they represent are to have an opportunity to influence their working conditions within the changing pattern of circumstances. Lacking this opportunity, work groups may act unconstructively, opposing proposals put forward by management.

Indeed the procedure may need to be broken down further if consultation is to succeed. The breakdown of work groups within many stewards' constituencies may create informal leaders. Stewards may need to consult with them if their groups are to be fully involved. Otherwise, 'unofficial' opposition may arise with unhappy consequences for proposed productivity deals.

Indeed, the implementation of such bargains greatly affects

the relationships between management and stewards. The crux of productivity bargaining is that management settles such problems, neglected over the years, as demarcation problems and inefficient use of labour, some points of dispute between management and unions being removed. Not all disappear; in a dynamic situation, this is scarcely possible. Nevertheless, the scope for steward bargaining may well be restricted as a result, leaving the steward less powerful. Members may apply pressure on him to justify his election by producing improvements. This could result, in time, in erosion of some of the control management regained through the productivity agreement. The full time official is also important here. Though it is possible to use him to restrain stewards and defend the agreement, doubtless such action would alienate workers while undermining the position of the official.

It is said that those workers with no 'restrictive practices' to concede in a productivity agreement will invent them. Also, possibly, those involved in earlier productivity deals will create new rigidities to justify the improved conditions another one would bring. In fact, the workgroup pressures expressed through stewards plus technological change lead to fluctuations in the pattern of plant agreements.

(5) The role of the full time officials

That stewards played a large part in determining the final shape of the plan reflects the trust felt in management and stewards by the officials. The ex-T & GWU branch secretary insisted that his discussions with stewards were detailed and, where agreement seemed likely, that information was quickly passed to the union officials for ratification. He avoided reaching agreements with the stewards alone, seeing that this would reduce the full time officials' support for the plan. They would have resented what appeared as agreements reached behind their backs. These threaten to undermine their status, and by introducing agreements locally with far reaching implications for future bargaining elsewhere could cause problems for the unions. The opposition of the full-time officials could, of course, have killed the plan.

While stewards are vital in such radical agreements, they act as union officers. Agreements reached concern their superiors, who must be consulted if lasting progress is to be made.

(6) Managerial skill

This discussion has touched on the ability of the managers in these negotiations. A further illustration suggests the very high quality of management necessary to succeed in such ventures.

The Employee Relations Department in the refinery faced the prospect of discussing the plan with a craft convenor who, largely because of his own enthusiasm for it, could not persuade his fellow stewards. They thought him too pro-management to protect their interests adequately. Management, therefore, sent two stewards to an IWS course on the Esso Blue Book. One was probably the most intelligent unionist in the plant. He was in favour of the plan, but much more cautious than the convenor. On returning, he was most knowledgeable about productivity bargaining. Being more acceptable to the other stewards than the existing convenor, he was elected to this position in the annual craft union elections. The ex-convenor resigned, being offered the position of supervisor. The new convenor was allowed, with his deputy who had accompanied him on the course and who was also extremely able, to spend fifteen months in full time consultations about the plan with management. It was he who patiently ironed out points of difference between his fellow stewards and management. Without him, management admitted, the plan would probably not have gone through.

Managerial skill was also displayed in the decentralization of the administration of the plan, so that departmental managers and supervisors had to aid its implementation. A research group studying the behaviour of supervisors at Refining found they were disgruntled because, they claimed, the stewards knew more about the plan than they did. Management, realizing that by discussing with stewards they had indeed created this situation and seeing the dangers of alienating supervisors, arranged weekend courses. Here, their supervisors were fully briefed about the scheme and its progress. Having done this, the management could rely on supervisory co-operation as the plan was introduced. Decentralization of the responsibility for implementation is inevitable if managerial initiative is to be fully rewarded. It is pointless for major ventures by top management to fail departmentally because supervisors cannot or will not effectively implement them.

A leading industrial relations expert from Ford's in the USA has observed, '. . . of all the management specialities, the personnel function is perhaps the one least capable of being effectively carried out solely by a corps of specialists. Practically everyone in management, at all levels, is dealing with people in carrying out his responsibilities, and thus is involved in implementing personnel policies and affecting, in greater or lesser degree, the nature and extent of personnel problems. Quite aside from that aspect, major decisions in this area of management responsibility usually have an important effect in other areas, and the reverse is often equally true. The labour relations activity functions most effectively as a built-in, continuous, fully integrated part of the total managerial effort.'[14] Positive labour policies need total managerial effort, not just a specialist one.

This study of the introduction of a productivity plan does, however, great credit to the management. British management is often compared unfavourably with those abroad. An example of criticism of the traditional approach of British management to labour utilization was contained in the *Financial Times* editorial on 21st December, 1964. Analysing the results of Professor Dunning's article in the *Philip Hill Higginson Review*, the editorial points out that Professor Dunning proves, taking the years 1958–62, that the average US returns on overseas investment were 10·2 per cent, compared with the UK's 7·8 per cent. The difference was greatest in Western Europe, the Commonwealth, and Britain itself. The editorial concludes that American firms are more rigorous in their investment decisions. It summarizes these findings thus: 'The implications of this study, even though tentative, could be wide ranging. One of the arguments advanced to explain Britain's weak performance has been the poor quality of British labour and its lack of effort. If so, then British investment in foreign countries with less troublesome unions, should show better returns. But these statistics show that the rate of return on British capital is no better—even if it is located in "industrious" countries, such as Italy and America, than in the UK. One cannot yet be sure, but the implication could well follow that it is management, and the quality of its decisions, which stands at the real centre of Britain's sluggish rate of growth.'

The above case study is an example of managerial initiative and success in labour relations, showing the way to better utilization of company resources through productivity bargaining.

(7) The gradual nature of the change

Planned changes in detailed working arrangements affecting routines of many employees is an exercise in management. It also tests the quality of the workers' representatives. Too much enthusiasm for and too little questioning of the scheme can jeopardize its success. Thus, the attitude of the original convenor at Refining threatened to alienate other stewards, concerned that their constituents' interests should be carefully considered. The successful convenor consulted slowly on the proposed changes, taking all interests into account. If such changes are to be introduced in British industry, the lesson of this study is that bargaining must be gradual.

Some problems of management

It is easy to point to deficiencies in management; it is necessary to gain balance by pointing out their difficulties. Certainly, collective bargaining presents many, the most intractable being to know when to submit to shop floor pressure and when to resist it. Whichever management does is likely to bring criticism from some interested party, yet there are few guides to what is correct. Closely connected is how management functions are to be reconciled with the increasing number of topics claimed as negotiable by stewards. Often, stewards negotiate on topics connected with production management, such as safety measures and incentive schemes, intrusive on management's right to manage. In practice, reactions to this problem help set the tone of industrial relationships in a factory. Again, the problem of what facilities to afford stewards is not easily resolved. A liberal attitude may further their success, which may be unwelcome to management, while curtailment leads to difficulties in collective bargaining. To quote one manager, 'Before we act in relation to our stewards we have a very complicated balance sheet to construct and interpret'.

These problems are exacerbated by personalities which, even in a good atmosphere, can easily produce friction. This is especially true if turnover of stewards is so high as to prevent the development of steady relationships with managers. Finally, management finds itself dealing with more bargaining in the workplace as the dynamic of industrial relations shifts there. Several managers declined to comment on where they drew the line of demarcation between stewards and officials in negotiations.

In conclusion, we must add that management's task is most difficult in collective bargaining. Though it is undoubtedly management's job to make decisions here, shaping the nature of industrial relationships, it is unrealistic to criticize without sympathy for the awkward situations it finds itself in.

References

1. *In Trade Union Officers, op. cit.*, p. 175.
2. *The Role of Shop Stewards in British Industrial Relations, op. cit.*, para 19.
3. Seear, Nancy, 'Relations at Factory Level', *Industrial Relations: Contemporary Problems and Perspectives*, ed. B. C. Roberts, Methuen, 1962, p. 164.
4. Ross, Norman, *Workshop Bargaining: A New Approach*, Fabian Tract, No. 366, p. 12.
5. Flanders, Allan, *The Fawley Productivity Agreements, op. cit.*, p. 226.
6. Clegg, H. A., *Implications of the Shorter Working Week for Management*, B. I. M. Paper No. 1962, p. 13.
7. Flanders, *op. cit.*, p. 237.
8. This section is based on discussions with management and shop stewards at an oil refinery. We are deeply grateful for their co-operation, but a guarantee of anonymity prevents mention of their names.
9. Flanders, *op. cit.*, p. 217.
10. See Flanders, *op. cit.*, pp. 107–37.
11. Flanders, *op. cit.*, p. 164.
12. Royal Commission on Trade Unions and Employers' Associations. Research Paper No. 4, 1967 p. 6.
13. It is a commonplace that management is inclined towards efficiency and employees towards security, though this generalization is not equally applicable in all cases. Management here were recognizing what Jack Barbash states. 'The problem of industrial relations, then, arises out of the tensions between the employers' application of

rational pressures and the workers' resistance to these pressures through his protective devices'. See *British Journal of Industrial Relations*, March 1964, p. 72.

14. Denise, M. L., 'The Personnel Manager and his Educational Preparation', *Industrial and Labour Relations Review*, October 1962.

10

Recent Trends and the Future Role of Shop Stewards

The problems associated with stewards are related to wider ones stemming from changes in both union organizations and industrial management. Their present power can be partly attributed to the rigidity of our industrial relations institutions, thus allowing stewards' roles to develop pragmatically. This is especially true of bargaining, where favourable conditions for workplace bargaining have provoked no general structural reforms to cater for this development. Thus, the stewards' role has grown. The unions have seldom resolved the dilemma of how to maintain their authority and appeal without foregoing workplace opportunities, while many managers have responded with expedients, seeking to avoid stoppages or other sanctions. The atmosphere has been permissive, many would claim excessively so. The functions of old procedures and institutions have been eroded, to the point where fundamental changes in the machinery of industrial relations are necessary, but have not been forthcoming.

Yet, this pragmatism and flexibility have brought advantages to both sides, though there is occasionally concern over the now powerful position of stewards. Assessment raises the question of how the existing situation can be rationalized, and perhaps formalized. Whether the process needs formal consolidation or whether further evolution along present lines is best concerns not only unions and managements, but also the government worried about the collective bargaining system. If a new direction is necessary, a longer term view of the direction of the whole industrial relations system is implied. Decisions over whether workplace bargaining is to be promoted or to be checked are involved. The answer rests ultimately on the structure thought most likely to reconcile union members' demands for higher standards of living, better security, and higher status with company and government concern over competitiveness and prices.

The coincidence of a buoyant economic climate since 1945 with both managements' and unions' preference for informality has often led relationships to be based on opportunism. Managements often resent the effects of the internalized system—though they have helped foster it. It holds advantages for them, but when its disadvantages appear the tendency is to call on the old procedures. Similarly, stewards have preferred internal relationships, while also retaining access to, and relying on, the 'reserve' power of their unions. It is significant that, for many managers and stewards, external alliances are now supplementary, rather than primary as before.

Although many managements have well intentioned policies to improve labour relations internally, thus enhancing the role of workplace representatives, generally the level of labour management appears low. Despite the pressures, or perhaps because of them, only rarely have firms scrutinized these relationships as closely as, for example, products or markets. 'Research and development' has been non-existent, with a few exceptions, and though each plant is a different problem, some commentators have resignedly called for the same externally imposed 'solutions'. Too many managers have taken the absence of strife as indicating all is well, while market considerations or anticipated difficulties of changes have dissuaded others from regarding labour utilization as a useful field for their attention. Yet the successes in plant productivity bargaining have revealed simultaneously how malpractices have 'just grown', and how they can be removed by imaginative and well informed management. Stewards are usually involved in these negotiations; indeed they would be impossible without representatives on the same wavelength as the members. Thus, stewards are an essential element in one of the most encouraging features of contemporary industrial relations. It is paradoxical that the informal and fragmented understandings which these negotiations either formalize or remove were often built up by the same stewards and some of the managers who negotiate their removal.

Clearly, stewards must get the best for their members from the shopfloor situation, and if not met by a purposive management, with a long term design for workplace relations, then expedients proliferate. It is crucial to such reorientation that management and stewards leave the hazy world of stereotypes, establishing human relationships based on an acceptance of the other's rights and duties. This has been a feature of several productivity agreements.

Many aspects of the employment relationship, important to union members, cannot be regulated outside the workplace. Topics such as manning, day to day labour mobility, discipline, overtime allocations, work organization, and job demarcation cannot be regulated in detail by external collective agreements. Most are left to informality. They concern both management and employees, but are complicated by their implications of status. Attempts by workplace representatives to regulate them are usually resisted strongly, and they cause almost half the strikes in this country. The issues at stake here are, in microcosm, those of management prerogatives and of worker control. They indicate that work groups and their representatives want more than to influence the price of their labour, but to regulate its utilization. Often it is this encroachment by stewards of new topics rather than greater pressure on money matters, which many managers find most galling. These issues provide sufficient scope for active workplace representation, even in the absence of bargaining over financial matters, with which they are indirectly linked. Moreover, the importance of issues concerned with status, degrees of influence over work organization, styles of treatment, etc., may well increase. The effect on earnings may not be great, but their influence on labour costs is high.

For managements, the enhanced importance of stewards has brought both advantages and disadvantages. Some have welcomed the development, affording good facilities in the firm and developing good relations with stewards which have improved labour relations considerably. Many have utilized the opportunities afforded by the stewards' role to introduce innovations, but others ignore its possibilities.

Many managements deeply resent stewards' scrutiny of their decisions, with their attempts to circumscribe management freedoms, regarding the process as an endless stream of impossible demands. Typically, management strategy is defensive, rather than advancing their own interests. Managers regard facilities for stewards and agreements reached with them as privileges and concessions. Often, managers extend facilities far beyond the terms of national agreements, maintaining the illusion that they can be withdrawn by failing to regularize them. In consequence, agreements understate the role of stewards, the lack of realistic formal agreements further widening the gap between stewards and the rules of the industrial relations system.

Stewards also challenge the unions, though remaining indispensable in recruiting members, collecting dues, handling minor workplace problems, and as channels of communication. The challenge to the unions is essentially one of maintaining control and leadership without alienating the membership or stifling local initiative. The internal structure of unions, particularly the division of authority within them, was fashioned to the needs of industry-wide bargaining. As this has declined in significance since 1945, this structure might well be called into question. Certainly, the challenge from below is as much to unions as to management and the old collective bargaining structure. The primacy of national union executives is more appropriate to unions in industries where bargaining is restricted to that level, but is less justified where the industry-wide machinery has declined. However, practice differs; unions are indulgent of variations between rule books and reality, trusting to loyalty and tradition rather than close definition.

The unions have stressed the continued unity of their organizations, while allowing the acquisition of bargaining functions by stewards. This is accepted, rather than promoted. Unions may fear their stewards are not sufficiently skilled to deal alone with higher levels of managements, though officials may fear equally for their positions in organizations subject to power struggles. Clearly, an analogy exists with large business organizations, for example over the decentralization of decision taking, sections acting in their own interests, the ambition of individuals, etc. On the other hand, few trade unions can insist, on pain of sanctions, on the acceptance of instructions from above. Such obedience may be necessary to the career of a manager; it is not for most unionists.

Discussion of a union's control over its members provokes questions over the purposes of union organization, and the methods most appropriate to them. If it is primarily to advance the interests of its members, sectionally, unions clearly cannot do this only by industry-wide negotiations, which are typically multi-union and not comprehensive. Workplace representatives can negotiate with individual managements, lead opinion among members, and communicate shop floor opinion and problems to the union. Changes have been quicker at factory than at national level, and stewards have secured improvements, financial and otherwise, not possible at higher levels. Consequently, the workplace is a strong focus of members' attention, though the logic of the present formal system suggests it should be supplementary. Failure to acknowledge this change of emphasis has left unions and management ill equipped to regulate it. For example, workplace bargaining is somewhat secretive, opportunistic and piecemeal, its very status has affected its nature and results. Where managements have taken the initiative, as recently, the results have been rather different.

The steward, as a negotiator representing constituents, draws strength from his ability to carry his members with him, though the unions' failure to acknowledge this has left their members with no defined workplace unit in which to express their views. Union democracy is based on branches rather than the more meaningful workplace or workshop. Some unions have brought members closer to the union externally by encouraging shop or factory *organization*, rather than catering for their *representatives* and relying on residentially based branches. This emphasis is found in the printing unions, being also advocated in a NUFTO handbook. In both cases, workplace representatives attend periodic shop meetings,

212

giving members an opportunity to hear reports from their representatives and to raise topics. However, such facilities are rare, but they do much to prevent representatives and their constituents losing touch. Such checks are valuable to firms and unions believing in extended communications, and accepting the representational role of stewards.

Closer association of stewards with the unions is a difficult problem. Evidently, stewards build up this relationship if useful functionally, rather than merely being a duty. If stewards respect their local official, being satisfied with his interest, they are less likely to take action before consultation or to ignore his advice. If union committees and officials yield information and advice, problems are more likely to be referred to them than if the only reason for doing so is a clause in the rule book. More full time officials, able to specialize, is one way of building up this confidence. Another would be union research officers at district or company level to match managements' specialists, by disseminating information to stewards. Certainly, stewards want more information about affairs in their companies, finding it difficult to obtain it from management. Without this, their actions may be, and may seem, misguided if not selfish. If the local union office was a source of information on company, district, and national matters it would strengthen the link between stewards and their unions. Similarly, union policies might appear more realistic to members if stewards could present the views of members to the union executive. Some conflict may remain between the sectional interests of work groups and the overall interests of the union and its members. However, improved communications and education would explain the reasons for the differences, permitting different solutions in different circumstances.

Much depends on whether the unions want to stimulate or restrain the development of workplace representatives. The question of training, for example, involves not only the intention of the two sides, if managements are involved, in shop steward training, but also the functions of a steward. Few training officers operate without detailed job descriptions, yet that of the steward is particularly difficult to define. They are important communicators, but also decision-takers, and are more than simply custodians of constituents' established rights. Their quality is crucial to both unions and management, yet both often hold back from assisting stewards, the implications being either unknown or feared. Stewards may move away from both, and their autonomy is feared by both. If the workplace is to become the acknowledged centre of industrial relations activity, with the possible exception of negotiations on minimum conditions, the most urgent problem is how to 'integrate' members in the workshops, particularly representatives, into the unions' structures. Some unions have been successful in this, but there is scope for new organization and communications systems. These will be particularly necessary if acceptance of stewards' facilities, and increased training, are not to separate them from their constituents, thus loosening their leadership positions. It may never be possible to avoid occasional 'premature' sanctions by work groups, but in formalizing the steward's role, loss of sympathy between members and stewards must be guarded against. The steward's very proximity to work groups is what makes his role important.

The intractable problem is of union structure. Company bargaining emphasizes the need for inter-union co-operation, which joint steward organizations amply demonstrate. Inter-union hostility is a blot on our industrial relations system, structural and behavioural changes being necessary if the unions are to supervise workplace bargaining closely. One union has proposed direct communication from multi-union workplace committees to national negotiating committees. The independence of joint stewards committees from union supervision is a problem, and will be until schemes of joint supervision or industrial unionism are established. The three largest unions have begun to improve relations under TUC initiative. Amalgamations are more numerous, and presumably the Report of the Royal Commission[1] will not be without influence on this issue.

The challenge from below threatens the traditional industrial relations system in many ways. For example, the internalization of dealings between management and employees enhances the roles of stewards and labour relations specialists at the expense of employers' associations. Decentralization of important if fragmented bargaining has emphasized work-place rather than union loyalties among union members, inter-union stewards committees and combine committees have impeded united union leadership, while enhanced bargaining strength at factory level limits management freedoms. In acute situations, both unions and management have been unable to coerce or persuade members and employees to follow their advice, and unofficial strikes have increased. These trends, and their implications, cause concern, being all the more significant against the challenge from above of government responsibility for the economy, particularly for incomes policy. The incomes policy accentuates the weakness in the existing structure, making a solution to the challenge from below a prerequisite for the incorporation of new ideas at higher level. Indeed, perhaps the most significant feature of post-war changes has been the increasing gap between wage rates and earnings. Thus, the major problem facing the industrial relations system is to reconcile plant bargaining with industry-wide bargaining machinery, and reconciling both with the 'national interest'.

Much workplace bargaining is piecemeal; it is initiated principally by stewards, advancing by arguments based on comparisons and precedent. Its results are haphazard, often inflationary, and further complicate already untidy wage structures. The intricacies of wage differentials are exacerbated by multiple union representation and sectional claims. The process is graphically described as wage drift. The word is appropriate for it lacks conscious direction and erodes as well as supplements industry-wide agreements. Indeed, post war developments have emphasized the workplace rather than national committees as the place where effective decisions are made, and where labour costs are determined. These developments, taken with government concern with cost-push inflation, have placed collective bargaining at a crossroads. Events have shown that the traditional bargaining structure has lost significance; consequently, attempts to influence collective bargaining solely through these bodies are inadequate. Governments have striven to link growth in earnings and in productivity, but this has occurred in plant or company-based productivity agreements, rather than industry-wide settlements. This suggests that it is here that such relationships can best be achieved.

Practices leading to underemployment of labour are often peculiar to individual factories, and there are variations in the ways they are operated and defended. While some restrictions derive from union rules, e.g. apprenticeships, the more significant are those developed into custom and practice, often fossilizing practices which management introduced initially. Thus, modification of these obstacles to efficient labour utilization rests primarily with the men they protect, i.e. rank and file members, rather than the union as such. There is a better opportunity of implementing changes if the groups' representatives, shop stewards, are involved, rather than expecting them to rely on remote union officials. Most recent productivity agreements have involved both, but the workplace representative is vital in persuading men to accept fundamental changes. Such bargaining allows a closer association between improvements in productivity and in earnings, external criteria being played down. If workplace bargaining became open and systematic, and industry-wide negotiating subsidiary rather than vice versa, then productivity aspects might be incorporated specifically, which is seldom feasible otherwise. Excessive manning, overtime, and high labour costs probably stem more from plant practices than from national negotiations, and utilization can be tackled more effectively in the plant. There are always exceptions; on the railways, for example, many practices are regulated nationally by officials and a single employer.

However, decentralized bargaining presents problems as well as offering advantages. Even when taking the form of productivity bargaining, it is suspected by employers' associations, not wholly from self-interest. They consider that it encourages workers to devise new restrictive practices 'for sale', that productivity agreements are inflationary even if at first 'self-financing', for its rewards are spread by coercive comparisons more rapidly than its productivity aspects. Such negotiating units weaken both union and employers' organizations, while single plant productivity bargaining is slow in improving efficiency across the industry. They could, often, be more efficiently achieved nationally, if implemented fully at plant level.

Nevertheless, decentralized bargaining has numerous advantages in practice. It is easier to initiate, and implement at this level, partly because the negotiators also supervise its operation. It provides a method of bringing order into plant labour management and indicates management initiative. Negotiation locally with union officials and stewards has improved labour–management relations, resulting in better work organization, communications, and enhanced mutual trust. Some managements have, at last, brought the quality of labour management up to the standards of other managerial functions. The significance of productivity agreements is not simply their economics; they also create the opportunity for a new basis for relationships, with changes in the mechanisms for conducting them. Stewards are deeply involved in negotiating productivity agreements, and more so in their implementation. This implies a continuing role, even though the removal of complex wage structures, slackening of craft demarcation, job flexibility, and above all consolidation of earnings into basic rates may change the character of the steward's role and the issues he deals with. Indeed, changed management philosophy is a prerequisite of such agreements. For example, stewards negotiating with managements within a 'productivity framework' might need previously withheld company information to reach a bargain. Such agreements are possible only where good relations exist, improbable where management holds a traditional attitude to the stewards. Similarly, if union officials appeared to be negotiating over stewards' heads, rather than working together, this too would inhibit success.

Clearly, the plant has become the focus of industrial relations activity in many industries, and reforms in the system might proceed by acknowledging this, rather than in patching up the traditional machinery. The structure of bargaining affects its results, and with advances at some plants, a general promotion of such bargaining units might better serve the requirements of union members, managements, and governments. Structurally, this involves emphasizing the actual situation, not the traditional, enhancing the role of workplace representatives. Stewards would be front line negotiators, being fed information by union research departments and perhaps having access to company information during bargaining. Such negotiation might be related to the firm's situation, and such devious means of improving earnings as overtime be avoided. Thus, industry-wide agreements might continue to settle terms explicitly as minima, negotiated by both sides nationally to protect the lower paid—to whom they might be restricted. They might gain the status of Wages Council rates, i.e., become legally enforceable, but employers' associations would no longer regard their improvement by member firms as contrary to the spirit of the association.

Clearly, stewards' roles would be enhanced, more importantly if the decentralization was accompanied by the formalization of their roles, functions, and facilities in new procedure agreements. They would deal with additional matters handled within their factories, assisted by regular meetings with district officials, who would 'service' them rather than advise them as superiors. This would present the unions with an enormous problem of education and training, for stewards, though expert in factory practices and technology, could not be expected to gain the same bargaining skills without some instruction.

There are strong functional arguments for promoting the steward's role. The importance of work groups has been outlined earlier, and the steward's proximity to them suggests he is the best link with both unions and management. Extended workplace bargaining would enable work groups to participate more fully in negotiations important to them, and the involvement of their representatives in workplace changes might reduce suspicion and facilitate innovations. This structure would permit more meaningful participation in union affairs, and strengthen democracy within the unions. It would also enable participation in the processes of management, emphasizing more closely the interdependence of management and labour. External links with national unions will, however, prevent this interdependence becoming total dependence.

Amongst the major problems arising from this change of emphasis would be steward education and training, and multiple unionism at workplace level. Another is the large number of companies and establishments in the UK, despite the tendency for firms to become larger. The changes advocated fit more easily into the medium and large establishments, than into the small and very small. However, employees in these firms would be protected by a minimum wage rate which, if restricted to lower paid workers, might rise more rapidly than at the present. As we have seen, underutilization of labour is not peculiar to large firms; overtime is higher in industries with lower minimum wage rates. Our suggestions would have little effect on management or workers in establishments lacking effective workplace organization. However, it might involve difficulties for the government and other agencies concerned with incomes policy.

The difficulty is in information collection, for decentralization of bargaining would multiply the number of bargaining units. However, since workplace bargaining and wage drift are extensive under the present system, the problem already exists for central agencies, improvements being obscured in many ways and often not evaluated against any centrally determined criteria. Administratively, collecting information or enforcing principles centrally is difficult, and would be particularly so without the acquiescence of both parties. Determining whether wage and salary increases, job regradings, merit increases, changes in incentive schemes, etc., are 'justified', or increased overtime 'necessary' in the face of hostile managements and unions would be impossible even with strong legal powers. Wage drift and the negotiating activities of stewards are inextricably linked, and consequently any incomes policy will affect and be affected by shop stewards. Long term incomes policy, as opposed to short term crisis measures, must command general support to be effective. One suggestion is that representatives of national bodies concerned might join negotiations, or at least know the results before implementation. The early warning system of the Prices and Incomes Act does something to meet the latter point. It is unlikely that an open but unregulated system of plant bargaining could develop in this country, but while more bargaining units might appear to impede those responsible for incomes policy, the effects might well help them to their objectives. A smaller bargaining unit might be related better to internal efficiency, and though risks of inflationary settlements remain, e.g. those based on external comparisons, wage drift illustrates that these comparisons already take place either through management or through unionists locally. If we take the level of these comparisons as given, formalized plant bargaining seems more likely to provide an institutional framework which does more to inhibit inflationary settlements. Much depends on the economic and social climate, several Ministers having implied that the country's economy is to be run at a 'higher margin of spare resources' than in the past. Whatever the arguments for this, the result might be a slackening of pressure in labour markets.

If the actual increase in stewards' power is consolidated by formal recognition, this would be a fundamental change in industrial relations, and its underlying philosophy. This, over the last fifty years, has emphasized the importance of national agreements, regarding factory agreements as subsidiary. The failure to bring stewards within the formal framework has produced problems, though this development is characteristic of industrial relations and aids flexibility. An alternative to promoting the stewards is to increase the number of full time officials, though unions are slow in improving the ratio of such officials to members. Though this might increase contact between membership and officials, it might also create bureaucracy, driving members even further from the union. This gap between representatives and those represented is a danger in the formalization of stewards' roles. It must be guarded against if the emergence of a new intermediate unofficial layer is to be prevented.

Nevertheless, the need to extend the system into the workplace is apparent. With the development of incomes policy, such a move is likely, although its specific nature remains to be seen. The pattern is intricate suggesting that unions will find it difficult to standardize stewards' functions, a retrograde step in a system moving away from its previous rigidity. Most likely is that the system will continue much as before, trends apparent in a few progressive sectors will take a long time to be felt over the whole system. The variety of work situations ensures there is no single right answer, but that formalization and change will probably proceed on a company by company basis.

POSTSCRIPT: The Report of the Royal Commission on Trade Unions and Employers' Associations[1]

Since this chapter was written, the Royal Commission Report has appeared and we felt it would be of interest to compare our analysis and comments with those of the Donovan Commission. We have therefore added a synopsis of the Donovan Report as it applies to shop stewards. No comments are made on the Report, and a comparison between its recommendations and the foregoing analysis is left to the reader.

The central theme of the Report was that there were two systems of industrial relations, the formal i.e. the traditional, with its externally based institutions regulating relationships through industry-wide agreements, and the informal i.e. workplace regulation of work and pay by managers and shop stewards. The former was considered a façade, the latter the reality. The Commission's major recommendation was that the structure of collective bargaining should be reformed, and emphasis on industry-wide agreements be replaced by 'comprehensive, orderly and systematic' company or factory agreements. These proposals, if adopted, will affect the role of shop stewards, but our purpose here is to summarize the relevant parts of the Report rather than to predict its consequences.

In its analysis of workplace relations and shop stewards the Report relies on and quotes freely from its survey and published research papers. It enumerates the contemporary tasks of shop stewards, i.e. recruiting new members; maintaining members; in some instances collecting dues; responsibility for two-way communications between union and members, which is underlined by low attendance at branch meetings; representing the union to members and the members to the union; and, most important, helping to regulate workers' pay and conditions, and representing members in dealings with management. The absence of uniformity in stewards' duties is noted. A minority of stewards do not negotiate with managers at all, but over half negotiate with managers over issues of pay, and of hours—the most common being the level and distribution of overtime. About one third regularly represent their members on disciplinary issues, and other matters which some of them negotiate about include the distribution and pace of work, manning, transfers, introduction of new machinery and new jobs, taking on new labour and redundancy. The Report suggests that there are about 175,000 shop stewards in Britain, compared with about 3,000 full time trade union officials, and stewards now handle many times the volume of business conducted by their full time officers.

The Commission points out that the marked growth in the numbers of shop stewards since the war has not been accompanied by an equivalent growth in the numbers of full time officers. 'The evidence, therefore, is that there is obviously a shortage of full time officers at any rate in some unions.' The following table illustrates the effects of this on officials' ability to maintain close contacts with shop stewards.

Full Time Local Officers: Shop steward responsibilities and contacts

Name of union	Average No. of stewards for whom each officer is responsible	Average No. of stewards contacted in last 4 weeks	Proportion of shop stewards contacted in last 4 weeks
T & GWU	120	96	80%
AEU	477	132	28%
NUGMW	169	65	38%
ETU	232	94	41%
AUBTW	33	30	91%
All unions	172	89	52%

We should like to thank the Controller HMSO for permission
to reproduce this table

Despite these variations, the Commission's survey recorded that 87 per cent of district officers felt they had sufficient influence over the activities of shop stewards, and virtually all regarded the work done by stewards very highly indeed.

Stewards derive their authority from two major sources—the union and their constituents. Where stewards are mentioned in the union's rulebook something is usually said about the method of appointment, the body to whom the steward is nominally responsible, the duties of recruiting and retaining members, and collecting subscriptions. If the steward's representative function is touched on, little is said about it.

Most major unions have shop stewards' handbooks, which set out some of these tasks at greater length. The issues which fall within a steward's competence to handle are seldom spelled out, and he is often simply referred to the relevant industrial agreement, which is usually far from comprehensive. In fact stewards are concerned not so much with the application of industry-wide agreements, but with obtaining and retaining concessions in excess of its terms, and in establishing rights over issues not touched on in the agreement. Secondly, the power of stewards rests on their constituents, divided into work groups, which owe their strength not to their union but to, *inter alia*, full employment, management policies, and the reaction of British industrial relations institutions to post war developments. British managers have augmented the increased influence of the work group 'by their preference for keeping many matters out of agreements, by the inadequacy of the methods of control over systems of payments, by their preference for informality and by their tolerance of custom and practice'.

Managers do not, on the whole, want to formalize existing factory *understandings*, for example, the privileges and facilities of shop stewards. Concessions are made *de facto* rather than *de jure* partly because managers may wish to withdraw them when circumstances change (e.g. if a less co-operative steward were elected), and partly because senior management—particularly at board level—'would not be prepared to admit publicly that they had been forced to accept such modifications in their managerial prerogatives and formal chains of command'.

The Commission considers it is often inaccurate to describe shop stewards as 'troublemakers', and observes that stewards are not necessarily responsible for actions and behaviour at shop floor level. 'Shop floor decisions which generally precede unofficial strikes are often taken against the advice of shop stewards. Thus shop stewards are rarely agitators pushing workers towards unconstitutional action. In some instances they may be the mere mouthpieces of their work groups. But quite commonly they are supporters of order exercising a restraining influence on their members in conditions which promote disorder.' Management may rely heavily on their efforts to achieve this: the steward is more of a lubricant than an irritant. 75 per cent of works managers interviewed in the Commission's survey felt that stewards were fairly or very efficient as workers' representatives. The vast majority of stewards felt that managers were reasonable in their dealings with stewards. Finally, the Report quotes from Turner, Clack and Roberts' study of the motor industry[2] to the effect that 'strikes have been as common in plants where stewards' organization is weak and divided as where it is strong; and there is more evidence to suggest that senior stewards attempt to control the development of disputes and are pushed into stoppages from behind than they lead workers into such crises'.

Despite these positive features, the Commission made a number of recommendations relating directly to shop stewards. These included more comprehensive coverage in union rule-books, and agreed and realistic facilities to be set out in the proposed company or factory agreements. The Commission felt that union rulebooks did not reach a sufficiently high standard to allow stewards to perform their functions within the compass of the rules, and recommend that union rules should cover the following:

(1) The way in which stewards are elected

'If stewards are to become an integral part of formal structure of union authority provision should be made for the holding of an election where there is more than one candidate for the job.'

(2) The term of office

While no standard period is recommended, in view of the variety of circumstances wherever possible the period should be long enough to enable the steward to settle down in the job and acquire useful experience.

(3) The filling of casual vacancies
(4) The bounds of steward's jurisdiction

'The rules should try to give more guidance than is now usual about the action which a steward may take on his own authority or as a result of a meeting of members. This means establishing the relationship between such a meeting and the branch. It should be made clear that neither is entitled to take decisions which are at variance with those arising out of factory, company or industry-wide agreements to which the union is party.'

(5) Relations with other union officials and officers

'In factory based branches the offices of senior steward and steward should be combined wherever possible with those of branch secretary and branch committee member. The relationship of the branch to its local full time union officer should also be made clear, together with his right to attend branch meetings and inform those present on union policy and advice.'

(6) The place of the shop steward in the union's organization

'There should be a clear statement as to the authority within the union to which the shop steward is finally responsible and which can in case of need suspend or dismiss him from office.'

(7) Multi-union committees

The rules should not hinder the setting up of official multi-union committees at plant or company level.

In general, the Report charges boards of directors with a review of industrial relations *within* their companies, and recommends the conclusion of comprehensive company (or factory) agreements. They are advised 'to conclude with unions representative of their employees agreements regulating the position of shop stewards in matters such as: facilities for holding elections; numbers and constituencies; recognition of credentials; facilities to consult and report back to their members; facilities to meet with other stewards; the responsibilities of the chief steward (if any); pay while functioning as steward in working hours; day release with pay for training'. Given its emphasis on the conclusion of comprehensive company or factory agreements, and the re-orientation of both trade unions and employers' associations to facilitate this, the Commission makes many other recommendations which impinge on the role of shop stewards. It recommends that the number of full time union officials be increased to facilitate contact with shop stewards, and that the TUC and the unions pursue a policy of one union for each grade of work in a factory. Further, unions should base their branches on the workplace, and should meet there. They should provide recognized facilities for 'combine committees' in multi-plant firms to meet under union auspices. Training facilities for shop stewards should be expanded. Finally the emphasis on company (or factory) agreements is related to the need to link such bargaining with productivity, and the crucial role of shop stewards in detailed productivity bargaining is outlined.

The Commission recommended continued reliance on voluntary methods in industrial relations while the reforms it recommended were being introduced. The Report argued at length against the introduction of legal penalties as a deterrent to unconstitutional industrial action, although a majority did recommend a change in the law to restrict the protection afforded by Section 3 of the 1906 Trade Disputes Act and the 1965 Act to registered trade unions and employers' associations. This would enable employers to sue and obtain injunctions against the leaders of unofficial strikes, but its impact in practice may be limited.

References

1. The Report of the Royal Commission on Trade Unions and Employers Associations, HMSO, 1968.
2. H. A. Turner, G. Clack and G. Roberts, *op. cit.*, p. 330.

Appendix A
Statistics on
Stoppages of Work

The source of statistics concerning stoppages of work is the Department of Employment and Productivity, and unless otherwise stated the figures given have been derived from this source. There are a number of facts which must be taken into account in assessing these figures. The Department's published figures do not distinguish between strikes and lock-outs, or between official, unofficial, constitutional, and uncon-stitutional stoppages. Stoppages involving less than ten workers and those which lasted for less than one day are excluded, except where the aggregate number of working days lost exceeds 100. Moreover, it is widely acknowledged that by no means all stoppages are reported to the Ministry, and other forms of industrial action, e.g. overtime bans, go-slows, etc., are not included. The classification of single or principal causes is necessarily arbitrary. Finally, the days lost figures do not include time lost at establishments other than that at which the stoppage took place.

We would like to thank the Editor of the *International Labour Review* for permission to reproduce material from an article by one of the present writers, published in May, 1967.

Table A.1. Stoppages of work beginning in each year 1914–67

Year	Stoppages in year	Workers involved	Aggregate working days lost	Year	Stoppages in year	Workers involved	Aggregate working days lost
		(thousands)				(thousands)	
1914	972	447	9,360	1941	1,251	360	1,080
1915	672	448	2,970	1942	1,303	456	1,530
1916	532	276	2,370	1943	1,785	557	1,830
1917	730	872	5,870	1944	2,194	821	3,700
1918	1,165	1,161	5,890	1945	2,293	531	2,850
1919	1,352	2,591	36,030	1946	2,205	526	2,180
1920	1,607	1,932	28,860	1947	1,721	620	1,400
1921	763	1,801	82,270	1948	1,759	424	1,940
1922	576	552	19,650	1949	1,426	433	1,820
1923	628	405	10,950	1950	1,339	302	1,380
1924	710	613	8,360	1951	1,719	379	1,710
1925	603	441	8,910	1952	1,714	415	1,800
1926	323	2,734	161,300	1953	1,746	1,370	2,170
1927	308	108	870	1954	1,989	448	2,480
1928	302	124	1,390	1955	2,419	659	3,790
1929	431	533	8,290	1956	2,648	507	2,050
1930	422	307	4,450	1957	2,859	1,356	8,400
1931	420	490	7,010	1958	2,629	523	3,470
1932	389	379	6,430	1959	2,093	645	5,280
1933	357	136	1,020	1960	2,832	814	3,050
1934	474	134	1,060	1961	2,686	771	3,040
1935	553	271	1,950	1962	2,449	4,420	5,780
1936	818	316	2,010	1963	2,068	590	2,000
1937	1,129	597	3,140	1964	2,524	873	2,030
1938	875	274	1,330	1965	2,354	868	2,932
1939	940	337	1,350	1966	1,937	530	2,395
1940	922	299	940	1967	2,116	732	2,783

Table A.2. Strikes in the coal industry, and elsewhere
(Stoppages beginning in each year)

Year	Number	Total %	Days lost %	Number of strikes outside the coal industry
1945	1,306	57	23	987
1946	1,329	60	20	876
1947	1,053	61	37	668
1948	1,116	63	24	643
1949	874	61	39	552
1950	860	64	31	479
1951	1,058	61	20	661
1952	1,221	71	38	493
1953	1,307	75	18	439
1954	1,464	74	19	525
1955	1,783	74	29	636
1956	2,076	78	24	572
1957	2,224	78	6	635
1958	1,963	77	13	666
1959	1,307	62	7	786
1960	1,666	59	16	1,166
1961	1,458	54	24	1,228
1962	1,205	49	27	1,244
1963	987	48	16	1,081
1964	1,058	42	13	1,466
1965	740	31	14	1,614
1966	553	29	5	1,384
1967	399	14	14	1,717

Table A.3. Strikes outside the coal industry*

Industry	1953–54–55		1963–64–65	
	Total	Average	Total	Average
Electrical machinery apparatus and goods	38	13	268	89
Non-electrical engineering	140	47	522	174
Motor vehicles and cycles	145†	48	459	153
Construction	251	84	651	217
Shipbuilding and marine engineering	209	70	286	95
Port and inland water transport	159	53	263	88

* Owing to changes in the Standard Industrial Classification, these industries are not strictly comparable between these two periods, but such definitional variations have not greatly affected the figures in the industries mentioned.

† This figure includes aircraft.

National Figures, excluding coal industry

     1953–54–55   Total = 1,600   Annual average = 533.

     1963–64–65   Total = 4,161   Annual average = 1,387.

i.e. 160 per cent increase in ten year period.

Table A.4. Number of stoppages of work outside the coal industry by cause 1959-66 (Stoppages beginning in each year)

Wages	1959 No.	%	1960 No.	%	1961 No.	%	1962 No.	%	1963 No.	%	1964 No.	%	1965 No.	%	1966 No.	%
(a) Claims for increases	216	28	420	36	399	33	343	28	362	34	531	36	642	40	429	31
(b) Other wage disputes	129	16	172	15	181	15	175	14	136	13	159	11	182	11	224	16
All wage disputes	345	44	592	51	580	48	518	42	498	46	690	47	824	51	653	47
(c) Hours of labour	6	1	37	3	22	2	8	1	17	2	23	2	44	3	26	2
(d) Demarcation disputes	31	4	48	4	50	4	58	5	58	5	58	4	60	4	55	4
(e) Disputes concerning the employment or discharge of workers (including redundancy questions)	174	22	186	16	242	20	276	22	215	20	249	17	301	19	275	20
(f) Other disputes mainly concerning personnel questions	44	6	51	4	46	4	102	8	32	3	47	3	41	3	44	3
(g) Other working arrangements, rules, and discipline	123	16	161	14	183	15	164	13	167	16	279	19	260	16	255	19
(h) Trade union status	42	5	63	5	69	6	100	8	73	7	97	7	69	4	59	4
(i) Sympathetic action	17	2	25	2	25	2	24	2	15	1	16	1	12	1	14	1
All causes	782	100	1,163	100	1,220	100	1,242	100	1,075	100	1,461	100	1,611	100	1,381	100

Table A.5. Days lost due to stoppages per thousand persons employed in mining, manufacturing, construction, and transport in various countries in 1955-64

Country	Average for 10 years	Average for 5 years	Average for 5 years
	1956–65	1961–65	1956–60
Switzerland	5	10	—
Sweden	7	4	10
West Germany	45	34	56
Netherlands	49	16	81
New Zealand	113	144	81
Norway	259	212	306
U.K.	288	238	338
Finland	289	318	260
France	301	342	260
Denmark	326	772	549
Australia	359	352	366
Japan	389	304	474
Belgium	437	130	744
Canada	581	556	606
Ireland	632	1,008	256
India	666	436	896
Italy	885	1,202	568
USA	1,020	744	1,296

(Source: International Labour Office, as published in the Ministry of Labour *Gazette*, October 1966. This should be seen for statistical notes.)

Table A.6. Number of stoppages per million employees in various countries

	Country	Yearly average over 5 years 1959–63
1.	Switzerland	0·14
2.	Sweden	0·58
3.	India	0·78
4.	Norway	0·89
5.	South Africa	0·98
6.	Belgium	1·4
7.	Netherlands	1·8
8.	Denmark	1·8
9.	Finland	2·4
10.	Japan	2·5
11.	Canada	4·7
12.	United States	5·2
13.	Ireland	6·4
14.	New Zealand	8·1
15.	United Kingdom	10·2
16.	Italy	15·7
17.	France	19·1
18.	Australia	33·2

(West Germany's figures not available.) (Source: International Labour Office.)

Appendix B
The Education and Training of Shop Stewards

The investigations from which much of the material contained in this appendix was gained took place in 1963 and courses may have been changed in the intervening period.

Reasons for training shop stewards

(1) Trade unions

Developments since the Second World War have made stewards a powerful force in many unions. Consequently, the unions have a *prima facie* interest in developing not only the level of stewards' skills and information, but also their loyalty to the union and its policies. This reason seems to account for much of the subject matter of many courses given by the unions. They normally deal with the union's history, structure, and policies, and the role of the steward and the contents of agreements. Most union run courses emphasize the traditions and unity of the union, and the interdependence of its officers attempting to win the allegiance of those attending. The enhanced importance of stewards as bargainers and the often wide gap between their education and that of managers puts them at a disadvantage unless they are natural bargainers. Thus, the unions have an obvious reason for ensuring that their representatives and members do not suffer as a result, and the courses often include bargaining exercises as well as outlines of the principles of negotiating.

Naturally unions, within the limits of scarce resources, want to train *all* their officers to improve their performance and effectiveness. Consequently, most do not regard the steward as a distinct entity, but rather as a voluntary officer who may rise to such higher union office as branch secretary, chairman, or full time official. Thus, his education and training are part of an overall scheme within the union, rather than specifically equipping him for his present role. The unions are often suspicious of external courses which may stress the steward's distinctive role rather than seeing it as part of the union machine. This point was emphasized in conversation with TUC officials. Organizers of such courses may include subject matter within the responsibilities and duties of a steward ranging wider than a union wishes. Unions are interested in training stewards, but not to stimulate a widening of their powers and responsibilities. However, not all unions train their stewards; to our knowledge, only twelve provide courses specifically for stewards.

(2) Management

The reasons why many managements prefer to deal with stewards have been given in the text. Undoubtedly, many feel more confident when dealing with representatives they employ than with a union official. In-company steward training may foster this situation, for information given to stewards about company piece rates, bonus schemes, work study practices, and other issues peculiar to the company makes stewards better placed as bargainers in itself, and improves their position as against officials unlikely to be briefed in such detail. Managements often find themselves dealing with stewards whether they positively sought it or not, because of frequent non-availability among full time officials at short notice. Given that managements do negotiate with stewards, they obviously prefer representatives who understand their language and who can be moved by facts. Education in the background to management policies and the techniques they employ is one way of achieving this, in removing resistance arising from ignorance rather than from fact. This is probably the main reason for managements providing training courses for stewards. Managements may also hope that they will create a rapport between stewards and management, and a wider knowledge showing itself in an enhanced respect for constitutional methods.

(3) Academic bodies

Many bodies have become involved in steward education and training through their more general activities in adult education. Partly through co-operation with the WEA, university extra-mural departments have expanded considerably since 1945, and many are active in union education. Some, such as London and Nottingham, devote themselves mostly to broader educational work, while others such as Oxford run training courses in topics specific to stewards' vocational needs.

Many technical colleges and colleges of further education are also engaged in this work. Contacts with local industry have led through management courses to an interest in union education, and naturally to those most likely to benefit from further education, the shop stewards.

One major problem for academic bodies is lack of sufficient staff with knowledgeable experience to teach the subjects. This is an obstacle to rapid expansion.

Some courses available to shop stewards

As Professor Roberts has observed, in *Trade Union Government and Administration*, 'There is no clear division between education and training. What is really involved is the problem of what subjects should be taught, how they should be taught and who should teach them.' He goes on to say that both the narrow training and broad liberal educational aspects are essential, 'the one to make effective and efficient trade unionists in the narrow sense, and the other to develop the future leaders of the trade union . . .'.[1]

Education is partly concerned with training the mind, and those institutions concerned with broader education rather than specific training are helping to equip stewards. A steward must think clearly to marshal facts and arguments, and express himself. Education helps him do this while liberal studies simultaneously provide perspective.

The courses divide into four categories.

(1) Externally based general background courses

These include courses giving stewards background information in his job. Subjects taught include the responsibilities and duties of a steward, industrial law, the Factory Acts, work study, self-expression or clear speaking, union history, communications, and negotiating procedure.

Sponsors of these include Slough College of Further Education, Grays Thurrock Technical College (Essex), Luton College of Technology, Wolverhampton and Staffordshire College of Technology, and Crawley Technical College. Other bodies include Supervisory Training Services Limited, Burton Manor, William Temple College, and Holly Royde College.

(2) Union or company based background courses

Union Courses. When organized by the unions, these courses normally include instruction on the history of the union, structure, policy, practice in negotiating with explanatory talks, making speeches, industrial agreements, the role of the steward, the Factories Acts, and work study. Unions operating such courses include the T & GWU, NUGMW, AEF, USDAW, ETU, CAWU, AUBTW, DATA, TWU, NUTGW, NUVB, AUFW, and the NUS.

Management Courses. Managements also run courses of this type with information about the company, joint negotiating procedure, and agreements, the position and duties of the local representative, work measurement techniques, wages structure, company products and markets, and often outlines by specialist managers of their function in the company. Companies running such courses include the Esso Petroleum Company, the Imperial Smelting Company of Avonmouth, Motherwell Bridge and Engineering Company, Joseph Lucas Ltd., Michelin Tyre Company Ltd., British Visqueen Ltd., and ICI.

A few examples are known of joint ventures between union and management. The Unilever–USDAW course is well known, while Raleigh Industries runs a similar course drawing stewards from the unions represented in its plant. ICI also organize a three day course jointly with the unions covering general information on the unions represented in the firm and ICI.

237

(3) Intensive training in particular subjects

In some cases, specific subjects are taught. The best example is the Oxford University Extra-Mural Delegacy with classes for stewards on the Engineering Agreements, and the histories of the Confederation of Shipbuilding and Engineering Unions and the Engineering and Allied Employers' Federation. Short essays on these subjects are provided, to be used in eighteen two-hour afternoon sessions of discussion. Stewards come from the BMC group, the courses being held in local firms, Pressed Steel being the first, in January 1961. These courses have the advantage of being specific, with fairly precise objectives closely related to the job of those attending.

(4) Liberal education courses

London Extra-Mural Department and Nottingham Adult Education Department run courses for stewards in numerous firms locally, subjects including industrial relations, and also economics, industrial law, etc. Leeds, Nottingham, and Sheffield Universities have day release courses for the NUM. Courses last for two or three years, covering economics, politics, industrial relations, and communications.

Nottingham and Leeds also run day release courses of instruction in these subjects for stewards in local industry. Birmingham University runs courses of half a day per week for sixteen weeks for stewards. Working in conjunction with local companies, unions, and the WEA, it teaches industrial relations, economics, the industrial pattern of Birmingham, and the background to national, social, and economic problems. About twenty stewards attend each course.

There are, of course, other educational bodies offering liberal subjects to unionists. These include the WEA, which deals with thousands of stewards, Ruskin College, Oxford, some trade unions including DATA, some Adult Education Centres including Burton Manor, Cheshire, William Temple College, Rugby, and Knuston Hall Adult Education Centre, Wellingborough.

Stewards also attend other courses of general value, but this cross section describes educational opportunities for shop stewards.

Present coverage and an evaluation of training

Certainly, stewards can benefit from education and training, their roles including complex functions and problems. New stewards, especially, face difficulties in coping with them without outside help. This might come from inside the union movement, but also derive from outside educational bodies. The replies to our questionnaire showed that many stewards considered industrial relations and economics most useful. These subjects could be provided most easily by educational bodies outside the union movement, such as University Extra-Mural Departments, WEA districts, technical colleges, colleges of further education, etc. Certainly, they could expand their work, since the volume of such education and training in the UK is very small. A survey conducted by Mr D. F. Bellairs, which formed the basis of his evidence to the Royal Commission on Trade Unions and Employers' Associations, showed that of 356 eligible technical colleges only 5·9 per cent conducted courses for stewards, only three colleges having tutors wholly engaged in steward training. Sixteen had tutors engaged part time in such work. Courses are sparse, usually being presented one to three times during the academic year. Many were either evening or half day courses lasting from sixteen weeks, suggesting that the training is not extensive.

He estimates that about 9,000 union students participate in all courses, including those run by university extra mural departments, WEA districts, unions, the TUC technical colleges, etc. This is a minute proportion of all unionists (about 10 million) accounting for only 5 to 8 per cent of stewards in the UK, even if all 9,000 were stewards. It should be noted, however, that there is some conflicting evidence here. *The Training of Shop Stewards*[2] contains information to the effect that the TUC Working Party's survey reveals that 'even if the large element of postal courses and one day schools is excluded the total provision in 1965–66 by seven unions, the TUC, and public educational bodies amounts to 30,000 student places for workplace representatives. This is one place for every five workplace representatives covered by the TUC inquiry.' There clearly remains an enormous amount of work to be done in this field. Encouragement for shop steward education and training from the Industrial Training Boards would do much to stimulate the growth of courses provided that employers and trade unionists were prepared to offer their support. The Boards in shipbuilding and construction have already shown some initiative in this direction.

One recurring and difficult question in shop steward training is that of its objectives. The failure to reach wide agreement about these helps to account for the limited training provided. Management's objectives may be to promote among stewards a wider view of the structural and economic environment in which they perform, to clarify company policies and the mechanics of particular techniques, and to stress observation of procedural and other agreements. The unions may stress loyalty to the larger unit, solidarity, and co-ordination in all action, while providing advice about negotiating to avoid losing opportunities or reaching 'bad' agreements. Both, to a point, emphasize the steward's 'responsibility' to groups other than his constituents. This may draw him away from his members, and poses a problem of balance to the steward.

Little is known about the educational and training requirements of the stewards themselves. For example, which problems cause them most trouble, what kind of balance would they like between specific training and broader education? While many outside observers feel that the uncertainties of a steward's role cause problems, stewards themselves may not feel that this is a weakness.

The balance of responsibility for the initiation, organization, staffing, and finance of courses for stewards is undefined, and very different practices are to be found. Some consider it a union responsibility, others as shared by unions and managements. Others feel that the government should lead, or that the Industrial Training Boards should give it higher priority. On the other hand, the *effects* of training stewards remain largely unknown. More research and discussion is necessary, and greater resources diverted, if the quantity and quality of education and training are to be raised. Despite the uncertainty over the results of training, it is pessimistic to suggest it has no beneficial effects on relationships in the workplace.

References

1. Roberts, op. cit, pp. 334–5.
2. The TUC *The Training of Shop Stewards*, 1968. This booklet provides an interesting and up-to-date summary of the TUC's approach to shop steward education and training.

Appendix C
Questionnaire for Shop Stewards

This questionnaire is part of a university survey being carried out on the duties and responsibilities of shop stewards. The results of the survey will be kept completely anonymous and in no case will names or personal details be divulged. Please answer the following questions as fully as you are able and return questionnaire.

Date   Age   Union   Male or Female

1. What office(s) do you hold in the union?
2. (a) In which industry do you work?
   (b) What does your company make?
3. What do you do for a living?
4. Roughly how many people are employed at your place of work?
   - Over 10,000
   - 2,000 – 10,000
   - 500 – 2,000
   - 100 – 500
   - Under 100
5. Here is a list of trade union duties at the place of work. Please tick those with which you are concerned as a shop steward.

Pay problems	Shift work
Hours	Production queries
Safety	New works agreements
Demarcation	Holidays

Hygiene	Complaints about
Overtime	management
Union membership	Staffing
Observance of agreements	Apprentices
Joint consultation	Welfare of constituents
Branch meeting	Dues
Branch committee meeting	Discipline
Steward meetings	Work study
Job performance	Redundancy
Victimization	Suggestion schemes

Are there any other duties not mentioned above which take up your time? If so please list them.

6. Which of the above duties (or others) do you regard as most important (not necessarily taking up the most time) in your job as shop steward? List the seven main ones in order of importance.

7. How many hours a week do you normally spend on your job as shop steward?
   (*a*) Within working time.....................hours
   (*b*) In your own time   ....hours

8. How long have you been a steward? Give details of previous time as a steward also.

9. Are you subject to regular re-election?

10. Have you been opposed:
    (*a*) When first elected?
    (*b*) When coming up for re-election?

11. If you were to resign as shop steward do you think that there would be anyone else to take your place?

12. Why did you decide to stand for the position of shop steward?

13. For how many members are you personally responsible?

14. Give the steps in the bargaining procedure, i.e. if you have to negotiate with management what are the successive stages of management that you should deal with?
    E.g., Departmental foreman, Departmental manager, Personnel manager, etc.

    1st Stage, 2nd Stage, 3rd Stage, 4th Stage, 5th Stage. Would you always follow this? Yes/No. If not under what circumstances and at what stage would you vary it?

15. On which subjects do you negotiate with the foreman (or foremen) in the bargaining procedure?

Pay problems	New works agreements
Hours	Holidays
Safety	Complaints about
Demarcation	management
Hygiene	Staffing
Overtime	Apprentices
Union membership	Welfare of constituents
Observance of agreements	Dues
Joint consultation	Discipline
Job performance	Work study
Victimization	Redundancy
Shift work	Suggestion schemes

Are there any other matters not listed above on which you negotiate with the foreman? If so please put them at the end of the list provided.

16. How would you rate the general importance of the foreman in the procedure?

> Very important
> Important
> Neither important nor unimportant
> Not very important
> Not important at all

17. For what reasons did you rate the foreman so?

18. Have you taken part in any educational classes since you left school? Please tick the following where appropriate.

(1) Union day schools
(2) Union weekend schools
(3) Union summer school
(4) TUC schools
(5) University adult education classes
(6) University adult education weekend or day schools
(7) University adult education summer schools
(8) WEA classes
(9) WEA weekend or day schools
(10) WEA summer schools
(11) NCLC classes
(12) NCLC day schools
(13) Ruskin college

244

(14) Fircroft college

(15) London School of Economics

(16) Correspondence courses

(17) Evening institute classes

(18) Other classes

What subjects have you studied in these classes which have been helpful to you *as a shop steward*? List in order of importance.

19. What subjects would you like to study which would be helpful to you as a shop steward? List in order of importance.

20. Does the management place restrictions in your way which hamper you in carrying out your duties as a shop steward. Yes/No.

21. If 'Yes' what are these restrictions?

22. Has there been a case of victimization of shop stewards in your place of work during the last ten years. Yes/No. If 'Yes' could you describe it briefly?

23. When management quotes company information to you in support of their arguments do you:

> Accept it in every case
> Accept it in most cases
> Accept it in a few cases
> Accept it in very few cases
> Never accept it?

24. How do you get on with your departmental manager?

> Very well
> Well
> Neither well nor badly
> Not very well
> Very badly

25. Would you like to see more company information. Yes/No.

26. If 'Yes' what sort of information would you like to see?

27. How would seeing this information help you to fulfil your functions as a shop steward more successfully?

28. How would you use this information?

29. Does your firm have a joint consultative committee or committees? Yes/No.

30. If 'Yes' do you sit on it? Yes/No.
31. If 'No' do you regard the work of the representative who does as in any way interfering with your responsibilities as a shop steward? Yes/No.
    If 'Yes' in what way?
32. How often do you meet a full time official on union business? Please tick as appropriate.
    Once a week
    Once a month
    Once every three months
    Once every six months
33. Do you feel it necessary to meet a full time official often? Yes/No. If 'Yes', how often?
    Once a week
    Once a month
    Once every three months
    Once every six months
34. What subjects would you like to discuss with a full time official if you met him more frequently?
35. What ratio of branch meetings do you usually attend? Please tick the following as appropriate.
    Every one 1 in 4
    1 in 2   1 in 5
    1 in 3   1 in 6
    less than 1 in 6? Please state the appropriate number.
36. In what ways, if any, are branch meetings useful to you as a shop steward? List in order of importance.
37. Is your branch based on your place of work, i.e. do only members from your firm attend it?
38. What do you like about being a shop steward?
39. Would you like to become a supervisor, (a) In your own firm? Yes/No. (b) In another firm? Yes/No.
40. Do you think that you would like to become a full time union official? Yes/No. If 'Yes' please give reasons why in order of importance.
41. What changes would you like to see made at your place of work in order to improve industrial relations? List in order of importance.
42. Do you sit on a Shop Stewards' Committee? Yes/No.
43. If 'Yes' how often do you meet?

44. What subjects does the Committee discuss? List in your estimation of importance.
45. Do you think that such a Committee is useful. Yes/No.
46. If 'Yes' for what reasons?
47. Is there anything else you would like to add?

Index

249

Duties, responsibilities and attitudes of shop stewards, survey of, 74–8, 87–115: company information, 100–1; election, 94–5; factors affecting stewards, 99; joint consultation, 102; questionnaire, 87, 242–7; reasons for standing for steward's position, 93; relations with management, 95–9; relations with supervisors, 109; relations with union, 102–3; results of survey, 87–8; size of constituency, 88–93; stewards and education, 104–5; survey compared with Royal Commission's Survey, 109–15; time spent on steward's duties, 93

Early growth and development of shop stewards, 22–38: administrative duties, 23–4; in coal mines, 25; in engineering industry, 23–5; in printing industry, 23, 25; Shop Stewards' Movement, 26–34; Second World War and after, 34–8; increase in numbers, 35–8
Education, stewards and, 104–5, 218, 234–41
'Effort bargains', 155
Election of stewards, 41–55, 94–5
Electricity supply industry, unofficial stewards' organization in, 122
Employers' associations, 192–3
Engineering and Allied Trades Shop Stewards' National Council, 36, 122
Engineering Employers Federation, 33, 37, 80, 131, 136
Engineering Industry three year agreement (1964), 165–6
English Electric, 129
Erratic groups, 67–8, 71, 76
Esso Blue Book, 197, 199–200, 203
ETU (Electrical Trades Union), 74, 87, 88, 138, 199: and inter-union co-operation, 62; and stewards' negotiating role, 62; area officials, 58; election of stewards and senior stewards, 48, 54, 60; eligibility, 50, 55; rulebook, 48–50; steward committees, 118; stewards' conference and meetings, 59–60; stewards' duties and functions, 60, 61; stewards' responsibility to full-time officials, 57

Fairfields, facilities for convenors, 132

Fathers of the chapel (FOC), 3, 23, 25, 50–1, 58: Imperial Fathers, 135–6; payments to, 56
Fawley productivity agreements, 157: Blue Book, 197, 199–200, 203
Financial Times, 204
Firth Brown stewards, 123
Fixed period agreements, 146–7
Flanders, Allan, 66, 74, 196: on overtime, 157–8
Ford's, 123, 129, 133, 204: combine committee, 121, 120, 138; Joint Works Committee, 119; NJNC, 139; strikes, 184
Formalization of stewards' roles, 82–5, 218, 220: full time officials' attitude to, 83–4; functional arguments for, 218; management's attitude, 83
Fox, Alan, 133
Friendly Ironmoulders' Society, 23
Full employment, 145
Full time union officials, 13, 15, 56, 57, 102–3, 184, 222: and formalization of stewards' role, 83–4; hours of work, 84

Gallacher, William, 29, 30
Gallup Poll on internal communications between unions and members (1959), 63
General Strike (1926), 31, 34
Gilbreth, Frank, 66
Glasgow and District Engineers' and Boilermakers' Association, 24
Gouldner, A. W., 75, 181
Government intervention in national agreements, 147
Government Social Survey, 110
Grievance procedure, 176–7, 179, 185–6
Guild Socialists and Shop Stewards' Movement, 29

Hamblin, A. C., 97
Handbook of Social Psychology (ed. Lindzey), 5
Handbooks and manuals, stewards', 5, 41–64, 223–5
Hawthorne experiments, 66, 73
HDEU (Heating and Domestic Engineers Union), 74, 198: and shop stewards, 54; communication with stewards, 60; eligibility, 55; stewards' duties, 60

Hosiery Workers Union, 88: and shop committees, 59, 118; and stewards' negotiating role, 62; system of seniority, 60
Hours of work, stewards and, 162. *See also* Overtime

ICI, unofficial National Joint Committee, 121
Incentive schemes and rates, 153–5
Incomes policy, 219
Independent Labour Party, 29
Industrial conflict, stewards and, 169–88: bases, 169–73; conflict theory, 73–4, 171–2; control of conflict by stewards, 184–5; grievance procedures, 176–7, 179, 185–6; management and, 178–80, 185–6; role of stewards, 180–7; unofficial strikes and unofficial action, 173–80
Industrial Training Boards, 240
Industrial Welfare Society, 199, 203
Industry-wide negotiating procedure, value of, 143–4
Information: collection of, 219; stewards and, 100–1, 130, 193–5
Inman, Mrs. P., 35
Institute of Personnel Management, 148
International Labour Review, 227

Jacques, Elliot, 5
Jaguar, facilities for convenors, 132
Jefferys, James B., 37
Job evaluation, 159
Joint consultation, 102, 125, 147
Joint shop stewards committees (JSSC), 19–20, 48, 119–20, 124, 126–8, 130, 131, 136, 138, 139, 186: educational function, 127; fund raising, 127; officers and executive committees, 126–7
Jones, R. S., 145–6, 177

Kirkwood, David, 29
Knowles, K. G. J. C., 173, 174
Kuhn, James W., 185: on explicit plant bargaining, 79; on primary groups, 69–72, 74, 76

Lenin, 30
Lerner, Dr Shirley W., 123, 126, 129, 150, 162
Local full time officials, 58–9. *See also* Full time officials
London Airport committee, 138

London Building Works Joint Sites Committee, 122

McCarthy, Dr W. E. J., 71, 110, 149, 185, 191, 192: on formalization of stewards' roles, 83
Management and shop stewards, 15–17, 95–9, 163–4, 189, 206, 208–11, 223–4: and formalization of stewards' roles, 83; and enhancement of stewards' power, 15–16; and industrial conflict, 178–80, 185–6; case study, 196–205; co-operation, 73–4; defensiveness of managements, 192–3, 211; employers' associations, 192–3; importance of stewards to management, 189–91; level of labour management, 209; managerial approach to collective bargaining, 191–5; need to provide more information, 193–5; overtime, 196; personalities, 206; personnel managers, 190–1; positive management, 196; preference for stewards, 148; relations with convenors and senior stewards, 131–4
Marquand, Judith, 129
Marsh, A. I., 37–8, 72, 74, 118, 125, 145–6, 177
Marx, Karl, and Marxism, 28, 31
Mayo, Elton, 66–7
Merit payments, 159–60
Miners' Association of Great Britain, 15
Miners' Federation of Great Britain, 31
Mines Regulation Act 1872, 25
Morris Engines stewards' committee, 120
Motor industry: disintegration of industry-wide stewards committee, 122; Joint Labour Council, 82; 'unofficial-unofficial' strikes, 75
Munitions of War Act 1915, 27
Munns, V. G., 192

NACODS (National Association of Colliery Overmen, Deputies and Shotfirers), 88, 90
National agreements, 143–4, 146–7: government intervention in, 147
National Board for Prices and Incomes, 168
National Workers' Committee Movement, 28–30
NATSOPA (National Society of

Work groups and shop stewards—*cont.*
theories, 67–73; effectiveness of stewards, 72; erratic groups, 67–8, 71, 76; formalization of stewards' roles, 81–5; groups in industry, 66–7; Hawthorne experiments, 66, 73; significance of primary group theories to stewards, 79–82; socio-psychological forces, 70: stewards' leadership and its acceptance, 14–15; strategic groups, 68, 71; 'un-official-unofficial' strikes, 75

Workplace bargaining and shop stewards, 142–68: arguments of equity, 165–6; bargaining techniques, 164–7; bonuses etc., 160; collective agreements, 144, 146; consultative procedures, 147; 'custom and practice', 166; 'effort bargains', 155; financial topics, 152–60; fixed period agreements, 146–7; full employment, 145; government intervention, 147; hours of work, 162; incentive schemes and rates, 153–5; industry-wide negotiating procedures, 143–4; informality, 149; job evaluation, 159; managements' preference for stewards, 148; merit payments, 159–60; overtime, 155–8, 162; payment by results, 147, 153–5; personnel specialists, 148–9; procedure facilities, 145–6; range of bargaining, 160–4; reasons for development, 145–9; redundancy, 162; stewards' bargaining powers, 79–81; trade union and shop steward status, 162; use of precedent, 166–7; wage drift, 149–53

Workplace relations, evaluation of system, 112–13

Works Committees, 119–20

PRINTED BY COX & WYMAN LTD.
LONDON, FAKENHAM AND READING